They Did Not Have Horns

The Viking Kings of Norway

Borghild Sande

Eva Mildred Mykleby Pearson

They Did Not Have Horns

The Viking Kings of Norway

from about 760 AD to 1066 AD
and the royal kings from 1066 AD to the present

Eva Mildred Mykleby Pearson

Norbakk Press
St. Paul, Minnesota

They Did Not Have Horns—The Viking Kings of Norway—A Historical/Genealogical Book of the Viking Kings of Norway

Other publications: *I Remember! I Remember! Your Viking Heritage*, 1989; *Viking Kings of Norway* Chart, 1995.

Excerpts reprinted from *Heimskringla: History of the Kings of Norway* by Snorri Sturluson, translated by Lee M. Hollander. Copyright ©1964. Courtesy of the University of Texas Press.

Printed in the United States of America

Book design: Dorie McClelland
Viking Ship illustration: Annette Sohljell
Viking King illustrations: Richard Hubal

They Did Not Have Horns: The Viking Kings of Norway
Includes glossary, maps, bibliography, index of personal names, reference to places, alphabetical and chronological list of battles. The accompanying chart includes:
1. A comprehensive family tree of the kings of Norway from six generations before King Harald I Fairhair to the present.
2. A detailed chart of King Harald I Fairhair to Queen Margrete (c872–1412)
3. Up-to-date information and family tree of kings from 1905 to present, including King Harald V or Norway
4. Many petty kings not always listed in regnal lists of Norwegian kings
5. List of Danish kings who ruled Norway from 1405–1814.
6. List of Swedish kings who ruled Norway from 1814–1905
7. Known children born to the kings and the order of their births
8. Known mistresses and their offspring
9. Nicknames to facilitate identification
10. Marriages and intermarriages between many of the royal houses of Europe
11. Many coat of arms

Publisher's Cataloging-in-Publication Data
(Provided by Quality Books, Inc.)

Pearson, Eva Mildred Mykleby
     They did not have horns: the Viking kings of Norway from
     about 760 AD to 1066 AD and the royal kings from 1066 AD
     to the present / Eva Mildred Mykleby Pearson — 1st ed.
         p. cm.
     Includes bibliographical references and index.
     Preassigned LCCN: 97-95075
     ISBN 0-9618227-2-4

     1. Norway—Kings and rulers—Biography. 2. Kings and
rulers—Genealogy. 3. Norway—Genealogy. I. Title.

DL444.1.P43 1998   948.1'092
                             QBI98-198

To the twelve* wonderful men in my life, with whom
I want to share my love of the history of our forefathers,
the Viking Kings of Norway.

*My husband, four sons, and seven grandsons.

Contents

Norway's 110-Year Civil War, 1130–1240 AD   83

Norway's Golden Years, 1240–1405 AD   133

*Petty kings and pretenders. Often not listed in regnal lists. See preface.

PREFACE

The period in history during which the Vikings made the greatest impact on Europe is often called the Viking Age—roughly between 875and 1066. The following centuries also saw many changes in the rule of Norway.

Several years ago, one of my Norwegian cousins, ceremoniously (but with "tongue-in-cheek") presented me with several pages of genealogical lineage indicating I was a direct descendant of King Harald I Fairhair, the first king of Norway. With my many years of experience as a genealogist, I decided it was time to look for information about my distinguished famous ancestor. With the assistance of our local library, I was presented with a copy of the original leather bound *Heimskringla*, by one of the great Icelandic saga writers, Snorri Sturluson. I have been a student of Viking history throughout most of my adult years, and I was intrigued with the exciting events of the Viking era portrayed in this book.

It was difficult to follow the lineage from the text, so I decided to find a genealogical chart of the Viking kings which would help me. I canvassed book stores, libraries and professional people, but could not find one to my liking. I finally consulted with Lars Løberg, Vice Counsel with the Norwegian Embassy (in Minneapolis, Minnesota, from 1989 to 1992). He was thoroughly versed in the subject, having a Ph.D. in Norwegian history. I was inspired and motivated by his vast knowledge of the history of Norway, and he constantly urged me to continue my work. However, he knew of no chart with the thorough information I wanted. He encouraged me to proceed with the chart I was creating, a large 24" x 36" genealogical/historical chart of the Viking kings of Norway. I designed and created an informative chart which has been sold separately and been received with much enthusiasm.

The Viking kings with their many adventures made interesting reading, but I felt it would be good to have a single book with a brief history of each of the kings who had ruled in Norway. After many months devoted to research at our local libraries, as well as the University of Minnesota and other college facilities, I took it upon myself to write the book. I have emphasized the wives, children and family life of the kings rather than their battles. It was interesting and rewarding work, and it is my wish that others will enjoy reading about the Norwegian Viking kings. It can be read in one sitting, or the chapters on the various kings may be read separately.

Many others have contributed to the writing of this book, and it would be impossible to name them all. I also want to express my gratitude to Liv Dahl, Editor of *Viking* magazine; Dr. Odd Lovoll, King Olav V Professor of Scandinavian American Studies at St. Olaf College; Dr. Kathleen Stokker, Norwegian Language Professor at Luther College; Dr. Michael Metcalf, Director of International Studies, University of Minnesota; and Associate Professor, Mariann Tiblin, purchaser of Scandinavian books for Wilson Library, University of Minnesota, to name a few. Jon Schweitzer, Instructor at the Los Angeles Family History Center Library, Los Angeles, California, was also tremendously helpful, particularly with dates and documentation.

The Viking ship on the book cover and chart is used with the permission of Annette Sjohjell, a gifted artist (of Norwegian heritage) from Hagensburg, British Columbia in Canada. The illustrations in the book are by Richard Hubal of St. Paul, Minnesota. My thanks to all of these people and also to my very special sister, Opal Hedberg, not only for her assistance in the checking of my material, but most of all for her cheerful but persistent motivating spirit.

It would not have been possible to keep track of the vast amount of information about the kings were it not for my very helpful friend, my computer. I also received considerable help from Norwegian friends on the Internet. The technical communications/electronic help and assistance I received for the production of the chart was made possible with the capable assistance of Nancy Hereid, Computer Analyst, and her daughter, Britt. I have also had help and encouragement from many cousins and friends while on numerous trips to Norway and the other Scandinavian countries.

The financial assistance from grants from the Sons of Norway International was most appreciated. Finally, my sons and their families are to be commended for their patience and understanding, and particularly my spouse, who has been especially tolerant and helpful; my midnight to dawn working hours are not easily understood by everyone.

Eva Mildred Mykleby Pearson

Key

It will benefit the reader to study the following abbreviations used throughout the book.

All dates are AD unless otherwise noted
b. – born
d. – died
c – ca, circa, about
  e.g. b.1172 d.1199 (40 yrs.) or (c40 yrs.)
      b. d.1199
      b.4 Jan 1172 d.11 Jun 1199
      b.Jan 1172 d.Jun 1199
      b.c1172 d.c1199
R. – reigned
      R.1182–1190
      R.c1182–1190

m. – married
      m. Sofie Larsdatter (if only one marriage)
        If more than one:
      m1) – first marriage
          e.g., m1)Sofie Larsdatter
      m2) – second marriage, etc.
          e.g., m2)Margrete Arnesdatter
√. – mistress or unknown mother

* – petty king (often not listed in regnal records)

The first information about each king gives the genealogical information, and lists parents, children, and additional lineage data that will be helpful to the reader.

The Viking Kings of Norway Genealogical/Historical Chart will enable the reader to follow the text with a better understanding.

INTRODUCTION

Is there any living man, king or prince, on land or water as bold as we?
No one dares to meet us sword with sword. Be we right or wrong, all
yield before us, plowman and merchant, horseman and ship.

A boast by a Viking chieftain in the year 866 AD. He was Ivar the Boneless, presumably because he was double-jointed. He led one of the first large raids on Kent, in southeastern England. So relates an early historian in the Anglo Saxon Chronicle, and so began the Viking era.

This book, *They Did Not Have Horns, The Viking Kings of Norway*, gives a short synopsis of the kings from several generations before King Harald I Fairhair, the first recognized ruler of all of Norway, past the Viking Age to about 1400 AD. At that time the Danes took over and it follows through to the present. Although we love to visualize the maurading Viking kings dashing into battle with their horned helmets, they were evidently never worn. Horned helmets were used in worship ceremonies, mainly by the nobles and the wealthy, as a ceremonial symbol when a boy became a warrior. The book deals more with the families, wives, children, and personal characteristics. The power and influence of Viking women is also evaluated. Historians have placed too much emphasis on the brutal savagery and battles of the Vikings, and not enough on the individual families. What each king contributed to bringing Christianity into Norway is also emphasized.

The genealogical, historical chart, in color—with a time line chart allows the reader to better follow the lineage of the many kings who descended from King Harald I Fairhair. An extensive Index of Names is included with comprehensive genealogical information of several thousand individuals who lived during the Viking period. According to the Forword in Snorri Sturluson's *Heimskringla*, there once was a genealogy of Viking kings compiled by the priest, Ari Thorgilsson the Learned (1057–1048)), an early historian. This was lost. I have tried to carefully reconstruct the genealogies of the Viking kings, as recorded in Snorri's manuscript.

The book includes information on sixty-one "kings, rulers, petty kings, and pretenders" who ruled (or thought they ruled), during this time, and six of Harald's ancestors who thought they were of royal blood and felt it was their right to be king.

Their exact number is controversial, due to the limited information available during this period. Every one of these individuals, however, is given a "short time in history" in this book and also on the chart.

As there is no official list of kings, the numbering system used is unique for this book and chart. It allows the reader a simple method of following the lineage and text.

The late Lee M. Hollander, a prominent translator of Norwegian sagas says that "it is difficult if not impossible to achieve consistency in the rendering of Old Norse names." Due to all these variations of the spelling of names, it was necessary to make a compromise. The decision was made to use whichever name would make it easier for the reader to follow the complex genealogical lines. For instance, St. Olav is easier than Olav II, and Harald I Fairhair is more descriptive than Harald I. Often names have been Americanized. It is hoped that this will simplify the general confusion of rule during this time, and make it easier to follow the genealogical "royal blood line" of King Harald I Fairhair.

In the appendix you will find a list of people, indexed according to their first name, as was customary for this time. The sequence used is that of the Latin alphabet with the three Norwegian letters with their nearest equivalent. There are also several maps, an index of places, battles (in alphabetical and chronological order), and a glossary of terms used during this period of history.

My main source of information was Snorri Sturluson's *Heimskringla* (Lee Hollander's translation). Various kenning prose was also used, with permission from the University of Texas, Austin. Much of the genealogical data is derived from *Heimskringla*, even though more recent historians doubt the accuracy of some of the information. A great deal of research was done before I decided to put it into book form, and although every effort was made to give credit to all sources, I apologize if any have been missed.

Pre-Harald I Rulers

c760–c872 AD

In the middle of the eighth century, the first signs of the Viking era were beginning to emerge in Norway. Small rulers from the powerful Yngling dynasty in northeastern Sweden traveled into Norway with their faithful followers. It was customary for the early settlers to form their ruling groups and have their sons carry on after them. One of the first to arrive was believed to be Olav Tree-Hewer, the great-great-great-great grandfather of King Harald I Fairhair, the first king of Norway. His family and kin were participants in the Battle of Lindisfarne, a small island in the North Sea, in 793 AD, the first Viking raid on foreign soil. These were small kings, often referred to as "petty kings" who ruled in separate areas and often fought with each other, determined to obtain more land and power. Six petty kings are involved in the first century before 872 AD which is the date most noted as the time when Norway became a country.

THE FIRST SIX PETTY KINGS are the ancestors of King Harald I Fairhair. The first one, Olav Tree-Hewer, is listed as "-6" and is six generations before King Harald; his son, Halfdan, is listed as "-5" and is five generations before King Harald, and so forth.

Olav Tree-Hewer
-6[1]

Olav Tretelgja,[2] Olof, Olav the Woodcutter, Olav, Olav I King of Vestfold[3]

Son of the Yngling (the royal family of Uppsula, Sweden) King Ingjald of Varmaland, Sweden (also called King Ingjald the Wicked), and Gauthild Algautsdatter.Olav Tree-Hewer is Harald Fairhair's (#1) great-great-great-great grandfather.

b.c670 d.c710 (c40 yrs.)
R.? c710
m.Solveig, b.c684, daughter of a Norwegian petty king,
    Halfdan Goldtooth of Soleyar (which is west of Varmaland)
        Children:
            Halfdan Whiteleg (-5), Prince Halfdan Olavsson of Vestfold,
                b.c710
            Ingjald, Prince Ingjald of Vestfold, b.c712

When Olav arrived in Varmaland—"warm land," so many people followed him there that the area was unable to support them. He cleared the forest with his axe and burned it down. The people of Sweden did not like his wood cutting and burning, so Olav moved further west. Poor crops and famine came to the area. It was customary to blame this on the king. Consequently many people surrounded the hall where he was living and burned him inside. In this way they "gave him to Odin," their pagan god, sacrificing him for good crops.

However, some of the people were wiser and thought the famine occurred because there were too many inhabitants for the area. Thereupon they captured Olav Tree-Hewer's son, Halfdan Whiteleg (#-5), and made him their leader and king. They then moved further west to Raumarike (now Romerike), an area to the south of Lake Mjøsa, in south-central Norway.

The story of Olav Tree-Hewer, as well as many of the kings that follow, may be fact or fiction, whichever you choose to believe.

1. Indicates he is 6 generations before Harald I Fairhair.
2. *Tretelgja* – tree cutter.
3. See map.

Halfdan Whiteleg
-5

Haivdan Hvitbein,[1] Halfdan Olavsson of Vestfold

Son of Olav Tree-Hewer (#-6) and Solveig (daughter of Halfdan Goldtooth of Soleyar). Halfdan Whiteleg is five generations before Harald Fairhair (#1). Halfdan is Harald Fairhair's great-great-great grandfather.

b.c710 d.c750 (c46 yrs.)
R.probably sometime during the period from 710–750
m.Asa Eysteinsdatter, b.c709, daughter of Eystein the Hard Ruler (King of Uppland and Jarl of Trondheim), and Solveig Halfdansdatter
    Children:
        Eystein Halfdansson (#-4), b.c730 d.c780 at Borre
        Guthroth, b.c738 d.c810 at Borre

King Halfdan Whiteleg was a powerful king. He had a white pine peg-leg, thus his name. He reportedly was from the royal family of Ynglings at Uppsula. He was raised in Soleyar by his maternal uncle, Solvi, and became king there. In about 740, he took over a large part of south central Norway, which included Raumarike, and was king of the Upplanders, and the first king of Vestfold. His brother, Ingjald, was king over Varmaland, a neighboring kingdom, but when Ingjald died, Halfdan took over control of that area as well.

Halfdan died of "a sickness," but lived to be an old man.[2] During the middle of the 8th century, Halfdan Whiteleg, and his son, Eystein, were buried near the famous temple at Skiringsal.

1. *Hvit* (or *kvit*) – white. *Bein* – bone.
2. Forty years was considered quite old during this time. The average life-span was about twenty-five years. War, disease, and famine occurred quite frequently, and a high percentage of babies died during their first year.

Eystein Halfdansson
-4

Øystein, Eystein the *Fart*[1], Eystein II

Son of Halfdan Whiteleg (#-5) and Asa Eysteinsdatter.
Eystein Halfdansson is Harald Fairhair's (#1) great-great grandfather.

b.c730 d.c780. (c50 yrs.) drowned
R. probably sometime between 750-780
m.Hild Eriksdatter, b.c732, daughter of Erik, the son of King Agnar, of Vestfold
    Children:
        Halfdan the Gentle (#-3), b.c750

Eystein was king in Raumarike sometime in the eighth century. His wife, Hild, had no brothers. Her father died during the rule of Halfdan Whiteleg (#-5). Then Halfdan and his son, Eystein took over the rule of all of Vestfold. When his father died, Eystein became king over Raumarike and Vestfold.

However, Eystein had his eye on Varna, an area across the fjord from Vestfold. At that time it was ruled by King Skjold, who was skilled in magic. Eystein took several warships and raided Varna. They killed cattle and took farm tools and whatever else they wanted, and then departed. When King Skjold came down to the seashore and saw what had happened, Eystein had already departed, but Skjold saw his sails in the distance. Using his magic skills, he took his cloak and blew into it. This created such a huge wave that the winging sail of a passing ship knocked Eystein overboard and he drowned. His men brought his corpse on board and he was taken to land and was buried next to his father at Borre, on the western shore of the Oslo Fjord.

1. *Fart* – fast or speedy.

Halfdan the Gentle
-3

Halfdan the Generous and Stingy of Food, Halfdan the Mild, Halfdan II King of Vestfold

Son of Eystein Halfdansson (#-4) and Hild Eriksdatter. Halfdan the Gentle is Harald Fairhair's (#1) great grandfather.

b.c750 d.c800 (c50 yrs.)
R.Halfdan the Gentle was king of Vestfold at some point in the 8th century,
    probably from c780 until his death in c800/802.
m.Liv (Lif, Lifa) Dagsdatter, b.c758, daughter of King Dag of Vestfold
    Children:
        Sigurd, b.c775 d.c810
        Guthroth, Guthroth the Hunting King (#2), b.c778 d.c840, murdered

Recent archeological findings are beginning to surface that indicate that the stories from now on, are not entirely mythical, as are, perhaps, the earlier ones.

Halfdan transferred the capitol of Vestfold further inland to Borre where he lived on a farm. Perhaps he considered this safer because of the hostile attitude of other petty kings nearby.

Although Halfdan was a great warrior and went on many Viking expeditions, it is said that he was not a significant "historical king." The sagas say that he generously gave his men their pay in gold rather than silver like other kings. He was stingy with food—*inn milde ok inn matarilli*, which accounts for his name.

Halfdan died of "a sickness." According to the Vikings, it was unfortunate to die a natural death. He is buried at Borri with his father. Today this area is a protected National Park with many beautiful oak and birch trees. However, in medieval times it was a royal cemetery, and many burial mounds are to be found here.

Guthroth, the Hunting King -2

Guthroth the Generous, Gudrød Veidekonge[1]

Son of Halfdan the Generous (#3) and Liv Dagsdatter.
Guthroth the Hunting King is Harald I Fairhair's (#1) grandfather.

b.c800 d.c840 (c40 yrs.) murdered
R.sometime between 800–840
m1)Alvhild, daughter of King Alfar of Alfheim,[2] who brought with her as
    dowry, half of her father's kingdom
        Children:
            Olav Geirstatha-Alf I, b.c810 d.c840. He had a son, Ragnvald.
m2)Asa Haraldsdatter, b.c.810 d.c850
        Children:
            Halfdan the Black (#-1), who later became the father of Harald I
              Fairhair (#1)

In about 793, the Viking raids on England began at the monastery at Lindisfarne. These were on a relatively small scale, with just a few ships and men making quick attacks and withdrawals. King Guthroth probably took part in a few of these raids. Guthroth's name is derived from the fact that he was a great hunter.

Guthroth's first wife was Alvhild. Her wealthy father gave her a dowry that expanded Guthroth's holdings to the extent that he had acquired a sizable kingdom. Their son was called Olav Geirstatha-Alf I. Alvhild died, and after her death, Guthroth set out to woo Asa, the beautiful princess in Agthir, the huge neighboring kingdom in southern Norway, which was ruled by her father, King Harald Redbeard. Guthroth sent emissaries to Agthir to ask for Asa's hand in marriage, but she refused. This infuriated Guthroth, and he set out with his warships and attacked Agthir without warning. King Harald Redbeard put up a heroic defense but both he and his son were killed. Asa was forcibly abducted and Guthroth took her back to Vestfold to become his wife.

The offspring of this marriage was Halfdan the Black (#-1), who was destined to be the father of Harald I Fairhair, the first king of Norway. However, Asa did not forgive Guthroth. A year after Halfdan was born, in about 840, Guthroth had his ship anchored in a bay and a great banquet was given for him by Asa. He got very drunk, and when it was dark he walked down to the end of the pier. A man leapt out of the darkness and drove his spear into him, and that was his death. The man, a page of Queen Asa, was killed immediately. The Queen did not bother concealing that she had planned the murder.

One of Snorri Sturluson's skalds[3] in *Heimskringla* wrote:

> With ease did
> Asa's evil
> errand-boy
> end the lord's life;
> and the prince,
> pierced to the heart,
> stumbling fell
> by Stiflu Sound.

Queen Asa

Asa coolly returned to Agthir and took over as Queen Mother and regent.

After Guthroth was murdered, his son, Olav Geirstatha-Alf I, about twenty years old, became ruler of his father's kingdom of Vestfold. He was probably about the same age as his spiteful stepmother. He was a great warrior and very able, exceedingly handsome, powerfully built and very tall. Apparently Olav died young and his son, Ragnvald, took over the reign.

In 1880 a magnificent ship burial was unearthed at Gokstad (this would be within the Vestfold region). All indications point to the fact that perhaps, just perhaps, the human remains of the Gokstad ship were those of Olav Geirstatha-Alf I.

Prince Ragnvald would have had the wealth to bury his father in such a fashion. It was said that Olav died from "a disease of the leg" and bone fragments that were found revealed that he evidently suffered from a leg problem, possibly osteoarthritis.

Little is known about Ragnvald, though there is a saga written about him. He probably was a great prince in his time. Ragnvald also must have died young, because the entire kingdom eventually became the property of his half-brother, Halfdan the Black.

In 1890 the Oseberg ship was excavated and it is quite certain that Queen Asa was buried there. It is impossible to know whether this story is myth or fact. There is probably a little of each, but the main idea is more than likely quite accurate.

1. *Veide* – hunt; *konge* – king. Hunting king.
2. At that time the name of the district between the present day rivers Glommer and Gota, in Trondheim.
3. Court poet. See glossary.

Halfdan the Black
-1

Halvdan Svart[1]

Son of Guthroth the Hunting King (#-2) and Asa Haraldsdatter. Halfdan the Black is Harald Fairhair's father.

b.c.830 d.c.860, died in a drowning accident
R.c.840–860
m1)Ragnhild, daughter of Harald Goldenbeard, king of Sogn
    Children:
        Harald, died at age 10
m2)Queen Ragnhild, daughter of Sigurth Hart, king of Ringeriki[2]
    Children:
        Harald I Fairhair (#1)

Halfdan was about ten years old when his father was murdered. He was raised in Agthir by his mother. He was large and strong, and had black hair, thus his name, Halfdan the Black. When he was eighteen years of age, he took over the reign of Agthir from his mother. His half-brother, Olav Geirstatha-Alf I, had ruled Vestfold ever since his father died. Both his mother and half-brother would have been about forty years old at this time.

Halfdan then demanded and received one-half of the kingdom of Vestfold, as his rightful paternal inheritance from his father. He became a mighty king. Olav Geirstatha-Alf I had a son named Ragnvald, who took over after him, and became a mighty prince. Both he and his father died young, after which Halfdan the Black became the ruler of the entire kingdom.

This would have made Halfdan a very wealthy king, which makes it all the more certain that it is his mother, Queen Asa who was buried in the famous Oseberg ship. The vessel was superbly carved from curled stem to stern with an intricate frieze depicting stylized animals struggling up from the water line. One historian wrote, "No one who has ever looked at the Oseberg ship can ever again think of the ninth century Norsemen as completely vile and soulless barbarians." An enormous amount of rich jewelry was also found on the ship.

Many Viking raids and battles followed and Halfdan gained control of many regions. At one time he was given a magnificent sword. The giving of gifts was customary and part of the Viking culture. Kings and chiefs rewarded their highest ranking followers with gold rings, gilded swords, and jewelry, and skalds were given precious gifts for writing splendid poems and sagas about the kings.

The sagas say that Halfdan the Black was married twice and both his wives were named Ragnhild. He also had a son by each marriage and each was named Harald. An interesting narrative is told of his romances.

Halfdan's first wife was the daughter of Harald Goldenbeard, who was king of Sogn at the time. They named their son after his grandfather, Harald Goldenbeard. Both Harald and his mother lived in Sogn with her father[3]. When Harald Goldenbeard died he left his kingdom to his grandson Harald. Ragnhild died the same year as her grandfather and Harald died shortly after. Harald was only ten years old.

Upon hearing of this, Halfdan the Black returned to Sogn and claimed the kingdom as "heir of his son." This was recognized and thus Halfdan the Black had added another kingdom to his growing realm.

Halfdan's roving eye soon fell on another Ragnhild—a woman of exceeding beauty and excellence—the twenty-year-old daughter of Sigurd Hart. Sigurd was a great warrior, stronger than any other man and also extremely handsome. One saga states that on one occasion, at age eleven, Sigurd killed a beserker and thirteen of his companions! A beserker is a warrior who fights furiously, often in his bare shirt, and "feels no pain."[4]

Sigurd was later killed and Ragnhild and her brother were kidnaped by Haki, one of Halfdan's enemies. Haki made plans to marry Ragnhild, but his battle wounds became infected, and the marriage was postponed.

Halfdan heard about this, and decided to take Ragnhild as his wife. He sent his troops across the lake to capture Ragnhild and her brother. They burned down Haki's house, put their captors in a carriage and took them across the ice-covered lake to Halfdan's kingdom. Halfdan had prepared a wedding feast for his marriage to Ragnhild. After the marriage, Ragnhild became a powerful queen, known as "Ragnhild the Powerful."

Halfdan the Black and Ragnhild had a son, Harald I Fairhair (#1), who was destined to become the first king of all of Norway. Queen Ragnhild had great ambitions for her son. It is said that one night she had a dream:

> As she stood in her garden she pulled a thorn out of her dress. She held it in her hand, and it grew and became a large tree. It struck root in the soil and lifted its branches high toward heaven. At the foot, the tree was blood red; farther up, the trunk was a shining green, and the crown was a snowy white.

This dream was later interpreted to signify that the great tree was her son, Harald I Fairhair, the first king of Norway. The lowest portion of the trunk that was red as blood meant there would be warfare. The section of trunk that was fair and green signified the flowering of his kingdom. The snowy white crown meant that Harald would become old and hoary. The branches and twigs of the tree told about his offspring who were to spread over the land. The saga interpretation was quite right—most of the kings of Norway during the next few centuries were descended from him. King Halfdan was perturbed because he did not have dreams, so he went to Thorleif the Wise to find out the reason for this. Thorleif told him that if he could not dream, he should go and sleep in a pigsty, and this brought results. He then had the following dream:

> He saw himself as having the longest hair of any man—in ringlets and reaching to the ground. Some reached to his waist and some to his knees. Some hair seemed to sprout from his head like horns.

He told Thorleif of his dream and it was interpreted to mean that Halfdan would have a great line of descendants. The different lengths of his locks showed that all would not be equal, but that there would be one who would be greater and nobler than all the rest. This, of course, was later to be the Holy King Olav (#9).

King Halfdan the Black was considered a wise man, a lover of truth and justice. He made good laws, which he observed himself and compelled others to observe. He fixed certain penalties for all crimes committed. His code of laws, called the Eidsiva Law, was adopted at a common *Thing*[5] at Eidsvold, where about a thousand years later the present constitution of Norway was adopted.

King Halfdan the Black later drowned while driving across an ice-covered lake in the spring. There was cow dung on the ice and this was warmed by the rays of the sun, and the ice melted. King Halfdan's carriage, with many of his followers, perished. His remains are said to be buried in a mound at Stein, Ringerike, where a little hill is still called Halfdan's Mound.[6]

Halfdan the Black lived to be thirty-seven years of age. This Halfdan became the ancestor of the royal race of Norway.

1. *Svart* – black.
2. The district northwest of the present city of Oslo.
3. During this time, it was customary for children to remain with their mother in her home.
4. Additional information is in the glossary on beserkers.
5. A government body, similar to Parliament. See glossary.
6. Author wishes you to note, that this places King Harald Fairhair, in the vicinity of Toten, Norway, and gives more authenticity to her rightful descent from King Harald I Fairhair!

The Viking Period

872–1066 AD

During the Viking period, the Norwegians joined forces with their Swedish and Danish brethren to raid and plunder vast territories in Europe. The first king during this period was Harald I Fairhair who was proclaimed king of Norway after his decisive victory in the battle of Hafrsfjord in about 872 AD. The next two centuries were filled with many battles between Sweden, Denmark, numerous countries in Europe, as well as neighboring factions in Norway. The Vikings were masters of the sea and the bows of the Norwegian ships were adorned with carved figures of dragons and wild beasts and their approach terrorized their enemies. By the beginning of the eleventh century, the raids were beginning to subside. By this time Christianity had virtually been accepted by most of Norway's inhabitants. Harald the Hard's defeat in 1066 AD in the Battle of Stamford Bridge brought an end to the Viking age.

Harald I Fairhair
THE FIRST KING OF NORWAY

Harald I Fairhair

1

The First King of All Norway

Harald Harfagr, Harald Lufa, Harald Finehair, Harald Mop-Hair, Harald Harfagri, Harald I Harfagre

Son of Halfdan the Black and Ragnhild (daughter of Sigurd Hart, King of Ringerike)

b.c850[1] d.c933 (c83 yrs.)
R.c872–930
Harald had at least eight wives/mistresses[2] and twenty-three (or more)
   Children—twenty sons and three daughters.
m1)Asa
   Guttorm (son)
   Halfdan the Black (son)
   Halfdan the White (son)
   Sigrod (son)
m2)Gyda
   Alof Arbot (daughter)
   Rorek (son)
   Sigtrygg (son)
   Frode (son)
   Thorgils (son)
m3)Svanhild
   Olav Geirstatha-Alf II (son)
   Bjorn the Chapman (son)
   Ragnar Rykkil (son)
m4)Alvhild
   Dag (son)
   Hring (son)
   Guthroth Skirja (son)
   Ingegerd (daughter)
m5)Snafrid
   Sigurd Hrisi "The Bastard" (son)
   Halfdan Halegg "Longshank" (son)
   Guthroth Ljomi "The Radiant" (son)

Ragnvald Rettilbein (son)
m6)Ragnhild
    Erik Bloodaxe (#2) (son)
m7)Thora
    Haakon the Good (#3) (son)
m8)Mother unknown
    Ingeborg (daughter)

Harald I Fairhair is acknowledged by historians as the first king of all of Norway. He inherited considerable property from his father, who died in a drowning accident when Harald was ten years of age. He also inherited his father's aggressiveness and his forceful pursuit of power.

He began his Viking career at age twelve, which was customary during this period of history. When he was fifteen, in about 865, he led his *bird* (followers)[3] across the mountain, with the guidance of his maternal uncle, Guttorm. Harald also gained the support of a powerful chieftain, Jarl Haakon Grjotgarthsson (son of Grjotgarth), who ruled over that part of Norway around Trondheim. Harald resided in Trondheim during the winter months, and set up his main estate there, called Hlathir. That same winter, when Harald was about sixteen years of age he married Jarl Haakon's daughter, Asa, and they had four children, which strengthened the relationship.

There were, however, many enemies. By combining forces, Harald and Jarl Haakon, began to bring the petty kings in the regions under their control. Jarl Haakon lost two sons in the fierce Battle of Solskjel in 866 and 867.

Another story always related to Harald was his ardent and passionate interest in Gyda. It is quite certain that he married Asa first, but Harald was noted for having a wandering eye. When he was in his late teens, he was enraptured by his love for Gyda, a young Swedish princess. He sent his emissaries to invite her to become his bride. (The whereabouts of Asa is anyone's guess!) She replied haughtily that she would not marry "a petty kingling," but wanted a man who controlled a whole country. Gyda was a wise princess and knew about the great kings in countries to the south. Gyda's answer only stirred Harald's ambitions further, and he vowed to conquer all of Norway. He swore that during this time he would neither cut nor comb his mop of beautiful blond hair.

After many alliances and battles, Harald, in 872, won a decisive victory in the battle of Hafrsfjord (near the present city of Stavanger), which usually is considered as the date of the unification of all of Norway. (However, modern historians place the date as closer to 900 AD.)

Harald again sent word to Gyda to ask for her hand. This time she willingly agreed to become his wife.

Snorri tells about Harald's haircut: "King Harald now went to the baths, and had his hair dressed; and Jarl Ragnvald of More clipped his hair, which had been unshorn and uncombed for ten years. Previously he had been known as Harald Lufa—Harald Mop-Hair, but Jarl Ragnvald now gave him a new nickname and called him Harald Harfagri, Harald FineHair, and everyone who saw him agreed that it was most appropriate, for he had a truly magnificent head of hair."

Harald's reign was not a peaceful time, as many aggressors from neighboring kingdoms did not want to give up their kingdoms without a struggle. Many of these men migrated to other shores where their opportunities seemed greater. One of these was Rollo,[4] who later became the Norwegian conqueror of Normandy. During the years that followed, numerous battles were fought, but Harald managed to remain in power.

Harald Fairhair resided on the large estates he controlled in central Norway, and his children usually resided with their mothers. Although he had some difficulties with his many sons, he was still able to rule with a firm hand. However when King Harald became eighty years of age, in about 930 AD, he became so disabled that it was not possible to journey about in the country and conduct the business of a king.

Harald then began to distribute his kingdom, and led his favorite son, Erik Bloodaxe, to his high-seat and gave him the power over all the land.

The Trondheim District he gave to Halfdan the Black, Halfdan the White, and Guthroth, and the people were pleased with this arrangement. Erik, however, was not too happy about this. After King Harald

Gyda

Fairhair's death, Erik was to occupy the Vik district, but the people of Trondheim favored Guttorm. Each son considered his area too small, and some of them went on plundering raids. On one of these expeditions Guttorm was killed, and on another Halfdan the White was killed. Erik Bloodaxe was responsible for the murder of almost all of his half-brothers, and the people of Norway hated him for this.

One winter Erik was being entertained in the north, and Halfdan the Black heard about this. He went there and surrounded Erik's house and burned it, but Erik had fled. Erik then went to King Harald Fairhair with this news and Harald was very angry, and planned to kill Halfdan the Black. A skald intervened between father and son, and a qualified peace was agreed upon.

Halfdan the Black occupied the king's high-seat and took over the government of the whole Province of Trondheim, and all the people agreed to that action. After the fall of Bjorn the Chapman, his brother Olav Geirstatha-Alf II, assumed the government of Vestfold and fostered Bjorn's son, Guthroth. Olav's son was called Tryggve. He and Guthroth were foster brothers of about the same age. Both were youths of great promise and the most energetic disposition. Tryggve excelled all others in size and strength. The inhabitants of Vik learned that the people of Horthaland had made Erik their overlord. They took Olav Geirstatha-Alf II, to be overlord of the Vik District, and he assumed the power there. This greatly angered Erik. Two years later Halfdan the Black died suddenly at a banquet in the Trondheim District. People said that Gunnhild Kingsmother,[5] Erik Bloodaxe's wife, had bribed a witch to prepare a poisoned drink for him. The people of Trondheim then chose as their king, Sigrod, another son of Harald and Asa.

Only three daughters are listed among Harald's many children. He married them to *jarls*[6] within his kingdom, and great families are descended from them.

Harald was probably the only king of Norway who was wholly heathen. However, he must have foreseen the coming of Christianity, when he sent his youngest son, Haakon, to be fostered, and later baptized, by King Athelstan, the Christian king of England.

In about 933, Harald Fairhair died of "a sickness" in Rogaland, and there stands a church. Close by the churchyard lies the mound of King Harald I Fairhair. In the middle of the mound is Harald's grave. One stone was placed at his head and another at his feet, and a slab was placed above him. It is there now, the burial spot of King Harald I, the first king of Norway.

Harald I Fairhair is remembered chiefly on two accounts: for creating a unified Norwegian realm, and for his romance with Gyda, by which he got his name of Harald Fairhair.

Harald was the greatest of the warrior chiefs who fought their way to power and wealth in the ninth century in Norway. He was the first who could, to any degree, claim to be the king of the whole country.

King Harald I Fairhair's Wives and Children

We cannot leave King Harald without taking a more intimate look at the interesting lives of his wives and children.

ASA: She was the daughter of Jarl Haakon Grjotgarthsson. All of Asa and Harald's children were brought up in the Trondheim area.

GUTTORM: Born about 884. He was the oldest of Harald and Asa's sons and had the defense of the Vik District under him. One day he sailed his warships out into the Oslo Fjord. When he laid anchor, Solvi Klofi (a king in More) came up and entered the battle and Guttorm was slain.

HALFDAN THE BLACK: Ruled, under his father, in the Trondheim area. Halfdan was born about 886. He had two wives—both named Ragnhild. He died suddenly at a banquet in the Trondheim District, and people said that Gunnhild Kingsmother[3] had bribed a witch to prepare a poisoned drink for him. The people of Trondheim then chose as their king, Sigrod, his younger brother.

HALFDAN THE WHITE: Ruled with his twin brother, Halfdan the Black, in the Trondheim area. Married Asa.[7] He was on a Viking expedition to England with his brother when he was killed in battle.

SIGROD: Became king of the Trondheim District after the death of Halfdan the Black, but was killed in a battle with one of his many half-brothers.

GYDA: Daughter of King Erik of Horthaland, Sweden. A young princess, a maiden of great beauty and high spirits.

ALOF ARBOT: She was Arbot, which means "Improver of the seasons and their produce." She married Jarl Thorir the Silent of Rognvald over More. Alof was the mother of Bergljot.

ROREK: (son)

SIGTRYGG: (son)

FRODE: (son) Was killed by a poisonous drink.

THORGILS: (son) Ruled over Dublin for some time.

SVANHILD: Dauther of Jarl Eystein.

OLAV GEIRSTATHA-ALF II: Also known as Olav Digerbein. He ruled in Viken, Raumarike and Vingulmark. Had a son, Tryggve, who became the father of King Olav Trygvasson.

BJORN THE CHAPMAN: He was a shrewd man of a calm disposition, and considered to have the makings of a good ruler. His father gave him control over Vestfold, and he apparently owned several ships and was known as a merchant (*kaupmann*). Bjorn did not engage much in warfare. He had a good marriage, and had a son, Guthroth. However, Erik Bloodaxe, his half brother, was determined to eradicate anyone who stood in his way in gaining full control of Norway. In about 927 he surprised Bjorn and his followers in the middle of the night and killed him and his men. The sagas say that Erik murdered him "with his own hands." The people of Vik were very angry about this, and hated Erik. Bjorn's son, Guthroth, and his cousin, Tryggve—two small "blue-blooded" boys—fled to Oppland and escaped Erik's wrath. (Anyone with royal blood was a threat to Erik Bloodaxe.) After King Erik fled to England, his successor, King Haakon I the Good (#3), brought the two boys back. They are both important in history: Guthroth was destined to be the grandfather of Saint Olav, and Tryggve the father of Olav Trygvasson. Guthroth ruled Vestfold during Haakon's reign (933–960), but was murdered by King Harald Graycloak, Erik's son, in 969. However, the following year, the Danish king, Harald Bluetooth accompanied by Guthroth's son, Harald Grenske, and Haakon Ladejarl (#5), took control again of Norway. Harald Grenske was made a "petty king" of Vestfold, but was to pay tribute to Denmark. Norway continued to be administered by petty kings until the arrival of Saint Olav.

RAGNAR RYKKIL: (son)

ALVHILD: Alvhild was the daughter of Hring Dagsson of Ringerike.
DAG: (son)
HRING: (son)
GUTHROTH SKIRJA: (son)
INGEGERD: (daughter)

SNAFRID: She was the daughter of Svasi of Finland. It happened that one winter, King Harald Fairhair went to visit Svasi's father. When he got there, Snafrid poured him a cup of tea and Harald was immediately taken by her great beauty and wanted to immediately "share her bed." Svasi objected unless they were married, and consequently King Harald and Snafrid were united. Harald loved her madly and they had four sons. Then Snafrid died, and Harald sat by her side and refused to have her buried. This continued for three years and the people were sorry for Harald because they thought he was bewitched.

Finally, a wise man convinced Harald that he had neglected his country and freed him of his sorcery. Harald relented and as they removed Snafrid's body "all kinds of worms, frogs and toads crawled out of it," and her body was burned. This brought Harald back to his senses and he returned to Norway and continued to rule his kingdom. Harald then refused to have anything to do with his sons by Snafrid, but later he accepted them. They all grew up to be gallant men, well trained in all accomplishments.

SIGURD HRISI "THE BASTARD" (SON): Sigurd had a son called Halfdan.

HALFDAN HALEGG "LONGSHANK" (SON): Slain in the Orkney Islands.

GUTHROTH LJOMI "THE RADIANT" (SON): One winter Guthroth was to visit his foster father, Thjotholf of Hvinir. His ship was fully manned as he journeyed north. A great storm came up, and his foster father warned him about taking out to sea. Guthroth stubbornly[8] refused to heed his advice and the ship sank and everyone on board perished.

RAGNVALD RETTILBEIN "THE STRAIGHT LIMBED" (SON): He learned magic and became a sorcerer. His father, King Harald Fairhair, did not like sorcerers. He warned Ragnvald, but then sent Erik Bloodaxe to Hathaland. Erik burned the hall where Ragnvald and about eighty wizards were gathered and all perished. Harald praised Erik for this deed.

There evidently were other wives and mistresses along the way because the sagas say that Harald Fairhair "put aside" eleven wives before he married Ragnhild. From one of the *Sagas*:

> The high-born liege-lord
> chose the lady from Denmark,
> broke with his Rogaland loves
> and his lemans of Horthland,
> the maidens of Halogaland
> and of Hathaland eke.

RAGNHILD: Ragnhild was Princess of Denmark. She was known as "Ragnhild the Powerful." To show his rank, and to establish himself as an equal to the kings in other countries, Harald Fairhair chose her as his queen, scorning (as the skalds say) women of lower birth. She was the daughter of King Erik of Denmark. She died three years after they were married. They had one son.

ERIK I BLOODAXE: So-called because of his fierce, bloodthirsty nature. He succeeded Harald Fairhair as king. Although Erik was not the oldest son, Harald gave him preference to his other sons because his mother, Princess Ragnhild, was the daughter of the king of Denmark. After his mother died, Erik went to be fostered by Hersir Thorir in the Fjord District and was raised there. Harald loved him more than all his other sons, and when he was twelve years old, gave him five warships and for the next four years Erik went on many raiding expeditions. Harald Fairhair eventually made him his successor to the throne.

THORA: When King Harald was almost seventy years old, he had a son with a woman called Thora Morstrstong whose kin lived on the Island of Morstr. She was of "good family," and was a most attractive woman. She was called the King's hand-maid. When their first child was to be born, she wanted to be with Harald. To accomplish this, she set sail on a ship belonging to Jarl Sigurd (Hlathajarl), and he accompanied her. When they anchored that night, near the land, Thora gave birth to her son on a slab of rock at the head of the pier. It was the custom to choose very carefully the person who was to sprinkle a newborn child with water and select a name for a child of noble birth. It was also necessary that this be done as soon as a child was born. This was a pagan ritual, and was similar to the Christian baptism. Thora chose Jarl Sigurd to perform this ceremony. Sigurd was a wealthy man and exceedingly wise. He also was married to Bergljot, Harald I Fairhair's granddaughter and therefore of a noble family. He chose Haakon, after his grandfather, Jarl of Hlathir.

HAAKON: He was destined to become King Haakon the Good (#3), the third king of Norway. He grew up to be handsome and of great size, and looked much like his father, King Harald I Fairhair.

UNKNOWN MOTHER: Probably a mistress:

INGEBORG: Snorri lists her as a daughter of King Harald I Fairhair. Ingebjorg married Jarl Halfdan. She had a daughter named Gunnhild, who had several sons, one of whom became the father of Eyvind Skaldaspillir, a renowned Icelandic skald.

Perhaps there were more wives, and very likely more children. We will probably never know, and it will remain a mystery like many of the events that occurred during the Viking period of history.

1. Various sources give Harald's birthdate as anywhere from 850 to 880.
2. During this time, it was not at all uncommon for men, especially kings, to have more than one wife/mistress; however, they did not live in the same household. It was customary for the children to remain with their mother at her residence.
3. *Hird.* See glossary.
4. *Rollo.* See glossary.
5. A name referring to the wife of Erik Bloodaxe, an aggressive and brutal woman.
6. See glossary for additional information on jarls.
7. Not to be confused with Harald I Fairhair's wife.
8. A strong Norwegian trait!

Erik I Bloodaxe
2

Eirik Blodoks, Erik Bloodyaxe

Son of Harald Fairhair (#1) and Ragnhild Eriksdatter

b.c895 d.954 at Stainmore, England (c59 yrs.)
R.c930–934
m.Gunnhild, Princess of Denmark, b.c914 d.c999 at about 85 years of age,
    daughter of King Gorm the Old and Thyre, Queen of England
      Children: 8 sons and 1 daughter
          Ragnvald
          Gamli
          Guttorm
          Harald (#4), later became king of Norway
          Ragnfred
          Ragnhild (daughter)
          Erling
          Guthroth
          Sigurd Slefa

Of all his sons, King Harald Fairhair loved Erik the best and held him in the highest honor, probably because Erik's mother was a Danish princess. When he was twelve years old, Harald gave him five warships. Erik went on raiding expeditions and was gone for four years. Then he left again for another four years, going as far as Russia, where he fought a great battle and was victorious. He was then about twenty years old.

Snorri relates this story, that was written by a skald (court poet) of how Erik met his wife, Gunnhild:

> In a hut, his men found a woman so beautiful that they had never seen the like of her. Her name was Gunnhild. "I have dwelt here," she said, "to learn sorcery from two Finns who are the wisest here in Finland. Just now they are gone on a hunt. Both want to marry me, and both are so clever that they can

follow a track like dogs, both on open ground and hard frozen snow. They run so well on skis that nothing can escape them, whether humans or animals, and whatever they shoot at they hit. In this way they have killed all men who have approached here. If they become enraged the ground turns about as they look at it, and any living thing falls down dead. Now you must not encounter them, if you value your lives, unless I hide you here in the hut. Then we shall try if we can kill them."

They agreed to that, and she hid them. She took a linen sack that they thought contained ashes. She put her hand in it and strewed the contents about the hut, both outside and inside. Shortly afterwards the Finns returned home. They asked who had been there. She said that no one had been there. The Finns thought it strange that they had followed tracks right to the hut but then did not find them. They kindled a fire and prepared their food. When they had eaten their fill, Gunnhild made up her bed. The last three nights passed in this wise that Gunnhild slept, but the others had kept awake with mutual jealousy.

Then she said, "Come here now, and each of you lie on his side of me." They were glad to do so. She put an arm around the neck of both. They soon fell asleep, but she roused them. Then they soon fell asleep again, and so soundly that she was scarcely able to wake them. They fell asleep again, and now she was not able to wake them by any means; she even set them up, but they kept on sleeping. Then she took two large bags and placed them over their heads, tying them fast under their arms. Then she made a sign to the king's men, and they leapt forward, killing them, and dragged them out of the hut. During the night there came such a tremendous thunderstorm that they could not leave, but in the morning they went to their ship, taking Gunnhild along and bringing her to Erik. Then they sailed south and Erik contacted Gunnhild's father (Ozur Toti) and asked if he could marry his daughter, and he consented. So Erik married her.

This story, as told by Snorri in *Heimskringla*, portrays Gunnhild as Ozur Toti's daughter. Most sources state she is the daughter of King Gorm of Denmark. The latter is probably true, but where did Snorri pick up the interesting story? Was he romanticizing? Surely, it seems that Gunnhild was regarded as having supernatural powers. Gunnhild was a very beautiful woman, shrewd and skilled in magic, friendly of speech, but full of deceit and cruelty. It is very probable that Gunnhild was sent to live with Ozur Toti to learn magic, and that he was then her foster father. We will let the readers make their own conclusions.

At about this time, Erik's father, King Harald Fairhair, appointed Erik to rule jointly with him, from 928 to 930, and then made him sole king in 930 AD. Erik was a large and handsome man, strong and of great prowess, a great and victorious warrior, but violent of disposition, cruel, gruff, and taciturn.

Erik's reign, from about 930 to approximately 934, was troubled and short. He was intensely jealous of his brothers and half-brothers, fearing they would gain control. He killed several of them—some historians say he was responsible for the death of all of his brothers. The first to fall was his half-cousin, Bjorn the Chapman, who was murdered in the dead of night. Bjorn's brother, Olav Geirstatha-Alf II, and another half-brother, Halfdan, were also murdered by Erik in 933, as they were plotting to defy him. Also in danger of their lives because of their potential claim to the throne, were his two nephews, Tryggve and Guthroth, but they escaped until Erik was exiled to England, at which time they returned to Norway to claim their rightful inheritances.

The severity of Erik's rule riled his subjects and he was overthrown and exiled by his half-brother, Haakon I the Good. This was in about 934, and Erik never returned to Norway. With a few troops who wished to follow him, he sailed west—first to the Orkney Islands. Then King Athelstan, the king of England, who had been a friend of his father, King Harald Fairhair, offered him a dominion in England. Erik took over as ruler of Northumberland in 948, and made York his home. Within a year his subjects drove him out, but he returned to York, and ruled again from 952 until 954. Soon afterwards he was killed in the Battle of Stainmore in England at about forty-four years of age.

Whether Erik contributed much to the entrance of Christianity in Norway is debatable. He is often cited as the being the last truly heathen king to rule in Norway. However, while he was in England, after he had to flee from Norway, he allowed himself to be baptized and he at this later date accepted Christianity. Apparently his wife and children were also baptized. This was according to the wishes of King Athlestan, who was a Christian and Erik needed to keep in his good graces at that time.

After Erik's death Gunnhild took over, and was determined that her sons would eventually regain control of Norway and become kings. She was driven out of England, and went to the Orkneys where her daughter lived. Later she returned to Denmark to be with her father. One of her sons, Harald (#4), did become king in 961, but had no male descendants. He was killed in an ambush in about 971.

"Gunnhild and her sons" as they were often called, played an important part in Viking history, so we will give you a little information about each. All of the sons were very handsome men, strong, and accomplished in bodily skills. They were cruel, but courageous, and great warriors and often victorious.

RAGNVALD—Ragnvald died at about age seven. He is not listed in *Heimskringla*.

GAMLI—After his father died in 954, the king of Denmark outfitted Gamli with a large army. They sailed to Norway to try to take over Norway from his uncle, King Haakon the Good (#4). However, Haakon received word of their approach, and after seeking council, decided to prepare for battle. He had only nine ships, and the sons of Gunnhild, with Gamli as their leader, had twenty ships. However, due to Haakon's excellent military strategy, the sons of Gunnhild saw their men fall, and turned and fled. All of the sons jumped into the water to escape, and managed to get back to their ships, but Gamli Eriksson died in this battle.

GUTTORM—The sons of Gunnhild sailed from Denmark. As they were approaching Vik, they made raids all along the Norwegian coast. King Haakon the Good (#3) heard about this, and gathered a large force and met them in a fierce encounter. Guttorm was killed in this battle by King Haakon. The other sons sailed back to Denmark where they remained for a long time.

HARALD II GRAYCLOAK (#4)—Harald became king of Norway in about 961. King Harald Bluetooth of Denmark had accepted Harald as his foster son and adopted him. He was brought up there at the court of the Danish king, Harald Bluetooth who was his uncle. King Harald Graycloak reigned for about nine years. He was killed in battle in 970 in an ambush laid by Jarl Haakon (#5) with the help of Harald Bluetooth of Denmark.

RAGNFRED—After one winter in the Orkney Islands, Ragnfred outfitted an expedition and sailed east to Norway. He fought with Jarl Haakon, and Ragnfred fled to his ships. He lost 360 of his men in this battle, and immediately sailed from Norway. Jarl Haakon restored Norway to peace and remained there that fall and winter.

RAGNHILD—The only daughter of Gunnhild and Erik. She married Arnfinn, Duke of Orkney, the son of Thorfinn Hausakljuf (Thorfinn "Skullcleaver" or "Skull-Splitter"), a prominent jarl in Denmark. He was murdered,and she married his brother Havard "Season-Prosperous," Duke of Orkney. He was killed and she married Jarl Ljot.

ERLING—Gunnhild taunted her remaining sons to regain the throne. "Let Harald and Erling remain in North More this fall. I shall go with you. Then all of us together shall try to see what will come of it." They followed this plan of Gunnhilds.

Harald and Erling sailed into the Trondheim Fjord with four ships and many troops. They set fire to Jarl Sigurd's house and it burned down with all of his company. This was in about 963. They then sailed to More where they stayed for a long time. Gunnhild now was responsible for the killing of another claimant to the throne.

GUTHROTH—Guthroth, with the help of Gunnhild, had been raiding in England ever since he fled from Jarl Haakon. In the summer of 999, when King Olav Trygvasson (#6) had been the king of Norway for four years, Guthroth came to Norway with many warships. He had sailed from England, and when he caught sight of land in Norway, he steered south along the coast line. There was less chance of meeting King Olav Trygvasson on this route and he sailed southeast toward Vik. When he landed, he began to fight and force people into submission, requiring them to acknowledge him as king. The people of the country saw that a large fleet had descended upon them, and they begged for peace and expressed their willingness to come to an agreement. They offered to have an assembly called and agreed to accept Guthroth as their king. Then King Olav Trygvasson's kin sailed north to Vik and one night came to the place where King Guthroth was being entertained. King Guthroth was killed there.

SIGURD SLEFA—Sigurd raped Hersir Klypp's wife, and Herser Klypp killed him. Another violent death in the family.

King Erik died in 954. Although one of his sons, Harald II Graycloak returned to Norway and reigned as king from about 961 to 970, he had no male heirs. By the year 999, Gunnhild and all her sons were dead. Gunnhild died at about age eighty-five and outlived all of her sons. Erik's genetic bloodline never again was able to take control of Norway.

Haakon I the Good
3

Hakon I, Hakon den Gode, Haakon Adalsteinfostre, Haakon Haraldsson

Son of Harald I Fairhair (#1) and Thora Morstrstong

b.c.920 d.961 (c.41 yrs.). killed in a battle at Fitjar, Norway, fighting King
    Erik Bloodaxe's (#2) sons
R.c.934–961[1]
√.Thora Mostaff
    Children:
        Thora
        (No male heirs)

Haakon was King Harald I Fairhair's (#1) youngest son, and reportedly also one of his favorites. He lived with his mother on the royal estates when he was young. However, with so many older brothers, Haakon's chances of succeeding to be king were slim, so Harald made a treaty with his good friend, King Athelstan of England, and send Haakon there to be "fostered" and educated. Children were often fostered to give them opportunities that were unavailable at home.

Haakon grew up in England, probably spending most of his time in the old royal city of Winchester. He was reared in the English courts and had as his companions a son of the king of Scotland and a prince from France who later became Louis IV.

Snorri says Athelstan had Haakon christened and taught him the right faith and good habits and "all kinds of learning and manners." He loved him much more than he did all his own kin, and so did everyone who knew the boy. He was later called Athelstan's foster son.

Snorri states, "Haakon was a young man, beautiful to behold, in a golden helmet and with a fine sword in his hand. He was the greatest in sports, bigger and stronger and more handsome than any other. He was wise, of fair speech, and a good Christian."

When Haakon was fifteen some Norwegians came to England, and told him of their dissatisfaction with his half-brother, Erik II Bloodaxe (#2), and no doubt invited him to Norway. Sigurd, Jarl of Lade[2], the most prominent man among Erik's opponents, probably originated the plan of getting Haakon to claim the throne, both because he had an affection for the boy and because he thought it a good plan for himself personally and for the country. Jarl Sigurd was a very shrewd man. Haakon accepted the invitation, and King Athelstan furnished him a fleet. He sailed to Norway and seized the throne from his half-brother, Erik Bloodaxe, who then fled to England.

Haakon the Good, as he became known, was Norway's first Christian king. Although he was the most powerful man in Norway, his efforts to introduce Christianity into Norway had little success. He was unable to instill the Christian faith on his native pagan country. He did, however, bring priests from England and built churches in the coastal area of western Norway.

Haakon was not successful in establishing Christianity, but he did manage to unite most of the country again and defend its independence. He established a naval defense, by which each of the coastal regions had to place a fully manned ship at the king's disposal for a certain period of time each year. He introduced a system of warning of approaching danger by means of bonfires on the mountain peaks. Within seven days this enabled Norway to have a somewhat advanced defense system. He also successfully developed codes of law and administration into various areas in Norway, including a court of appeals.

Haakon the Good was a great warrior, but he had to keep close watch over his country. He was concerned that Erik might reappear, but when he heard that Erik had died, and that Erik's sons had fled from England, he was no longer worried. However, one summer when he was residing in the northern part of Norway, he heard rumors that the Danes were causing trouble in the southern part, so he journeyed there with his army. When the Danes heard that Haakon had arrived, they fled, but King Haakon sailed after them with all his forces. A great battle followed, and King Haakon fought so valiantly that he advanced in front of his troops without either his helmet or coat of mail. A skald wrote a heroic poem about his brilliant victory. He later battled eleven enemy ships, and came out the winner, and after this, sailed up and down the coast, returning with considerable booty.

King Haakon was a most cheerful person, very eloquent, and most kindly disposed. He was a man of keen understanding and laid great stress on legislation. Haakon ruled wisely, both on land and sea. His popularity was responsible for his name, Haakon the Good. There were good crops in the land, and there was peace for both merchants and farmers, and they did not harm each other or destroy their neighbor's property. He apparently did not marry, but with a mistress, Thora had a daughter, also named Thora.

However, there was more trouble ahead for King Haakon. He heard that the sons of Erik Bloodaxe were invading the southern part of Norway. Haakon immediately put together a large force and sailed south. Both armies met on shore and fought a fierce battle. Haakon came to blows with King Guttorm, Erik's son, and many of his followers, but King Haakon won the battle. Haakon pursued the remaining sons of Erik into the open seas, and they sailed south to Denmark, and remained there for a long time.

The sons of Erik then began to engage constantly in raids on the Norwegian coast. In about 954, when Haakon the Good had been king for about twenty years, they gathered a large army and approached without warning. A fierce battle was fought and ended when the sons of Erik retreated, plunging into the water to escape to their ships. There, Gamli, Erik's oldest son, died, but the others survived and retreated again to Denmark. Harald, Gamli's brother, took over as head of Erik's sons after Gamli died.

After King Haakon had reigned for about twenty-six years, Harald Graycloak, Erik's son, unexpectedly attacked Norway with a large fleet of warships. The sagas say that the sons of Erik had six times as large an army as Haakon. The battle that followed was fought furiously, and the swords, javelins and missiles flew "as thick as a fall of snow." King Haakon was in front of his men—his helmet glittering as the sun shone upon it. As he reigned blows with his sword, he was suddenly struck by an arrow that entered a muscle just below the shoulder. However, the sons of Eric and their forces retreated, and they fled to their ships. Many were killed.

King Haakon returned to his warship, but his wound bled profusely and he knew that his death was near. He than called his friends to his side and said that since he had no male heirs, Erik's sons be notified that they would be kings over all of Norway.[3] He requested that they should show tolerance to his followers. On his deathbed, King Haakon the Good, asked to be able to live among Christians and do penance for his sins against God. Ironically, however, when he died he was given a pagan burial, in full armor, and sent on his way to Valhalla, "the glorious heaven of the heathen warriors." A *skald* wrote about King Haakon's last great battle, and about his welcome to Valhalla:

> Unbound against the dwellings of men
> the Fenris-wolf shall go
> before a king as good as he
> walks on that empty path.

Haakon the Good was forty-one years of age when he died and was the last of Harald I Fairhair's sons to rule.

---

1. Later historians state that his reign more reliably approximates 946-961AD
2. Jarl Sigurd was the father of Jarl Haakon of Lade (#5).
3. It is necessary to keep in mind that to be king you had to be a male descendant of a king. However, it is hard to believe that after fighting Erik's sons for over twenty years, Haakon was willing to bequeath Norway to them. But that is Snorri's version.

Harald II Graycloak
4

Harald Grafeldr, Harald Greypelt, Harald Grafell, Harald Gray-Skin, Harald Greycloak

Son of Erik Bloodaxe and Gunnhild

b.c935 d.970 (c35 yrs.)
R.c961–970
Probably not married, and had no sons

Harald was brought up at the court of his uncle, King Harald Bluetooth of Denmark, who accepted him as his foster son and adopted[1] him.

In 961, when Haakon the Good (#3) died, Harald, as the oldest living son of Erik and Gunnhild, returned to Norway as king, but it was not an easy time for him. For the past twenty-six years he and his family had been enemies of King Haakon I (#3) and many battles had been fought between them. It was necessary to reconcile the differences that existed between the various kingdoms. The chieftain in eastern Norway was Tryggve Olavsson, and in Vestfold, Guthroth Bjarnarson—both Harald's cousins who had to flee from Norway when Erik Bloodaxe (#2) reigned. In the Trondheim area Sigurd Hlathajarl was ruling, and this left the western part for King Harald Graycloak and his family.

King Harald Graycloak began negotiations. It was agreed that Tryggve and Guthroth would have the same kingdoms that they had under King Haakon. A similar agreement was made with Jarl Sigurd, and after that they hoped they had established peace.

All of the sons of Gunnhild had been baptized when they lived in England, but they had little success in establishing Christianity in Norway. Haakon the Good did make a sincere effort, but the time was not right. Harald Graycloak tried to rid

Norway of paganism, but his destruction of pagan sacrifices only brought him more hostility. In spite of his ruthless rule, he is credited with establishing the first Christian missions in Norway. However, when he prohibited the public worship of pagan gods, it brought opposition.

As time went on, Gunnhild was dissatisfied with the amount of power they had. She nagged her sons, insisting that they should at least regain power in the Trondheim district since Jarl Sigurd was not of royal blood. Her sons said this would be most difficult, so Gunnhild decided they would try to make more friends in the area, and get rid of Jarl Sigurd by other means.

Gunnhild was a scheming and clever woman. She managed to bribe Sigurd's friends with gifts and favors and consequently, in about 963, they turned against Sigurd and set his house on fire. Jarl Sigurd and his followers died. Sigurd's son, Jarl Haakon, immediately took over and maintained the reign at Trondheim, so Gunnhild's sons were still not able to collect any revenue from the province. As time passed, an uncertain friendship was established between Gunnhild's sons and Jarl Haakon.

A story relates how King Harald II got the name of Harald Graycloak. One summer a ship arrived from Iceland with a cargo of sheepskin cloaks. They steered into the Harthangerfjord because they heard there was a large gathering there, and they wanted to sell their wares. However, no one wanted to buy the cloaks. The skipper knew King Harald II and went to see him about his problem. Harald was a kindly disposed man and of a very cheerful disposition, so he boarded his skiff and sailed up to the skipper's ship. He asked if he could have one of the sheepskin cloaks and the skipper gladly agreed. King Harald flung the cloak across his shoulders, and immediately all of his men wanted similar cloaks. Consequently, the skipper happily disposed of all of his cargo, and from then on Harald was known as Graycloak. (Fashion was fashion—even then!)

One fall, the three remaining rulers of Norway, under King Haakon, got together at a secret meeting and agreed to be mutual friends. They were Jarl Haakon, Tryggve Olafsson, and Guthroth Bjarnarson. Gunnhild heard about this meeting and suspected treachery, so she arranged to have King Tryggve invited to join her son, Guthroth, on his ship.

Shortly afterwards, Harald Graycloak learned that Guthroth Bjarnarson was being entertained nearby. He sent his troops over and Guthroth was killed, along with twelve of his followers. Now Gunnhild had eliminated two more "blue blood" relatives from the picture.

Harald Graycloak was handsome, strong and excelled in athletics, as did all the sons of Erik and Gunnhild. However, Harald was not popular. He ruled harshly as his grandfather, Harald Fairhair, had done. He had killed the men whom he feared most—his own cousins, Tryggve and Sigurd, who were kings in the Oslo area. He also set fire to the house where the Jarl of Lade had his men gathered, and they died.

Harald Graycloak was almost constantly at war with Sweden and also with the Danes. He wanted to become a really independent ruler of all of Norway, and assume control over the Vik region, the section that the Danish king claimed. So the Danes plotted with Jarl Haakon, the exiled son of the murdered Jarl Sigurd. In the battle that followed in 970, King Harald Graycloak was killed. An ambush had been laid for him by Jarl Haakon, with the help of Harald Bluetooth.

Harald Graycloak is probably buried in Denmark.

1. In Lee Hollander's translation, Snorri uses the word "adopted," but it probably means Harald was fostered by King Harald Bluetooth and was raised in his household.

Haakon of Lade, Jarl
5

Hakon Jarl (Ladejarl), Jarl the Mighty, Haakon Sigurdsson, Haakon the Great

Son of Jarl Sigurd Grjotgarthsson, from the mighty Norwegian family of the Jarls of More from Trondelag, and Bergljot Thoresdatter, the granddaughter of Harald I Fairhair

b.c935 d.995 murdered (c60 yrs.)
R.c970–995
m.Thora Skagesdatter, daughter of Skage Skoptason. She was an unusually
   beautiful woman.
     Children:
         Svein (#8), b.c970 d.1016 (c46 yrs.)
            m.Holmfrid, Princess of Sweden
         Heming: b.c968
         Bergljot: b.c985 d.after 1050
            m.Einar Tambarskelfir
     Children (illegitimate) with unknown mothers:
         Ragnhild "Ingeborg," b.c 955
            m.Skopti Skagason. Skopti was Thora's brother.
         Erik (#7), b.c964 d.1024 (c60 yrs.)
            m.Gyda Sveinsdatter, Princess of Denmark. Erik was born before
               Haakon's marriage to Thora.
         Sigurd, b.c966 d.after 985
         Erland, b.c969 d.c955
         Erling, b.c973 d.c986
         Haakonsdatter, b.c978

For the next twenty-five years, no descendants of Harald I Fairhair claimed the crown in Norway. After King Harald Graycloak (#4) was killed, the Danish king, Harald Bluetooth, accompanied Jarl Haakon of Lade to Norway with a powerful fleet and took possession of the country without meeting any resistance. Old Queen Gunnhild, Harald Graycloak's mother, with her two remaining sons took refuge with her daughter, who was married to the Jarl of the Orkney Islands. Gunnhild's sons, however, continued to have frequent battles with Jarl Haakon. Apparently Guttorm, one of her sons, ruled in Vestland from about 970 until 974 when he lost a battle with Haakon and fled. Harald Bluetooth had made Haakon a jarl, and left part of Norway for him to rule. He kept for himself part of eastern Norway, but Jarl Haakon's great victory at Horundarfjord in 985 gave him a firm rule.

Jarl Haakon owed certain financial obligations and also military aid to the Danish king. The king soon found that the jarl was not as obedient and submissive as he had hoped. When Harald Bluetooth, the Danish king died, his son, Svein Forkbeard became king of Denmark and also claimed to be king of all of Norway. He sent a fleet of ships to battle with Haakon. However, Jarl Haakon was a bold and stout-hearted warrior and won a decisive victory. Many wild and heroic stories were told about this great battle, and Haakon was honored.

Before Haakon died a few small kings in the south were still under the watchful eye of Denmark, but in most of Norway a feeling of national unity could be detected.

Haakon was an aggressive heathen, and Christianity did not flourish. The people went back to their old pagan ways. The sagas say that King Harald of Denmark had forced old Haakon to receive baptism. This so humiliated him that he broke off relations with Denmark. Toward the end of Haakon's rule, heathen worship had virtually ended and Christianity was ready to take its place. Perhaps Haakon was the last genuine heathen to rule in Norway.

Haakon was disliked by many. Success had made him arrogant. His fraternization with many of the farmers' wives, as noted by his many children born out of wedlock, was also instrumental in his downfall.

It should be noted, however, that Haakon had many qualities of leadership; a good bloodline; shrewdness; briskness in battle and also a lucky hand in winning victories. He was a most cheerful person, very eloquent, and most kindly disposed—a man of keen understanding and laid great stress on legislation. Peace ruled over all of Norway facing the sea. A jarl controlled each of the sixteen districts. There were good harvests and peace reigned. Einar Skalaglamm's poem notes the heroic qualities of Haakon of Lade:

> Where else has it e'er been
> heard before that sixteen
> jarls did under one great
> jarl rule all of Norway?

Haakon was killed in 995 by one of his own followers; a thrall called Kark while hiding in a pigsty. So Jarl Haakon the Mighty met his end at about sixty years of age. He was, however, exceedingly generous to everyone and it was unfortunate that his life ended in such a manner.

Olav I Trygvasson
"The most beautifullest man in all the annals of Norway."

Olav I Trygvasson
6

Olav I Tryggvason, Olav I

Son of *småkongen* (small king) Tryggve Olavsson from Vika (an early name for Oslo) and Astrid Eriksdatter[1] from Jaren. He was the grandson of Olav Geiristha-Alf II, and great grandson of Harald I Fairhair and Svanhild.

b.c968 d.killed in battle on 31 August 1000 (32 yrs.)
R.995–1000
m1)Geira (From Germany), b.c971 d.c990
m2)Gyda (From Ireland), b.c975
    Children:
        Tryggve Olavsson, b.c993 d.1033[2]
m3)Gudrun Skeggesdatter, b.c975
m4)Queen Thyre Haraldsdatter of Denmark, b.c978, daughter of King Blaaten of Denmark. A sister of King Svein Forkbeard of Denmark. She had two previous marriages.
    Children:
        Harald, Prince of Norway, b.999 d.1000 (1 yr.)

Olav Trygvasson, in his short reign of five years, became one of Norway's most colorful kings. Snorri states, "He was strikingly handsome, very tall and strong, and excelled all others in the accomplishments told about Norwegians."

Olav's fast-paced life began even before he was born. King Harald Graycloak (#4) had killed Olav's father, Tryggve. Astrid, Tryggve's wife, was with child and knew that her life was in danger. King Graycloak had no heirs, and would be greatly concerned if she had a son who could have possible claim to the throne in the future. Astrid immediately picked up everything she could carry and fled with all the possessions. Her foster father, Thorolf Lousebeard, accompanied her and stayed with her at all times. He rowed her out to a small island on a lake and hid her with the others. This is where her son, Olav Trygvasson, was born. He was sprinkled with water[3] and given the name, Olav, after his grandfather. (This was Olav Geirstatha-Alf II, son of King Harald I Fairhair (#1) and his wife, Svanhild.) That summer, Astrid remained in hiding. When the weather became cooler, she started out again, accompanied by Thorolf and a few others. They traveled only by night through uninhabited places, so no one saw them. Finally they reached their destination, the estate of her father, who was an important chieftain in Sweden. He knew that her life was in danger, so let them hide in a small building. They stayed there during the winter and he provided them with the best food available.

It was not long before Gunnhild, King Harald Graycloak's mother, learned that Astrid and her newborn son, Olav, were in Sweden. She sent men there and insisted that they bring them back to Norway. This failed, but Astrid decided that it was not safe to stay in Sweden any longer and fled to Russia with Olav and her brother, Sigurd. There Olav was captured and separated from his mother. He was sold to a man called Klerk in exchange for a goat. Klerk killed Olav's foster father, Thorolf Lousebeard, and did not treat Olav well. Another man then bought Olav from Klerk for a good cloak. (This was in Estonia). His name was Reas, and Olav stayed with him and his wife, Rekon, and their son Rekoni for six years and was treated well. Later, Sigurd, Olav's uncle, saw Olav, and recognized him as the son of his sister, and bought him back.

One day, while Olav Trygvasson was in the market place, he recognized Klerk, the man who had killed his foster father. Olav hit Klerk with a small axe, and killed him. Fearing for Olav's life, Sigurd immediately took Olav to the Queen in the kingdom of Valdemar the Great in Russia. She and the king protected Olav and he stayed there for nine years.[4]

At age twelve, Olav followed the example of other ambitious young princes and nobles and began his career as a Viking. The Russians gave him a ship and the sagas relate many tales of his journeys and victorious raids to almost all the shores of Europe. First he plundered in the Baltic area, then the Netherlands. In 991 he was in England. His fame allowed him to secure a fleet of 390 ships for an attack on England. This was the Battle of Maldon in Essex (southeastern England) where he won a tremendous victory, but England bought peace with Danegold, a bribe,[5] in this case, 10,000 pounds of silver.

Olav remained in Ireland and England for some time and perhaps he was baptized there. He was also confirmed by the Bishop of Winchester, with the English king as a sponsor. Being a Christian was becoming fashionable. The sagas give him credit for the conversion of the Orkney Islands to Christianity, mostly by force, in 994. By this time, he had such a zealous interest in converting his people to Christianity that he gave up his Viking raids for good.

In 995 Olav heard that Jarl Haakon (#5), who had ruled Norway since 975, had been murdered in a pigsty by one of his own people, Kark, a *thrall*.[6] Olav was then about twenty-seven years old and at the height of his power. As the great grandson of Harald I Fairhair, and heir to the throne, he quickly decided to take advantage of this opportunity. He sailed north to Trondheim and was immediately acclaimed king when he arrived. As King Olav I, he gained control over most of the western part of Norway, but never even traveled into the interior.

Olav was, in reality, a very powerful Viking sea king, whose rule depended to a large extent upon his likable personality and presence. Snorri says that "Olav could play with three swords so that one was always in the air. Brave and quick-witted he was, too, and overflowing with cheer and generous friendliness. He was the proto-type of a national hero. However, he was also stubborn, relentlessly harsh and cruel to his enemies."

Olav Trygvasson was probably the most renowned Viking of his age. The story is told that young American boys playact and want to be cowboys. Norwegian boys all clamor to be Olav Trygvasson.

One report says that Olav was married in his early youth to Geira, a princess from Vendland (the early name for Germany). This may be true. Olav had been in Vendland only three years when Geira, was "stricken with a disease" which caused her death in 990. They had no children.

Olav then went to Ireland and married Gyda, a Dublin princess. Gyda was young and handsome. She was the sister of Olav Kvaan who was a king in Ireland from 938–980. She had been married in England to a powerful jarl. When he died she maintained herself in his kingdom. A certain man in her court asked to marry her, but she said she meant to choose her husband herself. She then called the men to come before her, and they were dressed in their finest clothes. Olav was there in his work clothes. Gyda came to him and said "If you care to marry me, I will choose you." "I shall not refuse that," said Olav, and they were married. They reportedly had one son, Tryggve. Not much is noted about him. Perhaps his mother died young, and Tryggve continued to live in Ireland with his grandfather. He may not have known about his royal bloodline until he was full-grown.

After Olav was accepted as king, he began to convert the Norwegians to Christianity. Here too, it was often by force. The people in the Trondheim area rejected the King's attempt to Christianize them, and the farmers rebelled. They had a large force, and a powerful chieftain, Jarnskegge (Ironbeard), who was the leader of this group. An assembly was held, and all the people were armed. King Olav, accompanied by a few of his men, entered the temple and knocked down the idol's pedestals. While the king was inside, Jarnskegge was killed in the front of the temple, by King Olav's men. Without a leader, the rest of the men decided to quickly accept Christianity, and all were baptized.

King Olav had houses built on the bank of the Nith River so that a market town could be developed there. He gave people land so they could build houses for themselves. He built a winter home for himself. He then tried to make amends with the blood relatives of Jarnskegge, and many farmers came to make a claim against him. In a strange settlement, it was also agreed that Olav was to marry Jarnskegge's daughter, Gudrun. The marriage was celebrated and King Olav and Gudrun "mounted the same bed." Evidently this arranged marriage was not to Gudrun's liking. She had revenge on her mind. On the first night, when the king had fallen asleep, she drew a knife and was about to thrust it into him, when he awoke. He wrestled the knife from her, and as Snorri nonchalantly states, "He got out of bed, and went to his men and told them what had happened." Just as nonchalantly, Gudrun also took her clothes and left. Nor did Guthrun ever again lie in the same bed with King Olav. A short marriage!

Snorri describes Olav as a "handsome man, with a great deal of charisma." It was also said he was "the most wildly beautifullest man in all the annals of Norway."

A little later, his eye fell on Queen Sigrid, known as Sigrid the Haughty, the widow of the king of Sweden. Sigrid was looked upon as a good match by Olav, and also by King Svein Forkbeard of Denmark, as both wanted more power. Olav asked her to marry him. (What happened to his Dublin princess, we know not.) He told Sigrid to "become a Christian." She refused. He struck her with his glove and shouted that she was a "heathen like a dog." Drawing herself up to her full height, she declared, "This will be your death," and she was right.

Queen Sigrid immediately married King Svein Forkbeard of Denmark, whose first wife had died. This brought about a close relationship between Denmark and Sweden.

Meanwhile, King Svein Forkbeard arranged for his sister, Thyre, to marry Burizlaf, a king in Vendland. However, Thyre absolutely refused to marry him because he was a heathen and was too old. Burizlaf insisted that the agreement be kept. Despite her wishes she was sent, most reluctantly, to Vendland and the wedding was celebrated. Thyre

Sigrid the Haughty

wept bitterly because she was among heathens, and refused food and drink for seven days. One dark night she escaped with the help of her foster father and returned to Denmark and then to Norway.[7]

There they were welcomed at Olav Trygvasson's court. Olav found her "hand-some and well–spoken" and they were married.

This, of course, displeased both her brother, Svein Forkbeard and his wife, Sigrid the Haughty. Sigrid still had revenge on her mind, and connived to get rid of Olav Trygvasson. She nagged Svein and her son, Olav, the King of Sweden to take a stand against Norway, which they eventually did. They set sail, and when Olav Trygvasson saw them approaching, he was not prepared. He put 200 armored men, far too many, on his beautiful ship, called *The Long Serpent*, and it capsized. When Olav saw the end was evident, he jumped into the sea and was drowned. Queen Sigrid, the Haughty, had her revenge.

This was the Battle of Svold, fought in 1000 near the island of Rugen in the Baltic Sea. It is listed as the most notable battle in the history of Norway since Hafrsfjord, and is considered by historians as the first date in Norwegian history that can be generally accepted as true.

Since there is uncertainty about how Olav Trygvasson met his end, we will relate another tale, to confuse the reader.

It seems that Olav's fourth wife, Queen Thyre, became discontented with Olav for not reclaiming her dowry from King Burizlaf. To prove his worth, as both hus-band and king, he sailed south with his cherished ship, the *Long Serpent*. It was the most beautiful ship in Norway, manned by the finest body of men that had ever been assembled. In this battle, the Battle of Svold, King Olav Trygvasson was killed.

We will let the reader decide which version suits his fancy. In either case, the short, but colorful life of Olav Trygvasson was brought to an end. He was just thirty-two years old when he died.

1. After Tryggve was murdered, Astrid married Lodin and had three children: Thorkel Nefia, Ingerid, and Ingegerd.
2. For additional information on Tryggve, see Chapter 11.
3. Sprinkling with water was both a pagan and Christian custom.
4. The account of Olav's mother's flight from Norway, his childhood and his slavery in Estonia is said to be fictitious by more recent historians, but Snorri gives a detailed description of this in *Heimskringla*.
5. A bribe. See glossary.
6. Thrall. Servant. See glossary.
7. It takes a strong Scandinavian woman to perform this feat after seven days of total fasting.

Erik, Jarl
7

Erik Haakonarson, Jarl Eirik

Illegitimate son of Jarl Haakon (#5) and an attractive mistress from Oppland in
central Norway

b.c964 d.c1024 (c60 yrs.)
R.1000–1115, abdicated
m.Gyda, b.c978, daughter of King Svein Forkbeard (Svein Tjugeskjegg) of
    Denmark
        Children:
            Haakon, Jarl, b.c998 d.c1030
                m.Gunnhild Vyrtgoernsdatter

Erik, his half-brother, Svein (#8), and many other prominent kinsmen fled from
Norway after Haakon (their father) was killed in 995. Jarl Erik went to Sweden and
was well received by Olav Stotkonung, the king of Sweden. Olav gave Erik and his
men the freedom of the country so he could maintain himself and his men.

After passing one winter in Sweden, Jarl Erik left for Denmark. He asked King
Svein Forkbeard for the hand of his daughter, Gyda, and they were married. They
later had a son named Haakon, who lived in Denmark.

During the winters Erik stayed in Denmark. He had a large following, and in the
summers they took their ships and went on many warlike expeditions. Numerous
raids and battles followed.

Erik participated in the Battle of Svold, in 1000, when Olav Trygvasson (#6) was
killed. He took possession of Olav's beloved ship, the *Long Serpent*, and much booty,
and sailed away with it. A *Heimskringla* saga states:

    Thither on Long Serpent
    sailed the helm-clad chieftain[1]
    bore it a bold crew—to

baleful storm-or-arrows.
After the battle, however,
eagerly took it over
Heming's[2] high-born brother[3]
hot raged sword-fight on it.

Upon the defeat and death of Olav I Trygvasson, Erik and his half-brother, Svein, returned to their inherited kingdom of Trondelag, as they were the sons of Jarl Haakon the Mighty, who ruled before Olav I Trygvasson's short reign.

Norway was then divided between Jarl Erik, Jarl Svein, Svein Forkbeard, the king of Denmark and Olav the king of Sweden. Jarl Erik and Jarl Svein took charge of most of Norway.

Erik and Svein ruled jointly for about fifteen years. They governed well and were loved by their people, with Jarl Erik having the most to say about matters dealing with government.

Although their father was a heathen, both Jarl Erik and Jarl Svein were baptized and accepted Christianity. However, while they ruled, they let everyone in Norway do as they pleased about their religious beliefs.

Toward the end of their reign, in about 1015, Erik received a message from his brother-in-law, Knut, king of Denmark. He asked Erik to take his fleet and go with him on his conquest of England. Knut wanted him with because Erik had achieved fame for his war deeds. One of these was the battle in which Jarl Erik and his young son, Jarl Haakon, defeated the Jomsvikings, a famous army of fighting Norwegians. The other was when Erik participated and won the Battle of Svold against Olav Trygvasson in 1000 AD.

Eric's adventurous spirit moved him to accept Knut's invitation. He abdicated and relinquished his sovereign rights in Norway to his seventeen-year-old son, Jarl Haakon. The very capable and famous Einar Tambarskelfir (named for his large quivering stomach), was his advisor. Young Haakon, however, was not recognized as a ruler. Jarl Erik joined King Knut and was with him when he conquered London. He stayed in England for some time and fought many battles. He planned to make a pilgrimage to Rome, but this never happened.

Jarl Erik died in England of a "loss of blood,"[4] perhaps in about 1024 (some historians quote an earlier date). He was about sixty years of age.

1. King Olav I Trygvasson.
2. Heming is one of Erik's brothers.
3. Jarl Erik.
4. A hemorrhage?

Svein, Jarl
8

Jarl Svein, Svein Haakonarsson, Svend Haakonsson

Son of Haakon, Jarl (#5) and Thora Skagesdatter. Ruled with his half-brother, Erik I (#7).

b.c970 d.c1016 (c46 yrs.)
R. 1000–1016
m.Holmfrid, daughter of King Erik "Segersall," King of Sweden
    Children: two daughters, no sons
        Sigrid Sveinsdatter, b.c995 d.c1016. m.Aslak Erlingsson in 1015, and
            had one son and two daughters
        Gunnhild Sveinsdatter, b.c999 d.after1060. m.Svein Estridsson, King
            of Denmark. They had a daughter, Princess Ingegerd, who mar-
            ried King Olav III Kyrre (#15). Gunnhild later married King Anund
            (Jacob) Olavsson of Sweden.

When Jarl Haakon (#5) was murdered in 995, his two sons had high hopes of becoming rulers in Norway. However, Olav I Trygvasson (#6) saw this as an opportunity to lay claim to his genealogical right as king of Norway. He collected his fleet and attempted a surprise attack on Trondelag, but had to retreat before the forces of Jarl Svein. A short time later Olav was able to gain control and was accepted as king.

Both Svein and his older half-brother Erik fled—Svein to Sweden and Erik to England. In this way, they felt they would have the support of both countries. During the next few years they gathered together a large army and prepared to attack Norway. King Olav was aware of their maneuvers, and waited for them to come. When they did attack, he finally decided to take the offensive. In the year 1000 he set out with a few ships, but was met with powerful forces. This was the famous Battle of Svold, the most notable battle in the history of Norway since King Harald I Fairhair's (#1) victory in the Battle of Hafrsfjord. King Olav fought against impossible odds, and met his death. After the battle both Svein and Erik returned to Norway, and took over control.

Now there were three countries involved in the rule. King Olav of Sweden divided Norway up between himself, King Svein of Denmark, and the two brothers. Svein had married the daughter of King Olav of Sweden, and Olav made Svein a jarl. He was given the area around Trondheim in Northern Norway to rule. The kings of Sweden and Denmark had enough to do in their own countries. Norway, for the next fifteen/sixteen years was governed by Erik and Svein, with Erik, perhaps, having the most to say. Jarl Erik abdicated in about 1015 to capture England. He left his seventeen-year-old son, Haakon, to take his place and rule his portion of Norway while he was gone. Young Haakon however is not usually listed as a ruler.

A year later, Olav II Haraldsson (#9), who later became Saint Olav, decided that he had a right to the throne. He was the great-great grandson of King Harald I Fairhair (#1), and therefore was of royal blood. On his voyage up the coast of western Norway he luckily captured young Haakon, Jarl Erik's son. He set him free on the condition he would leave Norway and never fight against him. This left a part of Norway without much supervision. Olav's timing was perfect and he was greeted and accepted as the leader in all territories along the coast.

In the meantime, Jarl Svein and Einar Tambarskelfir had ships and men enough to challenge Olav. Early in the spring, on Pentecost Day (the seventh Sunday after Easter), in 1016, their fleet met up with King Olav in the Battle of Nesjar in Folden Fjord. Jarl Svein was soundly defeated, and Saint Olav became the uncontested king of Norway.

Jarl Svein fled the country and died shortly after on a Viking tour. He never made any more attempts to regain control of Norway. He was about forty-six years of age. He left no sons, but his two daughters made good marriages.

The sagas say Jarl Svein was the handsomest man in people's memory.

St. Olav
Norway's beloved saint.

Olav II - Saint Olav
9

Olav, Olav II Haraldsson, Olav the Stout, Olav Big Mouth, Olav the Farmer, Hellig Olav, Olav the Fat

Son of Harald Grenske from Vestfold and Asta Gudbrandsdatter. He was brought up by Sigurd Syr from Ringerike, who Asta married after Grenske died. Olav is the great-great grandson of Harald I Fairhair (#1).

b.c995 d.29 Jul 1030 (c35 yrs.), killed in battle at Stiklestad, Norway. Shortly thereafter he was proclaimed a Saint.
R.1016–1028 and a short time in 1030
m.Princess Astrid[1] in about 1019, daughter of King Olav Skotkonung of Sweden. Her mother was Edla Wends, a mistress.
    Children:
        Ulfhild, b.c1020 d.24 May 1071
            m.Orduld, Duke of Saxony in November of 1042, had one son,
                Duke Magnus of Brunswick
√.Alvild, the little English hand-maid. She was from a "good family."[2]
    Children:
        Magnus the Good (#12) Illegitimate, later became king. b.c1024 d. 25 Oct 1047

Let us go back to Olav's parentage. You will recall at this time, the two little blue-eyed boys who had to flee from Norway to escape the wrath of Erik Bloodaxe and his sons. After the danger was over, the boys returned to Norway. One of these boys was Guthroth Bjornsson, who was the grandson of Harald Fairhair. The other boy was Tryggve, the father of Olav Trygvasson. Guthroth married a woman of "good birth." They had a son named Harald, and when Harald was young he was sent to Grenland, a district south of Vestfold, to be fostered by Hroi the White, a king's steward. Hroi had a son named Hrani the Widely-Traveled who was about the same age as Harald. After Guthroth's fall, Harald Guthrothsson was called Harald

Grenske, and gained a name for himself in Norwegian history. As you can see, Olav II had excellent parentage.

Olav had a half-brother, Harald. Asta had married Syr after Guthroth's death and they had a son. He was also named Harald, and later became King Harald III the Hard (#13) of Norway.

In about 1007 Olav started his Viking expeditions. He would have been about twelve years old at the time. This was the age when boys were legally considered adults, but they sometimes stayed home a little longer. Olav joined a ship commanded by his foster father.

During the next few years he became a leader, and spent much time on Viking expeditions. He also fought in the army of King Ethelred II of England against the Danes.

At age eighteen he was baptized in Rouen (Normandy). A couple of years later (1015), at about age twenty, Olav returned to Norway. He decided to dethrone Jarl Svein, who he felt was not a rightful heir to the throne, since he did not have royal blood. Svein's brother had just abdicated, and when Olav took over in 1016 he extended his power over many of the smaller kings. Snorri describes Olav as follows: "Olav was not of tall stature, but of middle height and of stout frame and great strength. His hair was of light chestnut color and his face, broad, of light complexion and ruddy. His eyes were unusually fine, bright and piercing, so that it inspired terror to look into them when he was furious. Olav was a man of many accomplishments. He was a good shot, an excellent swimmer, and second to none in hurling spears. He was skilled and had a sure eye for all kinds of handicraft work, whether the things were made for himself or others."

He was nicknamed "Olav the Stout." He was bold and ready in speech, matured early in all ways, both in bodily strength and shrewdness; and he endeared himself to all his kinfolk and acquaintances. He vied with all in games and always wanted to be the first in everything, as was proper, befitting his rank and birth.

For about fifteen years Olav II worked at Christianizing Norway, and many stories are told about this. He greatly increased the acceptance of Christianity and enacted a religious code in 1024 that is considered Norway's first national legislation. During this time he also fought numerous battles. He was victorious many times and considered a famous warrior. Snorri devotes many pages to the battles of St. Olav.

However, trouble was brewing. The nobles had grown increasingly jealous of Olav's power and of his policy of promoting men of humble birth, and the farmers were tired of his zealous methods. Also, Knut II the Great of Denmark (#10) was demanding his sovereign rights over Norway. Olav's answer to this was "I will defend Norway with my sword as long as I live and I will pay tribute to no man for my kingdom."

In 1028, Knut II the Great of Denmark, gathered together a large fleet and invaded Norway. The people deserted Olav, and he fled the country to the court of his brother-in-law, the ruler of Kiev. He took his four-year-old son, Magnus, with him, and young Magnus was raised in the courts. He later became King Magnus I the Good (#12).

In the meantime, Knut II had put a Norwegian jarl, Jarl Haakon, son of Jarl Erik (#7) on the throne in Norway and left to take care of his problems in Denmark. However, Jarl Haakon died shortly thereafter, and Olav decided it would be a perfect time to reclaim his right as king of Norway.

Olav returned in about 1030 and considered himself king, but was unable to get support from his people. The small army he managed to put together was no match in the ensuing battle of Stiklestad, which is remembered as one of the most famous battles in Norwegian history. The encounter took place on approximately the 29th day of July in 1030, and was probably the shortest battle in history, as it is said that it began about 1:30 in the afternoon and was over before 3:00 PM. His men desperately

St. Olav in his earlier years

shouted their war cry of *Fram, fram, Kristmen, krossmenn, konungsmenn!* (Forward, forward, Christ's men, cross-men, king's-men), but were immediately stopped. Olav fought ferociously, and it is said that the sky darkened, at the final moments when Olav lost his life.[3]

Olav's half-brother, Harald, accompanied Olav in this battle and was severely wounded, but managed to escape. Harald (#15) was only fifteen years of age at the time, and later became king of Norway.

Numerous stories of miracles began to appear. A wounded courtier who wiped the blood from the king's face and covered the body, had his own injuries instantly healed. A blind man, who that night accidentally rubbed his eyes with water in which the king's body had been washed had his sight restored. Olav's body was recovered, and his hair and nails continued to grow after his death. Many other miracles were told.

Olav in the years to follow, became the symbol of national independence, and was remembered for his attempts to unify and convert the country to Christianity. He was later canonized, and proclaimed a patron saint, the first in Norwegian history, Saint Olav.

1. The King of Sweden had three daughters, one legitimate and two "natural," and Olav wanted to marry the former, Ingegerd. This was very acceptable to Ingegerd, but it seems it was aborted by a tactless statement on her part. The king had been out hawking (shooting hawks), and had bagged five birds in two flights of his hawks. He boasted to Ingegerd, "Where have you heard of a king who has made so big a bag in so short a time?" To this Ingegerd tactlessly repled, "It was a good morning's bag to get five hawks, but it was a finer achievement that Olav, King of Norway, bagged five kings in a morning and won the whole kingdom." (Apparently, five small petty kings in Norway decided to meet and discuss the removal of King Olav. Olav heard about this and had his men set fire to the building, and the five kings perished.) The King of Sweden immediately forbade the marriage, and Olav married her sister, Astrid, the love child. Ingegerd married Yarolav I the Wise, grand prince of Kiev, and Holmfrid, the other daughter, married Jarl Svein (#8), one of the Danish viceroys in Norway. Astrid was the most beautiful, so Olav was compensated. End of love story!

2. See Chapter 12 for additional information on Alvhild and Magnus.

3. Astrologists now know there was an eclipse of the sun on August 1, 1030 AD and as the miracles of Olav began to be told, it is possible that the date of the battle was then, instead of the traditional date.

Knut the Great
10

Knut II, Knut den Mektige, Canute II the Great, Kanute II, Knud, Cnut, Canute

Knut was the second son of King Svein Forkbeard "Tjugeskjegg" and Gunnhild (from Poland).

b.c995 d. 12 Nov 1035 (c40 yrs.)
R.1016–1035 England
R.1018–1035 Denmark
R.1028–1035 Norway
√.Alfiva (mistress), b.c995 d.after 1040
    Children:
        Svein Alfivasson (#11), b.c1013 d.c1036, reigned after Knut the Great
        Harald Harfot "Hasenfuss," b.c1015 d.1040, ruled England until 1040
m.Emma of Normandy in 1017, b.c987 d.6 Mar 1052, Princess of Normandy,
    widow of King Ethelred of England
    Children:
        Hardeknut (Knut III), b.c1018 d.1042, became king of Denmark in
           1035, after Knut the Great died; became King of England in 1040
        Gunnhild, b.c1019 d.c1038. In 1035 she married Henry III, son of
           Roman Emperor, Conrad II. Gunnhild died two years later, proba-
           bly in childbirth.

Knut accompanied his father, King Svein Forkbeard of Denmark, to England in 1013 and helped drive King Ethelred II the Unready, out of the country.

In 1014 Knut's father died. Knut's older brother, Harald, became king of Denmark. After considerable warfare, Knut became king of England in 1016. However, in 1018, Harald died, and Knut also became became king of Denmark, as well as England.

While Knut was in England he met Alfiva, the daughter of a chief officer in Northumberland. With her he had two sons, Svein and Harald. Both later became Danish kings, and Svein also succeeded Knut as King of Norway.

In about 1017, Knut "sent away" his mistress/common-law wife, Alfiva, and their two sons. Why? King Ethelred died in 1016 and left a very desirable widow, Emma.[1] It is very likely that Knut saw his hold on England as being much more secure if he married Emma. Their marriage brought forth a son, Hardeknut (Knut III), and a daughter, Gunnhild.

Knut was the first Scandinavian to make a pilgrimage to Rome, and it was there that he attended the coronation of Conrad II and arranged for the marriage of Gunnhild, his daughter, to Conrad's son, Henry III, who was to become the future Royal Emperor. Sadly, Gunnhild died two years later, probably in childbirth.

Knut was king of both England and Denmark, and from 1028 to 1035 he claimed to be king of Norway. England commanded much of his time and attention, where he managed to keep peace. He was responsible for improving administration and law, and fostered the church. He also promoted education by founding many schools and and giving scholarships to able students.

Let us go back to Knut's personal life. His English Queen, Emma had two sons, Edward the Confessor, and Alfred, by King Ethelred. When Knut died in 1035, Emma tried to procure the crown for her son, Hardeknut. However, Harald Harfot, her step-son objected. A truce was formed and each received a part of England to govern. Hardeknut had to spend much of his time in Denmark, so Emma ruled for him in southern England. With Hardeknut in Denmark, Harald gained more popularity and took over the reign of all of England. He banished his step-mother, Emma, who returned to her home in Normandy. When Harald died in 1040, Emma returned, but her own son, Hardeknut, took all her wealth and she was forced to spend the rest of her life in seclusion in Winchester, England.

During the years that Knut the Great ruled, both Norway and Sweden tried to conquer Denmark, but were not successful. In 1028, Knut invaded Norway, and by this time, Olav II's popularity had reached a low point, and his followers deserted him and Knut became king of Norway, and the ruler of three countries. Olav, who later became St. Olav, fled to Russia, along with his four-year-old son, Magnus. He returned in 1030, and claimed he was still king, but was unable to gain sufficient support and was killed in the famous battle of Stiklestad.

Knut made his young son, Svein, a king (subking) to rule with him over Norway, but Knut spent most of his time in England, and they were unable to give the country much attention.

After Olav II's death, the grumbling grew against foreign rulers, so when Magnus, Olav's son was brought back to Norway in 1035, he was acclaimed king without much opposition. This ended the Danish rule for several centuries.

It is interesting to note that William the Conqueror based his right to the English throne on his relationship to Emma, who was the daughter of a Norman duke.

1. Emma married King Ethelred in 1002 at the age of fifteen and changed her name to Ælgifu when she arrived in England. They had two sons, Alfred and Edward the Confessor (so named because of his pious and religious lifestyle).

Svein Alfivasson
11

Knut's Son

Son of Knut the Great of Denmark, and mistress, Alfiva

b.c1013 d.1036 (23 yrs.)
R.1030–1035
Never married, no children

In 1030, Knut the Great (#10) designated his son Svein, as king (sub-king) of Norway. Svein was only seventeen years of age at the time and a child both in age and sense of responsibility. Knut had his own problems to take care of in Denmark, but Alfiva, Svein's mother decided she would assist Svein. She almost took over control of Norway. She was arrogant and unpopular and the Norwegians hated her.

The people that lived in Trondheim were blamed for the problems of Norway. It was here that Saint Olav was killed and they felt that the people had not given him the support he needed before his final battle. The chieftains decided to meet and decide what was to be done.

Another opportunist, Tryggve Olavsson[1] showed up on the scene at this time. He claimed to be the son of Norway's popular king, Olav I Trygvasson, and therefore of royal blood. Although Tryggve resembled Olav, he was probably the son of an Irish priest. By this time the Norwegians were tired of being ruled by Denmark and Svein's overbearing mother, and Tryggve was able to gather quite a number of followers, many from the northern area around Trondheim. Svein heard about this, but had problems gathering sufficient support for defense. Svein was a harsh and oppressive ruler, and many refused to join him because of their increasing dislike of the dictatorial rulers of Denmark, but he took the small army he had mustered and prepared for battle.

The fleets of Svein and Tryggve met in the Soknar Sound near the Island of Bokn. A violent battle took place. It was said that Tryggve hurled javelins with both hands at the same time, and he was, indeed, a most resourceful man. However, he was killed in this battle with many of his followers. A poem is written about this in *Heimskringla*:

> For fame eager, forth fared
> from the north King Tryggve,
> whilst Svein from the south forth
> sailed to join the battle.
> From fray not far was I.
> Fast they raised their banners.
> Swiftly then rang sword 'gainst
> sword began the bloodshed.

Another verse is quoted in *Heimskringla* praising King Svein:

> That Sunday morning, maiden,
> much unlike it was to
> days when at wassail women
> wait on men with ale-drink:
> when Svein the sailors bade his
> sloops of war to fasten
> by their bows, with carrion
> battening hungry ravens.

Svein continued to rule in Norway for a couple of more years. Then messengers from Norway, aiming to get back control, traveled to Russia and brought back little Magnus, the son of Saint Olav, and made him king in 1035.

Svein returned to Denmark, where he died the following year. He was only twenty-three years of age. Nothing more is said about his mother, Alfiva.

---

1. Not to be confused with Tryggve Olavsson, the son of Olav Geirstatha-Alf II.

Magnus I the Good
Acclaimed King of Norway at age ten.

Magnus I the Good
12

Magnus I Olavsson, Magnus den Gode, Magnus Olavsson

Illegitimate son of Saint Olav (#9) and Alvhild, his mistress; Stepson of Queen Astrid, Olav's Swedish wife

b.1024 d.25 Oct 1047 at Skibby, Denmark (23 yrs.)
R.1035–1047, King of Norway
  1042–1047, King of Denmark
  1042–1047, King of England
√.Mistress
    Children:
        Ragnhild, b.c.1043. Married Jarl Haakon Ivarsson of Denmark, and
        had one daughter

Magnus' mother was a little "English handmaid" named Alvhild. However, she was from a "good family," and very beautiful. It seems that when Alvhild went into labor, it was night. The only people present were some women, a priest, and the *skald* (court poet), Sigvat. After a difficult delivery, the baby was at death's door. The priest asked Sigvat to go to St. Olav (#9) and tell him about his son. Sigvat did not dare, because he had been forbidden to awaken the king. The priest then decided that it was imperative to baptize the baby because it might not live, so the baby was baptized and Sigvat named him Magnus. King Olav was furious upon hearing of the baby's birth. He did not favor the name, because it did not "run in the family." Sigvat replied that he had named him Magnus, after Charlemagne (Old Norse *Karlamagnus*), "the greatest man in the world," the Holy Roman Emperor. Then Olav forgave Sigvat.

Olav was exiled to Russia in 1028, and brought Magnus with him. Magnus was four years old at the time, and resided at the court of Kiev (now Russia) until 1035, and was fostered by Grand Prince Yaroslav I. At about this time the chiefs of Norway rebelled against the fierce rule of the Danes. They were tired of being ruled by another country. After a great deal of squabbling, a group of Norwegians went to Russia in 1035. The following summer they brought the ten-year-old Magnus back, and he was acclaimed king with little opposition from the Danes.

Snorri says that Magnus owed his throne to the loyal help of his stepmother, Queen Astrid, who obtained support for her son from Sweden.

How does a ten-year-old boy rule a country? Magnus had the help of Einar Tambarskelfir, a stout-hearted old chieftain who had controlled the armed forces for Magnus' father and was loyal to the young king.

When Magnus first became king, he punished the enemies of his father and took their land. Then he heeded the advice of his skalds, and from then on was known as Magnus the Good.

Snorri has this to say about Magnus: "King Magnus was of middle height, with regular features and light complexion. He had light blond hair, was well-spoken and quick to make up his mind, was of noble character, most generous, a great warrior and most valorous. He was most popular as a king, both friends and enemies praised him."

Let us keep in mind what was going on in the neighboring countries at this time.

When Knut the Great died in 1035, his control of Norway ended. One of his sons, Harald, became king of England, and a younger son, Hardeknut, king of Denmark in 1035. The two countries were afraid that a contender would invade their shores, and take over both countries, so they arranged a meeting between the two boy kings. This was in 1038, and both of the young kings were about fourteen years old. The decision was that Magnus was to remain king of Norway, but each king would be heir to the other. When one died, the other would take over both kingdoms.

Two years later, in 1042, Hardeknut died. According to the earlier agreement, Magnus laid claim to Denmark. He appointed Knut's nephew, Svein Estridsson, who Magnus had recklessly made a jarl, to rule under him. Magnus also became king of England, the only Viking to be the king of three countries.

This did not go unchallenged. Svein Estridsson decided to lay claim to his native Denmark. Although he had sworn loyalty to Magnus, he revoked his vows, and a fierce battle followed, with Magnus the winner. At about the same time, the Wends (Germans) invaded Denmark. Magnus and his Norwegian followers forced them to flee at the famous Battle of Lyrskov, near Slesvig. Magnus thereby gained great favor among the Danes.

In about 1045, another problem arose for Magnus (as though he did not have enough problems the way, it was)! Harald III the Hard arrived upon the scene from Constantinople and demanded his share of the throne. He was a half-brother to

Saint Olav, and thus an uncle (half-uncle?) to Magnus, and therefore claimed to have royal blood. Furthermore, Harald had fought side by side with Saint Olav in the famous Battle of Stiklestad, had traveled widely, and amassed a great fortune. At first, Magnus refused, but Harald went to Svein Estridsson for assistance. This frightened Magnus into accepting him as co-ruler. After this, both Magnus and Harald supported each other in their constant conflicts with Svein.

Now Svein, who was ruling Denmark under Magnus, was not happy with his position and challenged Magnus' sovereignty in Denmark. Magnus received the support of most Danes, and reportedly defeated Svein in a battle. However, in 1047, King Magnus died on board ship in Denmark during an attack against Svein, who then became the uncontested ruler of Denmark. Harald III the Hard (#13) took over as the sole ruler of Norway.

Magnus I the Good was one of the best loved of medieval Norwegian kings. He was only twenty-three years old at the time of his death.

Harald III the Hard
13

Harald Sigurdsson, Harald III, Harald the Hard, Harald Haardraade, Harald Sigurtharson, Harald the Stern, Harald Hardråde, Harald the Ruthless

Son of Sigurd Syr and Asta Gudbrandsdatter

b.c1015 d. 25 Sep 1066 (51 yrs.)
R.1042–1066
√.Thora Thorbergsdatter, b.c1015 d.aft.1050, daughter of Thorberg Arneson[1]
    Children:
        Magnus II, (King Magnus #14), b.c1045 d.1069
        Olav III, (King Olav Kyrre #15), b.1050 d.1093
m)Queen Illisif (also called Elizabet), b.c1032, daughter of King Jarizleif of Kiev and Ingegerd, daughter of King Olav of Sweden
    Children:
        Ingegerd, b.c1046, married King Olav Sveinsson (Olav I Hunger) of Denmark; then married King Phillip Hallstensson of Sweden
        Maria, b.ca.1049 d.25 Sep 1066, the same day and the same hour as her father, King Harald III. She was 17 years of age. One report states she was killed. This then becomes an unsolved mystery.

Both Harald III the Hard and St. Olav (#9) were great-great grandsons of Harald I Fairhair (#1). Their mother Asta was first married to Harald Grenski, and St. Olav was a child from this marriage. After Grenski's death, she married Sigurd Syr, and from this union Harald III was born. According to the sagas he had two brothers, Guttorm and Halfdan. He also had two sisters, Gunnhild and Ingegerd. Sigurd Syr was a grandson of Harald Fairhair's son, Sigurth Hrisi.[2]

Snorri tells a story in *Heimskringla* about how St. Olav tested his three half-brothers for leadership and gallantry, and noted Harald's leadership qualifications at such a young age:

One day while visiting his mother, Olav II found her three sons (his half-brothers) floating splinters of wood, which they called "warships," on a pond.

Then the king called Halfdan and Guttorm to him.

First he asked Guttorm:

"What would you like most to have?"

"A cornfield"[3] he answered.

"And how big would you like your cornfield to be?"

"I would like to have the whole headland jutting out into the lake sown with corn[3] every summer."

Now there were ten farmsteads on that headland, so the king answered:

"There would be a great deal of corn there."

Then the king turned to Halfdan and asked:

"And what would you most like to have?"

"Cows," he answered.

"How many would you like to have?" said the king.

"I would like," said he, "to have so many that when they went down to the lake to drink they would be standing all the way round the lake, as closely packed as they could stand."

"That would be setting up house on a large scale," said the king, "and you take after your father in this."

Then the king said to Harald:

"And what would you most like to have?"

"Warriors for my household," he answered.

"And how many would you like to have?" said the king.

"I would like," said he, "to have so many that they would eat up my brother Halfdan's cows at a single meal."

The king laughed, and said to Asta: "You are bringing up a king here, Mother."

This Harald, of course, was to become King Harald III (#13) of Norway!

Harald started his Viking raids early. In 1030, when he was fifteen years old, he accompanied his half brother, St. Olav, when he sailed to Norway in an attempt to regain his throne. Harald joined these warriors, even though St.Olav objected, saying that Harald was too young. St. Olav died in this fierce battle—the Battle of Stiklestad. Young Harald was wounded, but managed to escape.

Then Harald traveled east to Sweden, and found many of the men who had escaped from that battle. The following spring they got a ship and for the next fifteen years Harald made raids and fought in the Baltic, Greece and other countries in the east. He remained in Greece for several years and became the commander of the

Scandinavian guard under Zoe,⁴ who was Empress of Greece. During these years he fought battles in numerous countries, including Africa, where he remained for many years, acquiring great quantities of property and gold. Snorri describes Harald as follows: "Harald was larger and stronger than any other man, and so clever that nothing was impossible for him and that he always was victorious, wherever he fought; also that he was so rich in gold that no one ever had seen the like of it."

He spent a great deal of time in Africa, and when he acquired more wealth than he needed immediately, he sent it to King Yaroslav (king of Kiev) for safe-keeping. An immense amount of wealth accumulated there. It is said that by this time he had conquered 80 "strongholds."

To illustrate Harald's ingenuity during the Viking era, a story is told that he came to Sicily, and in his attempt to persuade them to surrender, he surrounded the city. However, it was protected by strong impenetrable walls and there appeared to be sufficient food and necessities so they could hold out against a long siege. Harald asked his "fowlers" (bird-catchers) to capture small birds that had their nests inside the walls. He tied pine shavings, soaked in wax and sulphur, to their backs, set fire to the shavings and the birds flew back to their nests—into the city, into the house thatches of reed and straw. So many fires were ignited that the people came out and begged for mercy. Harald generously gave quarters to all who asked for it, and made himself master of the city. Snorri states: "Harald was a handsome man of stately appearance, bold, daring and had a fighting spirit. He had light blond hair, with a blond beard and long, hanging mustaches, with one eyebrow higher than the other."

There are numerous stories of Harald's battles, but eventually he returned to Greece. He learned that Magnus I the Good (#15), had become king of both Norway and Denmark and decided to return and try to claim the throne for himself. When Queen Zoe learned he was leaving, she became very angry. She had him imprisoned for "misappropriating money"⁵ when he was chieftain over the Greek army. The sagas say that the real reason was that Harald planned to marry Maria, the daughter of Queen Zoe's brother, but Queen Zoe, herself, wanted to marry him. She had Harald imprisoned in a high tower—open at the top. During the night, a woman came and with the help of two servants, put up ladders to the top of the tower, let down ropes, and Harald escaped. This woman had been healed by St. Olav, and he appeared to her, and told her to free his brother from prison. This was another of the many miracles that were attributed to St. Olav, and later led to his sainthood.

After many victorious battles in Africa, Harald returned to Norway to contest the rule of his nephew, Magnus Olavsson (#12), St. Olav's son. However, in 1046, with the advice of counsel on both sides, Harald and Magnus came to an agreement—Harald was to rule jointly with Magnus, but Magnus was to be the superior, and Magnus in return was to receive half of Harald's wealth.

An uneasy relationship existed for a period of time, and in 1047 Magnus died. But before he died, he said he had a dream, that St. Olav told him that when he died, Harald Sigurdsson should become king of Norway, and Svein should get Denmark. Harald now proceeded to Norway with his army and was acknowledged as king in every district of Norway.

The winter after Magnus died, King Harald married Thora, the daughter of Thorberg Arnason. They had two sons. The older was called Magnus (#14), and the younger, Olav (#15). Both later became kings. Magnus married Queen Illisif, and they had two daughters, Ingegerd and Maria.

Denmark and Norway were still at odds, and many battles were fought between King Harald and King Svein of Norway. King Harald was a powerful and able ruler and extremely resourceful. No prince ever was his equal as to sagacity and wise counsel. He was a great warrior, skilled in arms, and was stronger and more dexterous with weapons than any other man.

Harald was also known for his influence over the Norwegian church, building churches and hand-picking bishops and other officials. He was also credited with the founding of Oslo. However, Harald goes down in history as a hard and stern ruler. He used his *hird* (warriors) against his own people, with fire and sword in a reign of terror lasting through three summers. Consequently he was called, Harald the Hard.

Harald is best remembered for his attempt to gain control of England. He sailed with a fleet of 240 large vessels, and after a fierce battle on September 25, 1066, was killed in the famous Battle of Stamford Bridge. This was the last and perhaps the greatest battle Norwegians ever fought on English soil.

This ended the life of Harald III the Hard, and brought to an end the Viking period. The descendants of King Harald III ruled for the next three generations.

If Harald III had won the battle at Stamford Bridge, would the Norwegians be the present-day rulers of England? Would we, in the United States, be speaking Norwegian?

1. It is debatable whether he was married to Thora, or she was his mistress. Historians also disagree as to whether Magnus and Olav are Thora's children or Queen Illisif's.
2. More recent historians dispute this claim.
3. *Corn* or *Korn* – grain. Corn was not grown in Norway due to its colder climate.
4. Queen Zoe the Powerful ruled Greece from 1028–1052
5. Some things never change!

Post-Viking Period

1066–1130 AD

The Viking raids were all but over. The kings were now putting their efforts into more socialistic ventures in order to improve their government. Other European countries were building bigger ships that could carry more merchandise for trading. Europe was in a state of economic expansion, and the Norwegians, with their expertise in trading, quickly joined the venture. This was a relatively peaceful and productive era in Norway, which continued until the outbreak of Norway's devastating 110-year Civil War in 1130.

Magnus II Haraldsson 14

Magnus II, Magnus Haraldsson, Magnus Sigurtharson

Son of Harald III the Hard (#13) and Thora Thorbergsdatter, nephew of Saint Olav (#9)

b.c1045 d.1069 (c24 yrs.)
R.1066–1069
√. Unknown mistress
    Children:
        Haakon Toresfostr (#16)

Magnus' father, King Harald III the Hard, died in 1066 during his momentous but fateful invasion of England in the Battle of Stamford Bridge. However, Harald had taken the precaution of proclaiming his son Magnus as king before he left.

After the first year of his reign, Magnus ruled with his brother, Olav Kyrre (#15). King Magnus governed the northern part and King Olav the eastern part of Norway.

There was a peace treaty between Norway and Denmark during the reign of King Harald III the Hard, but King Svein of Denmark stated this treaty was only in effect during King Harald's lifetime, and sent warships to Norway. However, the naval forces met and the kings came to an agreement by which peace was established between them.

Later, in 1069, while King Magnus was in Ireland, he became ill with ergotism, a fungus that sometimes grows on rye and other cereal grains, and died in Nitharos (Trondheim) where he was interred.

His short reign did not leave much information for historians, and in some lists of kings he is not included, but his reign was apparently relatively peaceful, and while he was king he was loved by all his people.

Olav III Kyrre
15

Olav III Haraldsson, Olav the Peaceful, Olav the Quiet, Olav Bonde, Olav Mundus[1]

Son of Harald III the Hard (#13) and Thora Thorbergsdatter

b.c.1050 d.22 Sep 1093 (c.43 yrs.)
R.1066–1093
m.Princess Ingegerd, in about 1070. She was the daughter of Svein Estridsson,
  king of Denmark. No children.
√.Thora Jonsdatter (mistress), b.c1050
  Children:
    Magnus, Magnus III Barelegs (#17), b.c1075, He succeeded his father.
    Sigrid Olavsdatter, a very beautiful woman, who was raped by King
      Sigurd the Crusader (#21) after a festival evening and forcibly made
      his mistress. Sigrid was also married to Sigurd Ranesson, a Norske
      lendsmann in Nordland.

Olav's father, Harald III the Hard, was married to Queen Illisif and they had two daughters. Harald also had two illegitimate children, Magnus and Olav, with Thora. Consequently, Olav had a brother and two half sisters.

Olav ruled jointly with his brother, Magnus, from 1066 to 1069, but after his brother's death in 1069, he became sole ruler. He guided the nation through one of its most prosperous periods, maintaining an extended peace rare in medieval Norwegian history.

Olav accompanied his father, Harald III the Hard, on his fateful invasion of England in 1066. After Harald's army was severely defeated and Harald was killed in battle, Olav obtained a truce, (thereafter he was often referred to as Olav the Peaceful) and left with twenty-four of the original 300 ships that landed. (Or possibly his name derived from the fact that at age sixteen, this was such a terrifying experience that, unlike his ancestors, he did not engage in any wars while he was king.)

In 1068 he concluded a peace treaty with the Danish King Svein II, by which the Danish king gave up his plan to conquer Norway and initiated a twenty-five-year period of peace.

Snorri makes this statement about Olav's appearance: "Olav was a large man in every way, and well proportioned. All are agreed that no one ever saw a handsomer man nor one of more stately appearance. He had flaxen, silky hair of great beauty, and a fair skin. His eyes were unusually fine, and his limbs well-shaped. As a rule he was a man of few words and spoke little at assemblies. But he was merry at ale and a great drinker, talkative and soft-spoken, peaceably inclined during his rule."

Olav III Kyrre also introduced into Norway many new ideas, manners, and cultures of the continental aristocracy. It was an old custom in Norway that the high-seat of the king was located in the middle of the long bench in the hall, and the ale was carried around the fire. King Olav was the first to have his high-seat placed on the elevated dais which ran across the hall, on one side. He was also the first to have rooms furnished with stoves, and have the floor covered with straw in winter (what a fire hazard!) as well as in summer.

Many new fashions also made their appearance. Men wore "court-breeches" laced tight around the legs, and some clasped gold rings around their ankles. They wore trailing gowns, laced with ribbons at the side, and sleeves five ells[2] in length and so tight that they had to be laced with straps all the way up to the shoulders. Also introduced were high shoes, embroidered all over with white silk, and some with gold laces.

Olav was evidently a very learned man and was the first Norwegian king who, himself, could read and write. Latin records were probably produced in Norway as early as about 1050. Snorri says that Olav the Peaceful could read the holy books. Undoubtedly these were in Latin.

Olav worked to give the Norwegian Church a more stable organization, making peace with Pope Gregory VII and Adelbert, archbishop of Bremen and vicar for the Scandinavian countries, who had been an enemy of Olav's father. Olav tried to follow the organizational model of the continental churches in Europe, but the Norwegian church was less influenced by Rome. Olav maintained personal control over the nation's clergy.

He then began a church building crusade, and during the time of his rule, the people of Norway were required by law to build and maintain these churches. To this day the Norwegian government builds and maintains their churches. He also built a small plain stone church as a shrine to St. Olav[3] (#9). A spring had burst forth there and he put the high alter directly above the place where St. Olav's body had rested the first night after the Battle of Stiklestad. Above the altar was placed the casket of the saint. This church was later replaced with the beautiful Christ Cathedral in Trondheim.

Olav encouraged urban growth by granting permanent areas to the four dioceses of the country. He founded several towns, including the city of Bergen in about 1070–75, which soon became an important trading center. Snorri states, "Olav set up a market town in Bergen; many rich men soon settled there and thither sailed merchants from other lands." Bergen soon became the largest, most important and most cosmopolitan city in Norway. This was the beginning of the Hanseatic[4] movement.

Olav Kyrre also encouraged the formation of "guilds" after the English model, to promote social security and sickness benefits. He strengthened the organization of the Norwegian Church. His reign was peaceful and he is credited with almost every phase of internal progress. He was much loved as a king and Norway grew greatly in wealth and honor during his reign.

Olav resided most of the time at his Haukebo palace in Ranrike in southeastern Norway. He had ruled for twenty-six years before he was "struck down by a sickness" and died there in 1093. He was about forty-three years of age. He was buried in the ancient Christ Church in Trondheim, the forerunner of the great cathedral at Trondheim. Earlier he had brought the bodies of Magnus I the Good (#12), his brother; and St. Olav (#9), his father, to be buried there. Thus it is the burial ground for three of the earliest and most able kings of Norway.

1. Probably means *den elegante,* referring to his continental tastes.
2. An old English measure of about 45 inches. It is inconceivable that the sleeves would be five ells long!
3. Genealogically speaking, Saint Olav was his uncle.
4. See glossary.

Haakon Toresfostre*[1]
16

Haakon Magnusson

Illegitimate son of King Magnus Haraldsson (#14) and unknown mother

b.c1064[2] d.1095 (31 yrs.)
R.1093–1094
Haakon was not married, and had no children.

When Olav III Kyrre (#15) died, his son, Magnus III Barelegs (#17) was named king in Vika, which later became known as Oslo. His nephew, Haakon, although illegitimate, gained control in the Uppland area and also claimed the throne for himself. He demanded the title of king and was given control over half the land, the same as his father King Magnus Haraldsson (#14) had while he reigned.

Haakon had been brought up by a prominent man, Thore of Steig (thus his name, Haakon Thoresfostre—fostered by Thore) in Gudbrandsdal and was first acclaimed king there. During the beginning of the winter of 1093-94, the two kings arrived at Nidaros (now Trondheim). They reigned together, uncomfortably, for a short time, and spent considerable time spying and worrying about each other. Both kings had troops in the area. It came close to war between them, but in the spring of 1094, Haakon died suddenly after an accident. He was crossing the Dovre mountains, when a ptarmigan (northern grouse) flew between the legs of his horse. The horse bolted and Haakon was killed.

Haakon was popular with his people because he relieved them of their land tax and also did not require them to give him *Yule* (Christmas) gifts, which had been necessary in the past. Snorri says he was gentle and kind to the people, and they grieved when he was killed. He was only thirty-one years of age.

1. * indicates a petty king. See kings in glossary.
2. According to Snorri, Haakon lived for only twenty-five years, so this date could be as late as 1070.

Magnus III Barelegs
17

Magnus Berrefott, Magnus Barefoot, Magnus Barfot, Magnus Styrjalder, Magnus the Tall, Magnus III Olavsson

Illegitimate son of Olav III Kyrre (#15) and Thora Jonsdatter, a mistress

b.c1075 d.24 Aug 1103 (28 yrs.) in Ulster, a Province in Northern Ireland
R.1093–1103
m.1)Margrete Fredkulla, "The Peach Maiden," in 1101 (at age 14), the daughter of King Inge I Steinkelsson the Elder of Sweden and Helen. No children.

Magnus had numerous children with known and unknown mistresses. Most were probably born before he married Margrete. All five of his sons eventually became kings of Norway.
Mistresses and children:[1]
√1)Unknown mistress. It was said she was a fine distinguished woman, though of "low birth."
  Children:
     Eystein I Magnusson (#20), b.c1094 d.c1122., married Ingeborg
        Guthormsdatter. They had one daughter, Maria, who married
        Guthbrand Skafhoggson. They had one son, Olav Ill-Luck.
     Thora Magnusdatter, Princess of Norway, b.c 1099 d.c1175, married
        Lopt Saemundarson, the father of Jon Loptsson, a powerful high-
        born chieftain in Iceland. Jon Loptsson was Snorri's foster father.
√2)Thora Guttormsdatter. She was of a "good line," but a hardhearted,unfeel-
  ing woman, b.c1072 d.c1103.
  Children:
     Sigurd the Crusader (#21), b.c1090 d.1130. Had several wives and
        mistresses and two known children: Magnus IV the Blind (#22) and
        Kristin Sigurdsdatter, who had several children. (See #21).
     Ragnhild Magnusdatter, b.c1096, married Harald Kestja of Denmark
        and had eleven children: Magnus, Olav, Knut, Harald, Bjorn, Eric,
        Sivard, Sven, Niels, Benedict, and Mistivint.
√3)Sigrid Saxeasdatter, b.c1085, daughter of Saxi of Vik, a chieftain in the district of Trondheim.

Magnus III Barelegs

"One should have a king for glorious deeds, not for a long life."

Children:
Olav (IV) Magnusson (#19), b.c1100 d.c1116
√4)Irin (from Ireland), b.c1075
Children:
Harald Gilchrist (#23), b.c1104 d.14 Dec 1136
√5)Thora Saxeasdatter (a sister of Sigrid Saxeasdatter), b.c1075, an act of adul-
tery by Thora since she was married to a priest at the time.
Children:
Sigurd Slembe (#24), b.c1100

After succeeding his father, Olav III Kyrre (#15), Magnus initially ruled jointly with his cousin, Haakon Toresfostre (#16). Haakon died the following year and Thore, his foster father managed to get another of his followers, Svein Haraldsson (#18), acknowledged as king in one area of Norway. In 1095, Svein lost in a battle with Magnus and fled to his native Sweden. This left Magnus as the sole king of Norway.

Magnus grew up in his father's court. Snorri states that as a lad he was handsome and gave much promise. He grew up to be exceedingly tall and wore a red doublet over his coat of mail. His long hair, as "pale as silk," fell down over his shoulders. He was known to have a fighting spirit, and was exceedingly fond of women. He was called Barelegs because he often wore Scottish kilts.

Magnus was considered a great warrior who consolidated Norway's rule in the Orkney and Hebride Islands and the Isle of Man, all now part of the United Kingdom.

In 1098, he launched expeditions to Ireland, and responded to Welsh pleas for help against the Normans by attacking Anglesey, an island off the coast of Wales, where he defeated the Normans. The Welsh people thought highly of Magnus for this accomplishment. Vidkunn Jonson of Bjarkoy accompanied him.

In 1101, Magnus attacked Sweden, but he made peace with the Swedish King Inge, and married his daughter Margrete. She was called "The Peace Maiden," and it was hoped the marriage would help solve differences between the two nations. She was only fourteen years of age at the time. They had no children, and Magnus died a couple of years later.

Magnus made another expedition to the western islands in 1102, visiting the Hebrides and Orkneys and the Isle of Man. The Norwegian control of the Isle of Man soon ended, but jarls who ruled the Orkney Islands recognized the sovereignty of the Norwegian king almost continually until 1468, and the Orkney and Hebrides dioceses became part of the Norwegian Church. By establishing closer relations with the islands Magnus stimulated trade with the British Isles.

In 1103, in a fight on an Ulster beach, Magnus was killed, after receiving three wounds. Vidkunn Johson was with the king to the last, when Magnus begged him to flee and save himself. Before he did this, Vidkunn killed the man who murdered his king, and was the last to leave the battle scene. Magnus' sons never forgot Vidkunn's heroism, and a son, Sigurd the Crusader (#21), had one of his sons fostered by Vidkunn, who lived to be a very old man.

The sagas say that he often proceeded incautiously when abroad. A statement by Magnus that is often quoted, "One should have a king for glorious deeds, not for a long life."

The people had to bear much expense because of Magnus' expeditions abroad, but he was greatly loved by his constituents. Even though there were a number of battles, it was a comparatively peaceful time.

Magnus Barelegs was a young man, not yet thirty years of age when he was killed. He had ruled for ten years and was the father of five future kings who were to rule in Norway.

1. The love-life of Magnus Barelegs is extremely complex. You will note the number of times the name "Thora" comes up. Thora was the name of his mother. He also had a mistress named Thora, who was the mother of two of his children. Another mistress was also named Thora and was supposedly the mother of Sigurd Slembe. Thora was also the name of his daughter.

Svein Haraldsson*
18

Sven Haraldsson

Son of Harald Flettir, of Danish origin

R.1095–1095

Toward the end of the eleventh century there were beginning to be more claimants to the throne. Both Magnus Barelegs (#17) and Haakon Thoresfostre (#16) appeared on the scene as soon as Olav III Kyrre died (#15) and they ruled together. However, since Haakon was killed shortly thereafter, this left Magnus as sole king.

Magnus Barelegs was an adventurous young man and was gone for long periods of time on raids. Steiger Thorir, a friend and follower of Harald III the Hard (#13), took advantage of these absences. He quickly found one of his followers, Svein Haraldsson, and managed to have him take over as king, along with Magnus.

Svein was Danish, a great Viking and warrior, and of noble lineage in his own country, but he had no genetic lineage to any Norwegian royalty. Steiger Thorir was now an old man, so he had Svein take over as leader of his band of henchmen. They collected forces and sailed north to Trondheim and won a battle with King Magnus' men. Magnus was on a Viking raid, but when he heard of the defeat, he summoned forces and also sailed toward Trondheim. A number of fierce battles followed and Steiger Thorir was captured and hanged.

Svein managed to escape and first fled out to sea, and then escaped to Denmark. This ended his short reign as a puppet king in Norway. From then on he continued to live in Denmark until he was able to make a conciliation with King Eystein I (#20), the son of Magnus III Barelegs. Eystein pardoned Svein and made him his cupbearer, befriended him and held him in great honor, but Svein never returned to Norway.

Although he claimed to be king for a period of time in 1095, he is often not listed in regnal lists.

Olav (IV)*
19

Olav Magnusson

Illegitimate son of Magnus III Barelegs (#17) and his mistress, Sigrid
Saxeasdatter

b.c1100 d.1116 (c16 yrs.). Olav died on 22 Dec 1115, but 1116 is usually
used as his year of death.
R.c1103–1116
Did not marry. Died young.

Olav was only four years old at the time his father died in 1103. According to
Norway's law called the "Divine Right of Kings," all the king's sons had equal rights
to the throne, whether legitimate or illegitimate. This resulted in much confusion
about legal rights since the kings during this time seemed to have their eye on many
women.

This was the case when Magnus III Barelegs died. He left three illegitimate sons:
Olav, about four years of age; Sigurd (#21), about thirteen, and Eystein (#20) at fifteen. They became joint kings upon the death of their father and their reign lasted
until about 1130, the longest rule by joint kings in Norway's history.

Olav, being the youngest, was under the control of his older brothers and never
took an active part in the government. Olav was of tall and slender build, handsome,
of cheerful disposition, affable, and popular.

Olav died in 1116 at the young age of sixteen. He reportedly was "attacked by a
disease." He apparently had no children. The three brothers had ruled for twelve
years at that time, and were loved by the common people. Snorri says, "They
grieved when Olav died." He is buried by Christ Church in Trondheim. He is sometimes not counted in regnal lists of Norwegian kings.

Eystein I Magnusson
20

Eystein Magnusson, Oystein I Magnusson, Augustine Magnusson

> Illegitimate son of Magnus III Barelegs (#17) and a mistress, Thora Jonsdatter. She was said to be of low birth, but a "fine, distinguished woman."
>
> b.c1094 d.22 Aug 1122 (28 yrs.)
> R.1103–1122
> m.Ingeborg, daughter of Guthorm, the son of Steiger-Thorir.
>   Children:
>   Maria, became the wife of Guthbrand Skafhoggson, and they had a
>   son, Olav Guthbrandsson, later called Olav Ill-Luck.[1]

When Magnus Barelegs (#17) was killed in 1103, Eystein I was the oldest of his three illegitimate sons, and at age fifteen took over the kingship with his thirteen year old brother, Sigurd (#21), and Olav (#19), age four.

By this time, the Vikings were no longer making raiding forages into other countries. Their journeys now were confined for the most part to trading and exploring. When they returned, the people praised them, since they "had acquired great fame and could tell of many events."

This news whetted the desire of a great many in Norway to undertake such a journey. Therefore they requested that since there were now three kings, one of them should be outfitted for such an expedition. Sigurd was the logical choice because he was the restless one. While he was gone, Eystein was to govern the country for the others.

Eystein served his country well, gaining territory from Sweden, encouraging trade, promoting internal progress and constructing royal dwellings as well as churches. He transferred the king's residence to modern Bergen in 1110, and made it the royal capitol of Norway, a status it enjoyed until 1299. He founded the two earliest abbeys in Vestlandet—those of St. Albans at Selje, and Munkeliv at Nornes. He also erected the beautiful St. Mary's Church in Bergen, which had been miraculously saved from the numerous fires that had ravaged the town throughout centuries.

Their rule was relatively peaceful, and is noted for being the longest joint rule in the history of Norway. Olav died at about age sixteen, so never took much of a part in the reign of Norway. After his death, Eystein and Sigurd divided the country between the two of them. Eystein kept the northern part and Sigurd the southern part. Eystein spent most of his time at Trondheim, which had become a progressive city under his guidance. People were also coming in greater numbers to visit the Shrine of Saint Olav (#9), and for their convenience, Eystein improved the roads over the Dovre Mountains. The Frostatling Law was also enacted during his reign, making many imports available for the people. A few of the items for trade that are mentioned are articles such as velvet, finely woven bed-curtains, eiderdown quilts, silver vessels, gold ornaments, precious stones, and even pet dogs.

Snorri states that King Eystein was strikingly handsome in appearance. His eyes were blue and rather large, his hair pale blond and curly. He was a man of middle height, wise and well-informed in all respects—both in the laws, instances, and history—and resourceful, eloquent, and well-spoken. He was of a most cheerful disposition, affable, pleasing in his ways, and beloved by all the people.

In 1122, Eystein was at an entertainment that was given for him, when he suddenly became sick and died (poisoned?). It is said that "over no man's body in Norway were so many men in sorrow" since the death of St. Olav's son, Magnus. He was thirty-four years of age.

Sigurd, the last survivor of the joint rule of the three brothers, then became sole ruler of Norway.

---

1. So named because his troops failed to win a battle, even though the enemy had been "delivered into his hands."

Sigurd the Crusader
21

Sigurd Magnusson, Sigurd Jorsalafarer, Sigurd I

Illegitimate son of Magnus III Barelegs (#17) and Thora Guttormsdatter

b.c1090 d.26 Mar 1130 in Oslo.(c40 yrs.)

R.1103–1130. Ruled with his brothers and took over as sole ruler when Eystein died in 1122.

√.Biadmuin, Princess Biadmuin. Her father was King Muikertach of Ireland. No children.

√.Borghild Olavsdatter, b.c1094, daughter of Olav-in-the-Dale, a wealthy and powerful farmer
  Children:
    Magnus IV the Blind (#22), b.c1115. He married Kristin (Christine), Princess of Denmark.

m1)Princess Malmfrida. b.c1090 in Kiev, Ukraine. Granddaughter of King Ingi Sveinkelsson of Sweden.Died sometime after 1137. She was the great-great-granddaughter of the king of England on her father's side, and the great-great-granddaughter of the king of Sweden on her mother's side. She had been married previously to Erik II "Emun" King of Denmark.
  Children:
    Kristin Sigurdsdatter,[1] b.c1126 d.c1178. Married Erling Skakke.

m2)Cecelia, this was an act of bigamy, as he was still married to Malmfrida. No children.

In 1103, when Magnus Barelegs (#17), died and his three sons took over, each got a part of Norway. Sigurd, a restless person, soon became bored and in 1107, when the people requested that one of the kings journey to other lands, Sigurd eagerly accepted the challenge. At age seventeen, he then became the first Scandinavian king to participate in the Crusades. He sailed away from Bergen with sixty ships and

10,000 trained men. (It is generally believed that these figures are often grossly exaggerated in the sagas.) He led expeditions to England, France, Spain, Sicily, Palestine and Jerusalem, and after this he was also known as Sigurd Jorsalafarer. Edvard Grieg later immortalized this voyage in his opera, *Sigurd Jorsalafarer.*

King Sigurth was a man of tall stature, and had reddish-brown hair. He was of an imposing appearance, not handsome but well-proportioned, brisk, of few words, and most often gruff, but a good friend, firm of mind, not inclined to talk much, well-mannered and high-minded. He observed the laws well, was generous, loved magnificence, and was renowned.

Sigurd considered himself a religious man. When he went to Jerusalem he brought back a fragment of the Holy Cross. It was his idea to impose tithes which provided a reliable source of income for the clergy. He also built monasteries and cathedrals, including the one at Stavanger, to strengthen the Norwegian Church. He traveled to Smaland in Sweden to convert its inhabitants, reportedly the last heathens left there.

While on his journeys, Sigurd had visited Ireland and while he was there he took Princess Biadmuin as his mistress. She was the daughter of Muikertach, the king of Ireland. However, when he left, she remained in Ireland and never came to Norway. They had no children.

Sigurd returned to Norway in about 1111, after his crusading. At this time there was a wealthy and powerful farmer living in the Borg area. He had a daughter named Borghild. She was very handsome and a wise and well-informed woman, and was constantly in the company of kings. Both King Eystein and King Sigurd spent considerable time there, and Sigurd did much to improve that market town. Borghild spent a great deal of time in the company of the two kings, and it was rumored that she was having an intimate relationship with King Eystein. She denied this and in order to prove her innocence, she agreed to *Jernbyrn*, the ordeal of "carrying hot iron."[2] She fasted to prepare herself. King Sigurd was away at the time, but when he heard about this he rode, in one day, what was a two day's journey, took Borghild away, and made her his mistress. Magnus (#22), who later became known as Magnus the Blind, was the offspring of this relationship.

At a later date, Sigurd married Malmfrida, who had royal blood from both Sweden and England. She had been married previously to Erik II "Emun" King of Denmark. As a result of this marriage, a daughter was born. Her name was Kristin, and she is often mentioned in history books, because of her marriage to Erling Skakke, a prominent man during this period.

About this time, King Sigurd evidently tired of Malfrida and fell madly in love with a "Lady Cecelia" while his wife, Queen Malmfrida, was still living. He wished to obtain the blessing of the church, but the Bishop of Bergen refused to marry him, because he was already married. Sigurd then persuaded the Bishop of Stavanger to perform the ceremony by offering him a vast sum of money so he could finish building his beautiful Cathedral of Stavanger (which still stands). Cecelia did not take her marital relationship and responsibility very seriously and finally deserted him on his deathbed.

In his later years Sigurd became mentally unbalanced and lapsed into periods of insanity. The sagas state that this was brought about when King Sigurd was being entertained in the Uppland District, and a bath was prepared for him. Baths, which were tented over, were often prepared for guests of high rank who traveled long distances. It seems that Sigurd saw a fish swimming in his bath, and this brought on such a fit of laughter that his mind was "unhinged." Consequently, Sigurd is often mentioned in the sagas as a "wild man."

Sigurd was about forty years of age when he became sick and died on the 25th of March in 1130. A story is told in the saga, *Morkinskinna*. It relates that shortly before his death, Sigurd had a dream that a shadow appeared far out in the ocean. It seemed to be a large tree with its roots stretching toward Norway. When it reached the shore, the many splinters drifted into every inlet. This dream was interpreted to signify that Harald Gilchrist and descendants were to rule in Norway. It is true that the blood line of Gilchrist was the one from which the future kings of Norway descended.

King Sigurd the Crusader had been a good king, and his constituents were blessed with both peace and good harvests during his twenty-seven year reign. Sigurd was the first of many kings to be buried in the great St. Hallvard Cathedral in Oslo.

King Sigurd's death marked the beginning of the 110-year devastating Civil War in Norway.

1. For more information on Kristin see index of names.
2. Ordeal by fire. See glossary.

Norway's 110-Year Civil War

1130–1240 AD

The devastating Civil War tore Norway apart. It began in about 1130 AD and lasted for 110 years. The question of succession to the throne was part of the problem, and it was bound to happen. Both legitimate and illegitimate sons had an equal right to the throne. During the Viking period the kings often died quite young and many sons were left to put in their claim. The Viking kings travelled to many lands on their raids and excursions. A mistress would often come forward, from another country, and relate to her son that he had royal blood due to an affair many years in the past. (It seems humanity does not change from one century to the next!) Consequently many "pretenders" and "petty kings" came from different parts of the country to lay their claim. If they passed the "ordeal by fire" or *jernbyrd*, they could claim royal blood. Also by this time,the people without land were becoming dissatisfied with the large landowners. They began to organize and became a significant power. Christianity and the church also gained more popularity and its financial position was strengthened. These factions led to many minor and major skirmishes within Norway for over a century. By the 1200s, the people were tired of war and were trying to reconcile their differences, and by 1240 Nor-way's 110-year Civil War was considered over.

Magnus IV the Blind
22

Magnus den Blinde, Magnus the Blind, Magnus Sigurdsson

Son of Sigurd the Crusader (#21) and Borghild Olavsdatter

b.c1115 d.12 Dec 1139 (c24 yrs.)
R.1130–1135 and 1137–1139
m.Kristin Knutsdatter, Princess of Denmark, b.c1118, daughter of Knut the
   Great (Knut Lavard), and a sister of Valdemar, King of Denmark. Her mother
   was Ingeborg, Princess of Kiev (now Russia). No children.

Magnus was only fifteen years of age in 1130, when his father, King Sigurd the Crusader (#21) died and he was acclaimed king. This marked the beginning of Norway's devastating 110-year Civil War. At this point perhaps Magnus should have been the sole king of Norway, as he was King Sigurd the Crusader's only son. However, while Sigurd was still living, an Irishman named Harald Gilchrist (#23) came forward and claimed he was the brother (half-brother) of King Sigurd. Sigurd reluctantly agreed to this relationship after Gilchrist passed the "ordeal by fire" test. In turn, he had Gilchrist promise not to claim the throne during his lifetime or the lifetime of his son, Magnus.

After young Magnus became king, Gilchrist immediately forgot his promise and laid claim to the throne. Magnus was forced to agree to the joint rule. There was hostility between the two, but for the first few years they ruled the land in relative peace.

Magnus did find time in his troubled life to find a wife; Kristin Knutsdatter, the Princess of Denmark. However, for whatever reason, the sagas say that Magnus "did not take to her," and sent her back to Denmark. Her relatives were greatly angered by this.

Snorri says that "Magnus matured early in stature and strength, and was handsomer than any man then living in Norway. However he was a man of haughty disposition, cruel, and a great athlete. He was much given to drinking, greed for money, was unfriendly and hard to get along with. It was his father's popularity that brought him the friendship of the people. It seems that Magnus picked some very undesirable habits at a very early age."

Many battles followed. Magnus won the first one, but shortly after that, Gilchrist defeated Magnus and had him blinded, mutilated and castrated to make him unfit to be king. He put him into a monastery where he remained for two years. The people of Norway were outraged by this incident, and felt justified when Sigurd Slembe (#24) appeared on the scene and murdered Gilchrist. Slembe claimed to be another of Magnus Bareleg's illegitimate sons. He obtained limited recognition as king, but in the meantime, Gilchrist's widow had quickly called together the *Thing*, and had their one-year-old son, Inge I Hunchback (#25) proclaimed king. Meanwhile, in northern Norway, three-year-old Sigurd II the Mouth (#26), another of Gilchrist's sons, was also crowned.

Magnus remained at the monastery while the three kings claimed the throne: Sigurd Slembe, and the two child-kings, Inge the Hunchback and Sigurd the Mouth. They battled for three years. Sigurd Slembe was unable to retain sufficient support for his own claim to the throne. To get a following, he took Magnus the Blind out of the monastery with hopes of installing him as king but to no avail.

With support from Denmark, Sigurd Slembe returned to Norway with thirty ships, eighteen of them Danish. They met twenty Norwegian ships led by the followers of the two infant kings. In the resulting battle in 1139, the Battle of Holmengra, Magnus was pierced by a sword. He cried, "This has come seven years too late," and died. The Danish ships fled back to Denmark. Sigurd was also brutally killed.

So ended the reign of both Sigurd Slembe and Magnus the Blind. Poor Magnus was only twenty-four years old when he died.

Harald Gilchrist
23

Harald IV Gilchrist, Harald Gilli, Harald IV Magnusson, Gille, Gilli

Son of Magnus III Barelegs (#17) and Irin, an Irish mistress

b.c1104 d.14 Dec 1136, murdered (c32 yrs.)
R.1130–1136
√.Beathack – Irish. b.c1110
    Children:
        Eystein II Haraldsson (#27), b.c1125 d.21 Aug 1157. m.Ragna
           Nikolasdatter
√.Unknown mistress (or mistresses)
    Children:
        Magnus Haraldsson,[1] b.c1125, was "diseased in his legs," died young.
        Maria Haraldsdatter, b.c1128. m.Simon Skalp, son of Hallkel Huk.
           Their son was Nikolas.
        Margrete Haraldsdatter, b.c1130. m.Jon Hallkelsson, brother of Simon
           Skalp
√.Thora Guttormsdatter, b.c1114, daughter of Guttorm Graybeard
    Children:
        Sigurd the Mouth (#26), b.c1133 d.10 Jun 1155. Had several mar-
        riages.
m1)Ingerid Ragnvaldsdatter "A Swedish Princess."[2] Her father was King
    Ragnvald Ingersson of Sweden.
    Children:
        Brigitha Haraldsdatter,[3] Princess of Norway, b.c1130. Had at least four
           marriages and many children.
        Inge I Hunchback (#25), b.c1135 d. Feb 1161, killed. Father of Jon
           Kuvlung (#34) and Harald Kongesson.

Before King Sigurd the Crusader (#21) died in 1130, Gilchrich came forward and claimed he was his half-brother and therefore was a rightful heir to the throne. Whether Harald actually had "royal blood," no one knows, but to prove his paternity, he did submit to a harsh "ordeal by fire," ordered by King Sigurd. Harald was to walk on nine red-hot ploughshares laid on the ground. He fasted to prepare himself for the ordeal, and then, led by two bishops, walked over them with his bare feet. After three days his feet were unburned. He had passed the test! King Sigurd reluctantly agreed to let him share the kingdom, as long as he didn't make any claim to the throne while he and his son Magnus IV (#22), were alive.

However, when Sigurd died in 1130, Gilchrist immediately forgot his promise and Magnus IV, the joint ruler, agreed.

Gilchrest was described "as a man of tall and slender stature. He had a long neck and rather long face, black eyes, and dark hair. He was alert and swift (in motions) and most often wore the Irish costume with short and light clothes. The Norwegian speech was hard for him to master; he often hesitated for words, and many ridiculed him for that. He was considered a worthless young man, addicted to strong drink and women. However he was affable, merry and gay, not haughty; and he was generous, so that he begrudged his friends nothing. He was open to advice, letting others give him counsel in whatever they would. All this made him popular and earned him praise."

This was not a peaceful reign, however, and there were many skirmishes between the two kings. In one battle in 1134, Gilchrist took Magnus prisoner. He had him blinded and castrated, in order to make him unfit to be king, and then had him shut up in a monastery.

The people, however, were upset with Gilchrist because of his treatment to Magnus. In the meantime, another half-brother, Sigurd Slembe (#24), arrived and put in his claim to the throne. The people approved when Sigurd killed Gilchrist when he found him in bed with his mistress, Thora. Gilchrist was drunk and slept hard. Sigurd plunged a dagger into his body. Gilchrists's last words were, "Why are you rough-handling me like this, Thora?"

After his death, his widow, Queen Ingerid, hastily called together the *Thing* and had their one-year-old son, Inge I Hunchback (#25), proclaimed king. Ingerid then married Ottar Birting, who was a staunch supporter of little King Inge. At the same time, in the north, another one of Harald's illegitimate sons, three-year-old Sigurd the Mouth (#26), so called because he had an ugly mouth, was made king. Thus Norway was ruled by two child kings.

Gilchrist had been sole king for only two years when he was murdered in 1136. He is buried in the Old Christ Church. For more than two decades his sons held the title of king of Norway. His reign was memorable only for violence and murder.

1. Magnus is listed in Heimskringla as the fourth son of Harald Gilchrist, so he may have been born later and had a different mother than Maria and Margrete. Magnus was "diseased in his legs." He lived just a short time but died a natural death.

2. Although Ingerid did not seem to have played any political role, she was the mother of some of the principal people during this critical time in Norwegian history.

Ingerid was first married to a Danish prince, by whom she had several sons who "left their mark" at that time. She could not, however, put up with her husband, so she ran away, disguised as a boy, and with a young male companion tried unsuccessfully to hide in Aalborg (a seaport in southeastern Denmark). Her Danish prince dragged her back, but when he died, she became a desirable widow. Harald Gilchrist then married her, and by him she had a son, Inge the Hunchback (#25), who later became king. They also had a daughter, Brigitha.

When she was widowed for the second time, Ingerid married Ottar Birting, who was a staunch supporter of Inge when he became king at age one.

After Ottar's death, she had, with a lover, Ivar Sneis, a son, Orm Kongsbror, who lived to make a great name for himself in national history.

Then she married a lendsmann, Arne Arnesson, and in this marriage she gave birth to the famous Nicholas Arnesson (1150–1225) who was a leader of the "Baglers", the rebel force in the later stages of the Civil war, when he was the Bishop of Oslo. With Arne she also had a daughter, Margrete, who had a son, Filippus Simonsson (#38), who later claimed the throne.

3. See Brigitha Haraldsdatter under Index of Personal Names'

Sigurd II Slembe
24

Sigurd Slembidjakn, Gadabout Deacon, Sigurd Slembi, Deacon Magnusson

Claimed to be son of Magnus Barelegs (#17). His mother was Thora Saxeasdatter, the daughter of Saxi in Vik.

b.c1100 d.12 Nov 1139 (c39 years)
R.c1136–1139
No record of marriages or children

During the last year of Harald Gilchrist's reign, Sigurd II Slembe appeared upon the scene, claiming to be Gilchrist's son. It is very likely, however, that he was the son of the priest, Athalbrikt. When he was young, he was "put to learning," and became a clerk and then a deacon.

Sigurd was a very talented and gifted man with great leadership qualities. He was brought up in Norway, but his own country did not recognize his abilities. The sagas say that as a youth he was a powerful and handsome individual, full of energy and ambition. His hair was rather thin, yet of good appearance. He was also recognized as a bold, resourceful, and unscrupulous young man. He was full of energy and ambition, but he had no "family name." Then his mother reluctantly revealed to him that King Magnus Barelegs (#17) had been her lover, and that Sigurd was really his son and of royal blood.

When Slembe heard this, he quickly quit his cleric/deacon position as it was no longer a necessity since he now had royal blood. He left Norway and traveled to many countries, including Jerusalem. While in Denmark he went through the "ordeal by fire" to prove his paternity, and passed. It was said that there were five bishops present to witness this occasion.

In about 1135, Sigurd went to Norway to visit his brother (half-brother) Harald Gilchrist, who was then king. It was now that Sigurd revealed his paternity to him and asked King Harald to acknowledge his kinship. Slembe then laid claim to the throne that he felt was rightfully his. Gilchrist refused to acknowledge him as a brother, and threw him in prison and charged him with murdering a chieftain in the Orkneys. Slembe made a thrilling escape, stole back to Bergen, broke into Gilchrist's bedroom and murdered him while he was sleeping with his mistress.

Upon his escape, Slembe took over the royal residence. However, the farmers would not allow this so Slembe retreated. Meanwhile, when Gilchrist was killed in 1136, his widow immediately brought forth their one-year-old son, Inge (#25), and he was accepted as king. In Northern Norway, Sigurd I the Mouth (#26), Inge's three-year-old half-brother was also acclaimed king.

To help his cause, Slembe then decided to take Magnus the Blind out of the monastery. With this move, he hoped that he would get the followers of Magnus to help him. For the next few years, Sigurd and Magnus battled the two child-kings, but they were unable to win any decisive battles.

In 1139, Magnus was killed in battle, and Sigurd Slembe was brutally tortured and put to death. The two boy kings, King Sigurd the Mouth and King Inge, aged six and four, continued their rule.

Sigurd Slembe is missing from many lists of Norwegian royal kings. However, there is some credence to verify his kingship for several years.

Many in Norway thought Slembe was a very capable individual, in every way, but he was pursued by bad luck. Sigurd II Slembe is buried at St. Mary's church in the town of Alaborg.

Inge I Hunchback
25

Inge Krokrygg, Inge Haraldsson, Ingi

The only legitimate son of Harald Gilchrist (#23) and Queen Ingerid from Sweden. She had other marriages and children.[1]

b.c1135 in Norway, d. Feb 1161 (c26 yrs.)
R.1136–1161, became king at age one
√. Unknown mothers. Probably not married.
    Children:
        Jon Kuvlung (#34), b.c1160
        Harald Kongesson, b.c1155

Immediately upon Harald Gilchrist's (#23) death, his widow, Ingerid, had their one year old son, Inge I Hunchback, proclaimed king. Meanwhile, another one of Gilchrist's illegitimate sons, three-year-old Sigurd the Mouth (#26), was acclaimed by the *Thing* as king in the North. Sigurd Slembe also claimed to be king at this time.

Inge was the youngest of the four sons of Harald Gilchrist. He alone, as the son of the Swedish Queen Ingerid, had the prestige of being legitimate, born in wedlock. He maintained the strongest claim to the throne against his father's illegitimate sons. Inge and Sigurd the Mouth reigned for about six years. At that time, an older brother, Eystein II Haraldsson (#27) came from Scotland, and was also proclaimed king at the *Thing*, and received a third of the kingdom. The brothers and their supporters then defeated the forces of Sigurd Slembe (#24) and the former ruler, Magnus IV the Blind (#22), who were both pretenders to the throne.

During this time the position of Inge was by far the strongest, and this period is often called the "Reign of Inge." When he was only two years old, one of his men carried him into battle and there he received his crippling injury, and received the nickname of "Inge the Hunchback." His disability proved to be advantageous to him. He was a good leader and found able men to work under him, and he leaned heavily on them. His followers also had a strong loyalty and warm affection for him.

Inge Hunchback

Became king of Norway at age one.

King Inge represented the interests of the higher nobles and clergy which later became known as the "Bagler" party.[2]

In *Heimskringla* it is said that Inge was tractable, gentle and an extremely handsome man. His hair was yellow, rather thin, and very curly. He was short in stature, and could hardly walk alone because one of his legs was withered, and he had a hump both on his shoulders and his chest. He was a kind and generous man and good to his friends. He let his chiefs share in the governing of the country, and was popular with the people.

One of his advisors was Erling Skakke Wryneck.[3] Erling was important in Norwegian history and much is written about him. His nickname, *Krokkrygg*, "crooked-neck" was derived from a wound from a slash by a saber. Erling also had the prestige of being married to Kristin, who had royal blood as the daughter of King Sigurd the Crusader (#21). Toward the end of Inge's reign, Erling drank heavily, became overly possessive of his power and lost favor with Inge.

As is usually the case when there are several leaders, trouble arose between the three kings. In about 1155, King Eystein and King Sigurd plotted to overthrow Inge. King Inge was informed of their plot, and his men killed Sigurth the Mouth in 1155. A couple of years later Inge's followers were blamed for the assassination of King Eystein. After Eystein's death, his son, Haakon the Broadshoulder (#28), became the ruler in that part of the kingdom.

Inge ruled for about five more years, and continuously fought off the advances of his half-brother, Haakon the Broadshoulder. Inge was finally defeated and killed during a battle with Haakon, on the ice between Oslo and Hovedøya. Kristin tended his body after he died. He is interred in the stone wall on the south side of St. Hallvard's Cathedral in Oslo. Inge was twenty-six years of age, and had been king for twenty-five years.

1. See Harald Gilchrist (#23) for additional information on Queen Ingerid.
2. See glossary.
3. See Chapter 29 for more information on Erling Skakke and Kristin.

Sigurd II the Mouth
26

Sigurd Munn, Sigurd II, Sigurd II Mund, Sigurd Haraldsson

Illegitimate son of Harald Gilchrist (#23) and Thora Guttormsdatter, the daughter of Guttorm Graybeard

b.c1133 d.c10 Jun 1155 (c22 yrs.)
R.1136–1155

Whether Sigurd the Mouth was ever married is debatable. However the following children claimed him as their father, and three of them became kings of Norway.

Mistresses and known children:
√.Mother unknown
   Erik, b.c1154 d.c1190. Erik was Sverre's "Jarl" at Viken, the area around the Oslofjord. Erik married Asta. Erik and his wife and sons all died of poisoning when living at St. Olav's Abbey in Tønsberg.
√.Mother unknown
   Cecelia Princess of Norway, b.c1153 d.c1185, first married Folkvid Lagmann of Sweden. While she was married to Folkvid she married Baard Guttormsson, and had a son, Inge Baardsson. Inge had royal blood through his mother, and she was anxious for him to be proclaimed king. However, she was accused of bigamy, and in order to refute this, she claimed that her Swedish husband, Folkvid, was just a lover. Inge II Baardsson (#39) did eventually become king. Cecelia was a "flighty and unprincipled" woman, and she presented the only evidence (probably false) for Sverre that he was her brother and therefore possessed "the hereditary divine right of kings." Cecelia apparently had personal reasons for wanting to remove Magnus V (#29) from the throne, and was not at all reluctant to lie, if it could accomplish her wish. With Magnus gone, her more immediate family would have a chance to be rulers. Two other children are listed for Cecelia, Haakon Galen and Skulle Baardsson (#45). However, Skulle was apparently the son of Baard Guttormsson's next wife and would have no royal blood whatsoever.

√.Kristin, daughter of Sigurd the Crusader (#21). Harald was a "love child" of Sigurd and Kristin before she married Erling Skakke.

Harald Sigurdsson, b.c1155 d.c1170. Erling had him executed at about age fourteen because he was afraid he would steal the throne from his own son, Magnus V.

√.Thora, b.c.1130, a servant girl and working woman of farmer Simon Thorbergsson

Haakon Broadshoulder (#38) b.1147 d.1162

√.Mother unknown

Sigurd Markusfostre (#30), b.c1142 d.1163

√.Gunnhild, wife of Unas the Combmaker from Bergen.

Sverre Sigurdsson (#33), b.c1151 d.1202

Sigurd the Mouth was only three years old when his father was murdered and he became king. He ruled jointly with another child king, Inge the Hunchback (#25), his half brother, who was only a year or two older. Sigurd ruled in the Trondelag area, and Inge ruled Viken in southern Norway; however, Inge definitely held the most power.

For three years civil war raged between their advisors and another king, Sigurd Slembe (#24), until Slembe was killed in 1139. Several years later, another older half brother, Eystein II (#27) came from Scotland and also was proclaimed king. For a period of time there were three kings ruling Norway. The relationship between the two original child kings, Sigurd and Inge, became more strained with time.

One tale from the sagas tell about Sigurd the Mouth in his youth. Sigurd and his followers were riding east in Vik and went past the estate of a wealthy man by the name of Simon Thorbergsson. As he rode through the yard he heard someone singing so beautifully in one of the houses that he wanted to meet her. He rode to the house and upon entering saw a woman standing by a handmill. As she ground the grain she sang with a most wonderful voice. The king got down from his horse and went in and "lay with the woman." However, when he was about to depart, farmer Simon got to know about this. The woman's name was Thora, and she was working for farmer Simon. When it became apparent that she was about to have a child, Simon had her work done by others. Later on she bore a son, and the boy was to become King Haakon Broadshoulder (#28). Haakon was brought up by Simon and his wife Gunnhild. Their sons, Onund and Andreas, were raised with Haakon, and they were so fond of each other that "only death could part them."

The sagas say that Sigurd had brown hair, was big and strong, rather stout, with small, but attractive facial features, except perhaps for his mouth.[1] He had a good command of the language and was a skillful speaker, but it is said he was ungovernable and restless. He reportedly was very fond of women, as can be seen from his many illegitimate children.

The followers of Sigurd were credited with being the pioneers of the movement that generations later won complete political victory as the "Birchlegs,"[2] under the leadership of Sverre.

In 1155, the two brothers, Sigurd and Eystein plotted to dethrone Inge Hunchback, under the pretense that, as a cripple he was not worthy to be king. Inge heard about this plot and Sigurd was captured and slain. He reportedly called in vain for mercy from his brothers, but to no avail. Snorri states that "so many weapons flew against Sigurd's golden shield that it seemed as though one were looking into a snowstorm."

King Sigurd was twenty-two years old when he died. it is interesting to note that of all of Harald Fairhair's twenty-three children, it is the blood line of Sigurd the Mouth, through his son Sverre, that carries through into the fourteenth century.

1. Possibly a hairlip.
2. See glossary.

Eystein II Haraldsson
27

Oystein II Haraldsson

Illegitimate son of Harald Gilchrist (#23) and Beathack from Ireland

b.c1125 d.21 Aug 1157
R.1142–1157
m.Ragna Nikolasdatter (daughter of Nikolas Masa), b.c1133, died sometime
    after 1161. When Eystein died, Ragna married Orm Kongsbror, the half-
    brother of King Inge Hunchback (#26). There probably were no children
    from this marriage, as the following are listed as illegitimate:
√.Mothers unknown
    Eystein Moyla (#32), b.c1145 d.1177
    Torleif Breiskjegg
    Daughter (Eysteinsdatter)

Inge I Hunchback (#25) and Sigurd II the Mouth (#26), mere children, were made kings upon Gilchrist's death in 1136. The country was torn by civil war. Six years later, Eystein II (#27) came to Norway from Ireland with his mother, who claimed Eystein was her son by Harald Gilchrist, and was entitled to part of the kingdom. Inge and Sigurd were in the eastern part of Norway at the time, and after much mediation it was reluctantly decided that Eystein was to have a third of the kingdom. During the following years, there was much jealousy and distrust among the three brothers, but there were also periods of extended peace.

Eystein is described as ungovernable and restless. He had black hair and a dark complexion. He was a little over average height and possessed a good mind and keen understanding. However, his greed for money and his stinginess made him unpopular with the people.

After becoming king, Eystein began an expedition to the west, raiding and conquering territory in both England and Scotland. Einar Skulason, a *skald*, wrote the following about the journey:

> Bit the king's sword
> Followed men their lord
> with all their soul
> at Hartlepool.
> Did ravens gloat.
> Many an English boat
> was cleared. Grew red
> swords with blood shed.

During the years that followed, there was much hostility and many skirmishes between the brothers. In 1155, Eystein II and his brother Sigurd planned to dethrone King Inge. Their plot was discovered by Gregorious Dagsson, a stanch supporter of King Inge, and he informed Inge of the plot. In the following battle, Sigurd was killed, in spite of his cry for mercy.

The two remaining brothers began to gather men and ships for a decisive battle. However, before war broke out, King Eystein was killed in Romerike under very tragic circumstances. It is said he was "chased into the woods and assassinated." To prove he was not a coward, he asked that they slash the mark of the cross between his shoulders. He was then brutally slain. This led people to believe he was a saint, and numerous miracles were said to have occurred at his grave. At the place where he was beheaded and blood touched the ground, a spring came up. Many called him holy.

Eystein is buried in Fors church, in the middle of the floor, with a rug spread over the grave site. Numerous people came to the church and claimed they regained their health from the water from the spring. Then his enemies poured a broth, made from a dog's urine, on the tomb, and the miracles stopped.

Eystein was thirty-two years of age at the time of his death.

Haakon Broadshoulder
28

Haakon II Sigurdsson, Haakon *Herdebreid*[1]

Illegitimate son of King Sigurd the Mouth (#26) and Thora, a servant girl

b.c1147 d.7 Jul 1162 (c15 yrs.)
R.1157–1162
Probably never married

Haakon's mother, Thora, was a servant girl of Simon Thorbergsson, a wealthy farmer in Vik. When Simon found out that she was carrying the child of King Sigurd the Mouth (#26), he relinquished her from her duties. Thora gave birth to Haakon there, and he was brought up in the household of Simon and his wife, Gunnhild. They also had two children of their own, Onund and Andreas, and all three were raised as brothers.

Haakon was a grandson of Harald Gilchrist (#23). At the age of ten, he was acclaimed king of the territory his father ruled. Inge the Hunchback (#25), had been sole king for several years, and had taken possession of property in the Vik area. He now proclaimed Haakon Broadshoulder as his enemy. However, after a battle between Haakon and Inge, the people accepted Haakon as king. This allowed him to have his paternal inheritance, one third of Norway, the same as his father had before him.

From the time he became king, at age ten, Haakon's life was filled with one confrontation after another. There were many battles between him and King Inge, with each winning and losing from time to time. However, in 1161 Haakon's men defeated and killed King Inge the Hunchback. At about age fourteen, Haakon then became the sole ruler of Norway.

However, upon Inge's death, Erling Skakke, a staunch supporter of King Inge, and a leading member of the Bagler group, rushed to get someone to take over.

They could not accept being ruled by King Haakon from the Birchlegs. Erling cleverly managed to get his own son, Magnus V Erlingsson (#29) to the throne. Magnus was five years old at the time, but Erling's wife, Kristin, was the daughter of King Sigurd the Crusader (#21), and claimed that by birth he was entitled to that rite.

Snorri says Haakon was friendly in conversation, playful and boyish in his ways and was loved by the people. He was a handsome, broad-shouldered young man, with a cheerful disposition, sociable, easy to get along with, and liked to be with young people.

His reign was not to last. In a fierce battle with Magnus in 1162, young King Haakon Broadsshoulder was killed. It seems a shame that history never gave him a chance to prove himself. He was fifteen years of age at the time of his death.

1. *Herdebreid.* Broad shoulder.

Magnus V Erlingsson
29

Magnus Erlingsson

Son of Erling Skakke and Kristin Sigurdsson (daughter of Sigurd the Crusader (#21))

b.c1156 d.14 Jun 1184 (c28 yrs)
R.1161–1184, reigned under regency until 1164
m.Eldrid Bjarnesdatter from Reim. No children from this marriage, however, the following children claimed Magnus V as their father
√.Mothers unknown:
   Kristin, b.c1174
       m. Reidar Sendemann, b.c1160
   Ingeborg, b.c1175
       m.Peter Steyper, b.c1165
   Sigurd Magnusson (#35,) also called Sigurd Kongsson,[1] b.c1180 d.1194
       R.1193–1194
   Inge II Magnusson (#36), b.c1176 d.1202 R.1196–1202
   Erling Stonewall (#42), father of Sigurd Ribung and Magnus. b.c1184
       d.1207 R.1204–1207
   Margrete, b.c1184

Magnus became king upon the death of Haakon Broadshoulder (#28). He was only five years old at the time, but was fortunate to have the capable assistance of his father, Erling Skakke.[2] He did not have royal blood on his father's side, as was usually required during this time, but his royal heritage came from his mother, Kristin, as she was the daughter of Sigurd the Crusader (#21).

Erling was determined to have Magnus remain in power. He was a great man during this period of history, but was a brutal and ruthless leader. It seems that Kristin had a "love-child," Harald, with Sigurd the Mouth (#26) before she married Erling. Harald and Magnus were about the same age, and were brought up together, as brothers. Although Magnus begged for the life of Harald, Erling had him executed (he was fourteen years of age), for fear he would put in a claim for the throne. Kristin was furious and immediately left Norway with a lover and settled in Constantinople where she had several more children.

Magnus V Erlingsson
On the shore of Nornes on the Sognfjord before the Battle of Fimreite

During this period of Norway's history, there were several claimants to the throne. One was Sigurd Markusfostre (#30), among the last of the anti-Erling party. He said he was the son of King Sigurd the Mouth (#26), and was acknowledged as a petty king in 1163, but was executed the same year.

Erling decided it best to legalize Magnus' claim to the throne, and in 1163 arranged to have him crowned in Bergen by Archbishop Eystein. Coronations had become popular in Europe, but this was the first coronation to take place in the Scandinavian countries. In order to get Magnus crowned, Erling had to "pay a price." This resulted in an agreement whereby Norway was virtually changed from hereditary to an elective monarchy, with the ultimate control over succession going to the bishops.

In 1170, Valdemar d. Store (#31) of Denmark also claimed to be king of Norway for a short period of time, but withdrew after mediating with Erling Skakke.

Sverre (#32) also caused Magnus many problems. He was a charismatic figure in Norwegian history, and was constantly at war with Magnus.

Several other "pretenders" came forward during this period. One was Eystein Moyla (#32) who claimed to be the sons of Eystein II Haraldsson (#27), and was acclaimed king in the Viken area. Eystein was the originator of the "Birchlegs," the anti-bishop party that was later taken over by Sverre. Eystein Moyla met his death when he was totally defeated by Magnus in 1177. This was the first battle in which young Magnus took a personal part and thereby gained glory.

Magnus was twenty-three years old in 1179 when his father Erling Skakke died. Erling had been the governing power at this time. During the next few years there were many battles and skirmishes between Magnus and Sverre. In the autumn of 1183, Sverre set up his government in Bergen and controlled the entire area between Rogaland and Sogn. However, the people of Sogn revolted when Sverre's sysselmenn[3] (followers) ordered food and drink for their personal consumption at a *Yule* (Christmas) Feast which they proposed to enjoy at Kaupanger. Most of Sverre's men were killed. However, the following spring, Sverre had his revenge and attempted a surprise attack on Magnus at Fimreite, off Nornes. Sverre won a complete victory. Many tales are told of this battle, and it is said that over 2000 men lost their lives on the banks of Fimreite, among them, Magnus, who was forced to jump overboard to his death.[4] Crafty Sverre had won yet another battle.

King Magnus' body was recovered and taken to Bergen for burial. He was twenty-eight years of age.

1. Several reports state that "Asa the Fair" was the mother of Sigurd.
2. See footnote, Chapter 25, for additional information about Erling Skakke.
3. *Sysselmen* were higher in rank than the regular Vikings. See glossary.
4. The writer visited this area many times. Her husband's mother was born and raised at Nornes. It is said that if you sit on the shores of the Sognfjord at midnight, when the wind sweeps down the fjord, you can hear the long mournful moans of the Vikings who died over 1000 years ago.

Sigurd Markusfostre*
30

Sigurd III Markusfostre

Claimed to be the son of Sigurd II the Mouth (#26)[1] and unknown mistress. Sigurd was fostered in the Opplands.

b.c1142 d.11 Sept 1163 (c21 yrs.)
R.1163–1163

Turmoil and great confusion continued during this period when King Haakon Broadshoulder (#28) was killed in 1162. Erling Skakke tried everything in his power to keep the reign of Norway in his hands. However, at this time another opponent arose, by the name of Sigurd Markusfostre, who claimed that he was a son of Sigurd II the Mouth (#26). He arrived in Hordaland (the Province in which Bergen is located) in 1163 and headed for Bergen. He probably believed that he would find it undefended. However, he was quickly captured and executed at Re in Vestfold in 1163. His foster-father, Marcus, was hanged on the same day. The anti-Erling party was now on its way out.

Sigurd is often not listed in regnal records, but is acknowledged as being a pretender, or king, for a period of time.

1. It seems rather doubtful that Sigurd Markusfostre was a son of Sigurd II the Mouth (#26) and had royal blood. During this time, the dates of battles and deaths, especially of kings, were more often recorded and accurate than the dates of birth. Therefore, Sigurd's death in 1163 is probably more accurate than his birth date, especially since he was illegitimate. Sigurd Markusfostre's birth date is listed as 1142 AD, but his father, Sigurd II the Mouth, would have been only 9 years old at the time. Perhaps Sigurd was born later. However, the tale of his battles indicate that he was at least in his late teens. Perhaps he was not the son of Sigurd the Mouth. Since he had no children, his royal blood-line did not continue, so maybe this is not of great importance to historians. We will let the readers make their own decisions.

Valdemar the Great
31

Valdemar d. Store, Valdemar I, Waldemar

Son of Knut Lavard (King Knut III Magnusson or Hardeknut) of Denmark

b.1131 d.1182 (51 yrs.)
R.1170–1170 in Norway
R.1157–1182 in Denmark
m.Sofia, a half-sister of Knut Magnusson (Knud III) and granddaughter of King
    Niels
      Children:
          Knut, b.1182, succeeded Valdemar the Great as King Knut VI, b.1163
              d.1202, R.1182–1202 in Denmark
          Valdemar II, in 1202 succeeded Knut VI as King Valdemar II Seier
              (#41), b.1170 d.1241, R.1204–1204 in Norway, R.1202–1241 in
              Denmark

Erling Skakke managed to put his son, Magnus V Erlingsson (#29) on the throne in 1161, thus keeping the Bagler movement alive. Haakon Broadshoulder (#28) was already king and served as a representative of the Birchlegs.

During the reign of Magnus, Erling found it advisable to seek the support in Denmark from Valdemar the Great, its new and powerful king. King Valdemar claimed the kingship of Norway for a short period of time in 1170. However, after mediation with Erling, Valdemar pulled out of Norway. Historians do not know what kind of an agreement was made when they met.

In Denmark, King Valdemar and his successors marked the beginning of a great period in Danish history. He consolidated a powerful kingdom, built churches and cities. It was the beginning of a period of economic, cultural and international growth for Denmark. Valdemar's reign was also a relatively peaceful time for the country, and he was considered a great Danish king.

Valdemar died suddenly in 1182, and was succeeded by his eldest son, Knut (as Knut VI) to the Danish throne.

Eystein Moyla*
32

Oystein Moyla, Eystein Meyla

Ilegitimate son of King Eystein II Haraldsson (#27) and unknown mistress

b.c1145 (perhaps later) d.1177 (c32 yrs.)
R.1176–1177
Probably never married

During the reign of Magnus V Erlingsson (#29), we also have another claimant to the throne—a young son of King Eystein Haraldsson (#27). He was called Eystein Moyla, (little girl or girlie). Snorri describes him as a "handsome little fellow, with a fair complexion and small features. He was not of a tall stature."

When Eystein discovered he was the son of a king, he went to Sweden and found his paternal aunt, Brigitha,[1] and her husband Birgir Brosa. He was in his early youth and received their support for his claim to the throne of Norway.[2] He stayed with them for a while and Birgir Brosa gave him some troops, ample money for subsistence and good presents before he left. King Magnus V. Erlingsson had been king for about thirteen years and they knew that he and his father, Erling Skakke, would not look favorably upon his demand.

Eystein decided to first go to Vik, and there many men were eager to join his group and make him king. They represented the poor peasants who were tired of being ruled by the upper-class group (Baglers). The band stayed in Vik during that winter and fought many battles. The sagas state that they ran out of money and their clothes fell off. They then used birch bark to wrap their legs to keep out the cold. From then on they were referred to as the "Birchlegs."

By this time the Birchlegs had grown into a relatively large army. They were tough and skilled with weapons, but usually pursued a headlong, reckless course after they had sufficient force to do so. Most of the time they had no counsel or obeyed no laws. Many of them just did what seemed best to them. They relied on their own bravery. As a result, the name "Birchlegs" was originally a title of disdain. Later the group was taken over by Sverre and it became an honorable title.

The Birchlegs remained in Vik for two years, and did not cause much concern to King Magnus. However, they then decided to sail up the west coast toward Trondheim. As they traveled, many proceeded to join them and Eystein's troops increased to about 2000 men. Many battles followed between King Eystein's Birchlegs and King Magnus and his followers. The final battle occurred in Re in the fall of 1177, where Eystein met total defeat. He was forced to take flight, ran into a house and asked for mercy, but the farmer killed him.

The date of Eystein's birth is not known, but he apparently died at a young age.

1. See Chapter 49 for additional information about Brigitha.
2. It was considered a duty and an obligation to claim the throne if you discovered that you had royal blood.

Sverre
Norway's brilliant military leader.

Sverre Sigurdsson
33

Sverre, Sverri

Son of Sigurd the Mouth (#26) and Gunnhild Sveinsdatter (who was married to Unas, a combmaker in Bergen at the time)

b.c1151, born on the Faeroe Islands, d.c9 Mar 1202 (51 yrs). Died "from a
  cold."
R.1177–1202
m1)Astrid Roesdatter, b.c1177, sister of King Knut Eriksson of Sweden), m.
   sometime before 1185, b.c1157
       Children:
               Cecelia Sverresdatter, b.c1177. m1) Kik Gregorius. m2) Einar Prest
               Ingeborg Sverresdatter, b.c1179. m1) Karl Sverkersson of Sweden
m2)Princess Margrete Eriksdatter, daughter of Erik IX Jedvardsson, King of
   Sweden and Christine Bjornsdatter of Jernside, Sweden
       Children:
               Kristin Sverresdatter, Princess of Norway, b.c1185 d.in child-birth;
                   m.Filippus Simonsson (#38) King of Baglers
               Erling, Prince of Norway, b.c1186, died young

Following children are listed as illegitimate with unknown mothers:
√.Mothers unknown:
               Sigurd Lavard, Prince of Norway, b.c1175 d.1202. He was
                   Sverre's oldest son. Sigurd was the father of Guttorm
                   Sigurdsson (#40).
               Haakon III, Prince of Norway, King Haakon III (#37). Reigned
                   from 1202 to 1204. Probably poisoned. m.Inga of Varteig.
                   Father of Haakon IV the Old (#43)

Sverre emerged from obscurity in about 1177 to lay claim to the throne. Whether he was a son of Sigurd the Mouth (#26) is debatable, but it seems that Sverre truly believed this to be true. He was a rebel, and after a generation of conflict in the twelfth century, he became a leader and was king until he died in 1202.

Sverre was to become one of Norway's most remarkable kings, and a brilliant military leader. He was also endowed with a sense of humor, a joy of life, and bold originality.

A little here about Sverre's background. It is said that he was the son of Gunnhild, a Norwegian woman married to a comb-maker in Bergen. When Sverre was four years old, she took him to the Faeroes where he was brought up by his uncle, who was a Bishop in the islands. Sverre was well educated and became an ordained priest at an unusually early age. However, after his mother told him that he was actually the son of the former Norwegian king, Sigurd II the Mouth (#26), he left for Norway in 1174 to claim the throne. He was about twenty-five years old at the time.

By 1177 he had become leader of the Birchlegs, rivals of the incumbent ruler Magnus V Erlingsson (#29). Before this, only a small group took part in Norway's Civil War, but now a larger number of the people participated. However, the war was largely confined to the Viken area, and Sverre's reign was a troubled one for the city of Bergen.

There were many battles and skirmishes between the Birchlegs with Sverri as their leader, and the Baglers with Magnus V in charge. One battle, The Battle of Fimreite, was of great significance. On June 14, 1184, Magnus sailed into Bergen and took the Birchlegs by surprise. Magnus told the people of Bergen that he would return after he defeated Sverre, who had proceeded up to Sogn. However, the tables turned and Sverre, a skillful military leader, won a complete victory. The battle was fought in the Sognfjord between Nordnes and Fimreite. The sagas say that over 2000 men were lost in this battle, including Magnus, who had been forced to jump overboard and drowned. This left Sverre as the sole ruling king in Norway.

In 1194 Sverre's coronation took place in the Bergen Cathedral. According to the sagas, he had been excommunicated, and consequently the bishops who per-formed the ceremony were also excommunicated. About this time Sverre made his celebrated "speech against the bishops," whereby he declared that the Church and the laws of the State gave him the right to influence the elections of bishops and appointment of chaplains. This expanded the power of the monarchy and limited the privileges of the church. There is controversy about the blessings from Rome, and whether Sverre caused papers to be forged. There are those who claim Sverre was "the greatest swindler of his time."

From 1194 until the time of his death in 1202, battles raged on all fronts, and blood was shed freely throughout Norway as the feud continued between the Birchlegs and the Baglers. From 1184 until his death in 1202, Sverre had almost complete control of Norway. There were brief periods during this time that Jon Kuvlung (#34), Sigurd Magnusson (#35) and Inge II Magnusson (#36) claimed to be king, but Sverre managed to remain as the foremost king and ruler.

Sverre spent the last year and a half of his life in Tønsberg, where he "picked up an infection," became ill and died. He was buried in the Great Christ Church in Bergen in 1202.

Sverre was a charismatic individual—one of the best known figures in medieval Norwegian history. By expanding the power of the monarchy and limiting the privileges of the church, he provoked civil uprisings that were not quelled until 1217.

Jon Kuvlung*
34

Reportedly the son of Inge the Hunchback (#25) and a mistress

b.c1160 d.1188, murdered
R.1185–88

During Sverre's (#33) reign, from 1177 to 1202, several claimants to the throne turned up. The first of these was Jon Kuvlung, who claimed to be the son of King Inge the Hunchback (#25). He began his revolt with a group of followers in about 1184, after Sverre's victory at the Battle of Fimreite.

Jon was a monk from the Abbey of Hovedøya at Oslo. He was nicknamed *Kuvlung* (*kuvl* = cowl, a monk's hood), due to his having discarded his cowl when he became king at the *Thing* in Tønsberg in 1185.

Jon had the support of both clergy and masses in Viken, over which he ruled for three years, while Sverre reigned in western Norway. He had considerable successes in battles against Sverre at Bergen and Trondheim. On one visit to Trondheim he captured it by surprise, and destroyed Zion (temple/church). However, he was defeated in 1187 at Jaren and fled to Tønsberg.

Sverre followed him in the autumn of 1188 and seized all of the *kuvlunger* ships. Then Jon and his *kuvlungers* marched overland to Trondheim and captured the castle, seized Sverre's ships and sailed to Bergen. However, Sverre, just before Christmas, in a battle near Bergen in 1188, killed Jon Kuvlung, who was buried in Maria Church in Bergen.

The followers of Jon Kuvlung dispersed and this was the end of the first attempt to found a "Kingdom of East Norway." The *kuvlunger* were then temporarily disbanded, with few remnants remaining.

Sigurd Magnusson*
35

Sigurd Kongsson

Son of Magnus V Erlingsson (#29) and unknown mother

b.c1180 d.1194
R.1193–1194
Probably not married

Another revolt against King Sverre occurred in about 1193, instigated by a band of rebels from the Orkney Island called "Island-beards" or *Oyskjegge*. They arrived unexpectedly at Tønsberg and quickly called together the *Thing*, and acclaimed Sigurd as king.

The following summer, King Sigurd assembled a fleet of ships under the capable leadership of Hallkel Johnsson. They arrived off Bergen in 1194. For some time, Sverresborg, Sverre's headquarters, was able to repel their attacks, but the town was eventually captured. Hallkel Johnsson felt they were in complete control, but Sverre, who was not at Sverresborg at the time of the attack, made another of his quick strategic moves and won a complete victory in the Battle of Florevaag.

The dead Island-beards were buried in a mass grave in Maria churchyard. King Sigurd was also slain in this battle and is buried in the Great Christ Church in Bergen. Hallkel Johnsson, a brother-in-law of Magnus Erlingsson (#29), was also given the honor of being buried there.

Historians usually consider Sigurd a "petty king," and he is often not included in regnal lists of kings.

Inge Magnusson*
36

Inge II

Claimed to be the son of Magnus V. Erlingsson (#29) and unknown mistress.
Inge and Sigurd Magnusson (#35) were apparently brothers or half-brothers.

b.c1175 d.1202
R.1196–1202
Probably not married

After the death of Sigurd Magnusson (#35), the Baglers needed someone to represent them. Inge Magnusson, brother or half-brother of Sigurd, laid claim to the
throne and was king for the Baglers who had stayed with Bishop Nikolas Arnesson's
party. The Birchlegs said he was Danish, but Inge claimed he was the son of Magnus
V. Erlingsson (#29), and great grandson of Sigurd the Crusader (#21) and therefore
had royal blood with a right to be king. (You will note that this was not from the
male line.)

Inge's reign was confined to the Viken area, and he did not cause Sverre much of
a problem. However, in 1199, Sverre attacked, and Inge lost the battle. In 1202 Inge
died at Helgøya, where he was killed by the local farmers.

Not much is said about Inge in history books, and he is not often listed in
regal lists.

Haaken III
37

Haakon Sverresson, Haaken the Younger

Illegitimate son of Sverre Sigurdsson (#33) with an unknown mistress

b.c1177 d.1204 (27 yrs.), probably poisoned
R.1202–1204
√.Inga of Varteig. Referred to as "The Peace Maiden."
  Children:
      Haakon IV (#43), born posthumously

King Sverre (#33) had made careful preparations for his only surviving son, Haakon, to succeed him. (Another son, Erling, had evidently died earlier.) Young Haakon was about twenty-five years of age at the time of his father's death when he took over as king. Haakon reigned only two years and although he was from Sverre's beloved Birchleg party, he did everything in his power to bring peace to Norway by bringing about a reconciliation with the Baglers. He supported the common people and was a firm leader, keeping his men under strict control. Haakon also did his best to make peace with the church leaders. The bishops returned to their former districts, and he guaranteed them many liberties which they had previously held. The people were tired of war and although vague, the agreement was helpful in keeping the peace.

The people were pleased with Haakon's leadership and the Bagler party continued to diminish. He was attractive, popular, and a well-meaning person—"He was a good man." King Haakon, however, did not have a cordial relationship with his stepmother, Margrete, Sverre's Swedish wife. She is sometimes referred to as his worst enemy. In order to keep control over her, Haakon had forbidden Margrete from going to Sweden with her daughter, Kristin. This infuriated Margrete. In an attempt at reconciliation, Haakon traveled to Trondheim in the winter of 1203-04. He asked his step-mother to join him at the Christmas feast. Margrete reluctantly agreed, and sat at the dais beside the king, with her daughter at her side, to King Haakon's great pleasure. Two nights later, Haakon suffered violent pains, and died suddenly on New Year's Day. It was said that his body was so blue and swollen it did not appear human. Was Margrete responsible?

All of Norway mourned King Haakon's death. After long years of warfare, he had brought a short period of peace. The people suspected Margrete of poisoning King Haakon's drink and demanded that she go through "ordeal by fire" to prove her innocence. She hired a deputy (emissary) to undergo the test for her, but his hands were so burned that they deemed Margrete guilty. The deputy was drowned, and they demanded that Margrete also receive the same punishment. She was saved by Haakon Galen who smuggled her back to Sweden.

As long as King Haakon III was alive there were no major hostilities, but his sudden death set the country again into a turmoil as to who was to rule. Shortly before his death, Haakon became infatuated by a well-born beauty, Inga of Varteig. Historians refer to her as "The Peach Maiden" as it was hoped she would further the quest for peace.[1] What was apparently not known when King Haakon died was that Inga was carrying his child. Therefore it wasn't until twelve years later that his son, Haakon IV (#43) was able to ascend the throne.

Haakon was twenty-seven years old when he died, and is buried in the Great Christ Church in Bergen.

[1]See Haakon IV the Old (#43) for more information on Inga of Varteig.

Filippus Simonsson*
38

Filip(pus) Simonsson, Philip Simonsson

> Son of Simon Karlsson and Margrete, the daughter of Harald Gille's (#23) queen, Ingerid Ragnvaldsdatter in her marriage with Arne Arnesson. Filippus was also the nephew of Bishop Nikolas and Inge Hunchback (#25)
>
> b.c1182 d.1217 (35 yrs.)
> R.1202–1217
> m.Kristin Sverresdatter, daughter of King Sverre (#33) and Princess Eriksdatter of Sweden. Kristin died in childbirth; one child; died shortly after mother.

When the brilliant Birchleg leader, Sverre (#33), died in 1202, he was followed by his son, Haakon III (#37). However, the Baglers had also acclaimed Filippus Simonsson, the nephew of Bishop Nikolas, as their king and he became the leader in the east. Filippus spent most of his time in Tønsberg, although Oslo was the capital; perhaps because he did not want to be so close to his overbearing uncle, Bishop Nikolas Arnesson. Although he is often not listed as a king, there are royal documents from that time, signed by Filippus, which have been preserved in their original state.

Upon the sudden death of Haakon III in 1204, trouble began to emerge again between the two factions. The Birchlegs quickly brought forth little four-year-old Guttorm (#40), Sverre's grandson, as a replacement for Haakon III. The leadership, however, was in the hands of Haakon Galen, Sverre's half-Swedish nephew. Guttorm, died within a few months after he was made king. Haakon Galen's wife, Kristin, was blamed for his death. She apparently wanted her husband to gain control and she would then be Queen of Norway. Haakon Galen tried to gain recognition as king, but was unsuccessful in his attempt.

The Baglers brought forth Inge II Baardsson (#39), and he became king in 1204. Erling Stonewall (#40) is also listed as a petty king during this period, but he was definitely subordinate to King Inge II. Upon Erling's death in 1207, Filippus was again recognized as the Bagler kings, in the east, while Inge II was supported by the Birchlegs. During these years, several others also claimed the throne for various lengths of time.

In about 1208 Bishop Nikolas suggested a meeting to bring both parties together. This met with the approval of the majority of Norwegians, as they had become tired of the long war. He suggested that Norway be divided into three areas under Filippus, Haakon Galen, and Inge II. It was also agreed that Filippus was to marry Sverre's daughter, Kristin, to cement relationships between the Baglers and the Birchlegs. Ingi II was to be the predominant king. Filippus, however, continued to be recognized as the Bagler king.

Filippus was considered a fairly descent fellow, with an attractive personality and was most popular. He did his best to tone down the excessive violence that his group, the Baglers, often initiated.

In 1209, Filippus and Kristin were married, and she brought her husband as a dowry a sizable piece of property. A few years later, Queen Kristin died in childbirth. The baby died soon afterwards, but outlived its mother. Kristin's mother, Swedish Queen Margrete, died a few days later, so Filippus was able to inherit all of Kristin's vast properties in Varmland and Vasterland, which he hurried to collect.

Again there was no heir with royal blood to the throne, so when King Inge II died in 1217, Filippus sent a message to Duke Skule that they divide the kingdom between them—otherwise he would resume the fighting. However, before the order was delivered, Filippus became ill and died at Tønsberg in July of 1217. Again the succession to the throne was under debate.

Filippus is often not listed in regnal records. He was probably about thirty-five years of age when he died.

Inge II Baardsson*
39

Inge II, Ingi II Bårdsson

Son of *lendmannen* Baard Guttormsson (from Reim in Trondelag) and Cecelia Sigurdsdatter, the daughter of Sigurd the Mouth (#26).

b.c1185 d.23 April 1217 (32 yrs)
R.1204–1217
m.Gyrid, b.c1190
    Children:
        Guttorm

Again there was no male heir to take over the cause of the Birchlegs, but they succeeded in electing Inge II Baardsson as king by virtue of his mother's royal blood. Although Sverre had always maintained that the king could only descend through the male line, this was not opposed.

The Bagler party continued to exist during this time, which resulted in many clashed between the two factions until 1208 when a temporary peace was made.

Inge II was a weak leader. Many others laid claim to the throne during the time he professed to be king. Both Haakon Galen and Skule Baardsson (#45), were advisors and had great influence over Inge II. They were strong leaders of the Birchlegs during this period.

In the autumn of 1207, King Inge II and Haakon Galen left with a large fleet, with a plan to drive the Baglers out of Bergen. They were not successful and Haakon Galen returned to Denmark.

Inge II died in 1217, and his half-brother, Skule Baardsson tried to be proclaimed king, claiming he was the personal heir of Inge, but was unsuccessful in this attempt. He did however, gain limited recognition as king some years later. (See #45). The Birchlegs put four-year-old Guttorm Sigurdsson (#40) on the throne after Haakon III (#37) died, but he died shortly thereafter.

Guttorm Sigurdsson*
40

Guttorm

Son of Sigurd Lavard (the oldest son of King Sverre) and unknown mother from the Faroe Islands

b.c1200 d.1204 (4 yrs)
R.1204–1204

When King Haakon III (#37) died suddenly in 1204, the Birchlegs quickly claimed the throne with four-year-old Guttorm Sigurdsson, the grandson of their beloved Sverre.

Guttorm was born in the Faroe Islands, and was fostered by Peter Styper and Einar Prest. Haaken Galen, Sverre's half-Swedish nephew, guided little Guttorm. He had been king for barely seven months, when he died suddenly. Haakon Galen's Swedish wife, Kristin Nikoladatter, *vart skulda for å stå bak dette nåsfallet*, was blamed for his death. Apparently Kristin felt that if little Guttorm was gone, her husband would become king and she would be the next queen of Norway.

Haakon Galen became the leading pretender, since there were no apparent heirs to the throne in the male line. However he was not acknowledged as a king, and the Danes again claimed control of Norway with Valdemar II (#41) as king.

Valdemar II*
41

Valdemar II Seier, Valdemar the Victorious

Son of Valdemar I (#31), King of Denmark and Sofia, Queen of Denmark

b.28 Jun 1170 d.28 Mar 1241 (c71 yrs.)
R.1204–1204 in Norway
R.1202–1240 in Denmark
m1)Helen Guttormsdatter
m2)Dagmar (Margarete) Princess of Bohemia
m3)Richsa, Princess of Saxony in 1202, b.1172 d.1204
m4) Berengaria, Princess of Portugal
    Children:
        Erik IV Plovpenny, King of Denmark, b.1216 d.1250 (c34 yrs),
            m.Jutte I, Prince of Saxony.
            Children:
                Ingeborg, married Norway's King Magnus the Lawmender
                (#46), and had four sons.
        Sofia, Princess of Denmark b.1217 d.1247 (35 yrs.)
            m.Johanne I Margrave
            Children:
                Kristin, married Norway's Magnus the Blind (#22)
        Abel, King of Denmark, b.1218 d.1252 (c34 yrs.)
            m.Mathilde, Countess of Holstein
        Christoffer, King of Denmark, b.1219 d.1259 (c40 yrs.)

Haakon Galen was unable to gain control of the throne after the death of Guttorm (#40). Valdemar II Seier of Denmark made use of this opportunity and laid claim to Norway.

Valdemar's reign marked a high point in Danish history, and his work at expanding the Danish control of the south Baltic coast left him little time to be involved to any great extent in Norway. After his death in 1241, Denmark entered a period of violence and decline that lasted for nearly 100 years.

Valdemar II is often not included in regnal lists of Norwegian rulers.

Erling Stonewall*
42

Erling Steinvegg

> Claimed to be the son of Magnus V Erlingsson (#29), who fell in the battle of Fimreite
>
> b.before 1184 d.February 1207
> R.1204–1207
> Probably not married, but when he died in 1207, he left two small infant sons:
>   Sigurd Ribung,[1] b.c1199 d.c1126
>   Magnus, b.c1199

In 1204 when Haakon Galen brought in little Guttorm, Sverre's grandson as ruler to represent the Birchlegs, the Baglers retaliated by gathering around Erling Stonewell. Erling's name "Stonewall" (*steinvegg* – stone wall) derived from the time Sverre (#33) persuaded his brother-in-law King Knut of Sweden to imprison him within stone walls on an island at Lake Vättern in Sweden. The Birchlegs claimed Erling was a "swindler," and not of royal blood; the Baglers claimed he was the son of Magnus V Erlingsson (#29).

It was 1204, and Erling was probably in his twenties at the time. He went to Tønsberg, which had become the royal capital of the "Kingdom of East Norway." In order to prove that he was the son of Magnus V, it was necessary for him to be subjected to "ordeal by fire." This was carried out by Bishop Nicholas Arnesson who wanted this done in the presence of Valdemar II, who had arrived at Tønsberg with 300 vessels on the 17th of June, 1204. (Valdemar assisted the Bagler movement.) Valdemar decided the manner of the ordeal and administered the oath, while the bishop determined its heat content and applied the hot irons. Valdemar also had the church surrounded by armed men during the critical moment when the bandages were removed. Erling passed the test, and the bishop remarked that he had never seen a hand come away so "unscathed"—and then they all sang *Te Deum Laudamus*. It was, of course, the bishop who was responsible for heating up the irons. He was aware that a solid relationship with Erling when he became king would be beneficial to him. There is little doubt that this kept him from making the irons too hot.

Erling was supposedly under the subjection of King Valdemar II, but this was as meaningless to Erling as was his father's, to Valdemar the Great. Valdemar also had too many problems of his own in Denmark, and was unable to pay much attention to what was going on in Norway.

The Baglers were now lords, with Erling as their king, and with Tonberg as their royal capitol. The "Kingdom of East Norway," was often at odds with the west. In 1205 they had to flee from their capitol when the Birchlegs succeeded in having Inge II (#39) proclaimed king. At the same time, the Baglers had attacked Trondheim, and Erling was acclaimed king there also, along with Filippus. King Erling Stonewall returned to Tønsberg for Christmas in 1206–1207, but died there in February. Although he apparently was not married, historians say he left two small sons, Sigurd and Magnus, when he died in 1207.

Erling was buried in the famous Round Church in Slesvig (Vestfold).

1. See Haakon IV the Old (#43) for more information on Sigurd Ribung.

Haakon IV the Old

Haakon's reign was called "The Age of Greatness."

Haakon IV the Old
43

Haakon the Old, Haakon Haakonsson, Håkon IV, Håkonarsonår

Illegitimate son of Haakon III Sverresson (#33) and Inga of Varteig

b.1204 near Sarpsborg, d.15 Dec 1263 (59 yrs.), on Orkney Island, now part
  of Scotland
R.1217–1263. Haakon was acclaimed king in 1217, but it wasn't until 30
  years later, in 1247, that he was crowned in Bergen.
√.Mother unknown
    Children:
        Olav: Illegitimate. b.1227 d.1240, only 13 years of age
m.Margrete, daughter of Skule Baardsson (#45)
    Children:
        Haakon, b.1232 d.1257. m.Richiza Birgirsdatter, Jarl Birgir's daughter
           from Sweden
        Kristin, b.1234 d.1262. m. Don Philip, Prince Don Philip of Spain
        Magnus VI the Lawmender (#46), b.1238 d.1280. m.Ingeborg
           Eriksdatter, daughter of King Erik IV Plovpenny of Denmark
√.Kanga the Young, Haakon also had two illegitimate children with Kanga
  before he married Margrete
    Children:
    Sigurd Haakonsson
    Cecelia Haakonsdatter. m1)Harald, King of the Isle of Man

Not known to the Birchlegs or the Baglers when Haakon III died in 1204 was that Inga of Varteig was with child. If it was a son, he would inherit the throne. It was a son and he immediately became a threat to the Baglers. He was named Haakon IV and was in constant danger of being seized and killed. In 1206, when he was only two years old, there was a flair-up of the civil war. They feared for young Haakon's life. Many stories are told of the events that followed when two loyal Viking follow-ers rescued him by bundling him up in the dead of winter and skiing him across the Dovre mountains. Their journey took them from Lillehammer to Trondheim where he was safely reunited with his mother, and triumphantly delivered to the court of the current Birchleg leader, King Inge II, where he spent his childhood.

This story is part of Viking history, and today is commemorated with Birkebeiner (Birchleg) Skiing races in Norway, USA and other countries.

In 1217 both King Inge II Baardsson and King Filippus died and thirteen-year-old Haakon was acclaimed king. There arose doubts as to his paternity, but his mother, Inga of Vertaig, successfully passed the "ordeal by fire," thereby confirming his royal heritage. Inga had rubbed her hands with the juice of *sempervivum tectorum* (house leek), and thereby her hands were unscarred. It is said that Norwegian house-wives, to this day, keep leaves from this plant in their kitchens as a burn remedy.

Jarl Skule (#45), Haakon's brilliant advisor, continued to control the government as he had done previously. For this he receiving a third of the royal income. Haakon placed great confidence in Skule who successfully protected Haakon for years against his enemies. However, their congenial relationship began to break up and in order to try to pacify Jarl Skule, Haakon married his daughter, Margrete. She was only seventeen at the time and he was twenty-one. In 1225 the wedding took place and they returned to Tønsberg, along with Inga of Varteig, the king's mother, and there they took up residence.

During Haakon's rule, Junker Knut (#44) also claimed the throne for a short period in 1226–1227.

At about this time the Baglers and the Birchlegs almost made peace with each other, but another rebel group, the Ribbungers,[1] gained control and took over Viken. Haakon and Skule supported each other in their battles against them. However, their leader, Sigurd Ribbung, died in 1226 and the rebellion was all but over.

The tension between Norway and Denmark continued to become more strained. King Haakon IV kept busy in Bergen, the capitol at that time. His relation-ship with Jarl Skule, who lived in Trondheim, worsened with time. Skule was a bril-liant advisor, but as he grew older his greed for power and prestige and his love for drinking finally led to an open revolt against King Haakon. Skule proclaimed him-self king in 1239, which ultimately led to a battle with Haakon which resulted in Skule's death in 1240 and ended Norway's devastating 110-year Civil War.

The next few years were relatively peaceful and Norway prospered. There began to be cooperation between the archbishop and the kingdom. In Haakon, Sverri's fam-ily in the direct male line was firmly established on the throne and was to continue to rule through a great century in Norway's history. The country came out of the internal conflicts, unified, and consolidated. It was as fully a developed national state as was to be found anywhere in Europe. Kingship had been at the center of the development. In Norway the conflicts were between kings and pretenders, while in the other countries it was chiefly between kings and nobles (powerful land owners). Haakon's strong reign gave the land peace and greatness. This royal power was the result of the support of both aristocrats who were both landholders and royal officials.

Haakon was also influential in promoting trading with other countries. He brought in more literary works, and this cultural trend was continued later when his son Magnus became king. They wanted the Norwegian courts to be comparable to other European countries. In 1262–1263, he also annexed Iceland and Greenland to the kingdom of Norway.

Margrete and Haakon had three children—two sons, Haakon, and Magnus (who later became King Magnus), and a daughter, Kristin. An illegitimate son, Olav, died at age thirteen, and no mention is made of the cause of his death. Haakon also had two illegitimate children with Kanga the Young before he married Margrete. Sigurd was the oldest, and not much is written about him. A brief mention is made about Cecelia, who married King Harald Olavsson of the Isle of Man; both were drowned off the Shetland Islands on their return from their honeymoon.

Haakon's fame travelled all over Europe. The king of Spain decided that it would be politically advantages for one of his sons to marry Kristin, King Haakon's daughter. When Haakon sailed home from a battle with the Danes he met a convoy with the Spanish Embassy on board. Their mission was to ask for the hand of Haakon's daughter. They were led by a priest. King Haakon invited them to spend the winter at Tønsberg and he would give them an answer by spring.

The Spaniards spent Christmas in Tønsberg and Crown Prince Haakon (son of Haakon IV), now in his mid-twenties, spent the winter with them. The young prince had returned from a campaign against the Danes. He became ill, and although he was attended faithfully by a doctor from the Spanish Embassy, he died, in about 1257. The king took his son's body to Oslo to be buried in St. Hallvard's church.

In the spring, the decision was made by King Haakon IV that his daughter, Kristin, was to go to Spain and she could choose which prince she wished to marry. She picked the youngest son, Don Philip. It was a magnificent wedding, held on March 31, 1258. However the marriage was not a happy one. It is easy to see the culture shock of young Kristin, leaving her people, language and climate and locating to Spain. Kristin died in 1262, probably in childbirth. She was but twenty-eight years of age. It is believed she is buried in Spain on the Castilian plateau.

Magnus (#46) was the last son of Margarete and Haakon IV. Haakon named him joint king with him, and had him crowned on the day Magnus married the Danish

Princess Ingeborg in 1261. It was hoped this union would end hostilities between Norway and Denmark, but this did not prove to be the case.

King Haakon's last visit to Tønsberg was in 1262. From then on, he and Magnus V used Bergen as their capitol city. However they had helped Tønsberg achieve great power. In about 1230, he and his son, Magnus had built forts at Slottsfjellet in Tønsberg and the city was of greater national and military importance than Oslo. They also built a wall around it with gatehouses and a dwelling. Slottsfjellet had been fortified in the 1160s, and was thought to be impenetrable. It was not until 1299 when Haakon V built Akerhus in Oslo that Oslo took over as the prominent city and capitol. For many years numerous pilgrimages were made to St. Michael's church in Tønsberg.

King Haakon IV's reign is considered to be the beginning of the "golden age," and came to be known as the "age of greatness." He ruled prosperously, and defended his possessions in the Hebrides Islands by an expedition to Scotland in 1263. He died there on the 15th of December, 1263. He was temporarily laid to rest at Kirkwall, but later brought to Bergen. On the 22nd of March in 1264, he was buried beside his father and family in the Great Christ Church. The burial was attended by Queen Margrete, Queen Ingeborg, and his son, Magnus, who delivered the oration.

King Haakon IV was fifty-nine years old when he died.

1. See glossary.

Knut, Junker*
44

Knut, Jarl Junker Knut

Son of Haaken Galen and unknown mistress

b.   d.1261
R.1226–1227
m.Ingerid Skulesdatter, daughter of Skule Baardsson (#45), and sister of Queen
   Margrete, wife of Haakon IV the Old (#43)
No children noted for this marriage

After Sigurd Ribbung died in 1226, his successor, the rebel leader, Junker Knut, took command of the Ribbungers. He marched into Romerike and was acclaimed king at Eidsvoll in 1226. However, the people of Viken did not recognize his claim to the throne, and put together a large group of followers to oppose him.

Knut's troops were almost annihilated when they marched into Oslo, but Junker Knut escaped. In a later major battle with King Haakon IV the Old (#43), he saved his own life by swimming ashore.

Haakon finally pardoned him and in 1234 gave him the title of *Jarl*. He was given Trondelag in "fief," and King Haakon and his court often visited him. Knut remained his loyal friend and servant for the rest of his life. Knut was married to Ingerid Skulesdatter, the sister of Queen Margrete, King Haakon IV's (#43) wife. No children are noted from this marriage.

Junker Knut was a cultured man but had a passion for drink that weakened him. He died in 1261, and was the last member of the royal household to reside permanently in Trondheim. His reign, from 1226–1227, was short and brutal, and he often is not recognized on regnal lists.

Skule Baardsson*
45

Jarl Skule, Duke Skule

Son of Lendman Baard Guttormsson from Rein and Ragnhild Erlingsdatter. Skule was a king's "Heir" from 1217–1223, *Jarl* from 1217–1236, *Hertung* from 1236–1239 and *Junker* from 1217–1236, titles used during this period of history. He was finally given the title of "Duke," a new title.

b.1189 d.May 1240 (51 yrs.)
R.1239–1240
m.Ragnhild, b.c1190
    Children:
        Margrete, b.c1205, m.Haakon IV (#43), b.1204
        Ingerid, b.c1215, m.Junker Knut (#44), b.c1214
        Ragnfrid
        Peter (adopted)

Thirteen-year-old Haakon Haakonson (#43) claimed the throne in 1217. This was contested by the church because of his illegitimate birth. His rival, Jarl Skule Baardsson also laid claim, but did not have royal blood in his veins.

Haakon was finally recognized as king, but Jarl Skule had a strong following and for the next six years caused King Haakon a great deal of trouble. During this time Skule held almost complete power in East Norway.

Battles continued from time to time between Skule and King Haakon. To Skule's discredit, he was responsible for keeping the Civil War smoldering. Several attempts were made for peace settlements, and at one such meeting it was agreed that Haakon was to marry Skule's daughter, Margaret, in hopes that this would prevent further bloodshed. Haakon did everything in his power to win Skule over, and gave him one title after another, and finally the title of "Duke." This was the first time this title had been used in Norway. Skule also was given control over northern Norway.

Skule and Ragnhild were married in about 1209. Their four children were Margrete, Ingerid, Ragnfrid and Peter. Peter is listed as adopted, and may have been an illegitimate son of Skule. Ingerid eventually became the wife of Junker Knut (#44). Not much is said about Ragnhild in history books. However, she accompanied her daughter, Margrete, to Tønsberg in 1238, when Margrete and King Haakon's son Magnus, was born.

Snorri described Skule as a tall, slim man, with light brown hair.

In 1230, Haakon IV established his capitol at Bergen and permitted Skule to take over the control of Trondheim. Skule's greed, however, would not permit him to be satisfied until he became king. In 1239 Duke Skule "touched the Shrine of St. Olav," and took the title of "King" for himself. King Haakon would not hear of this and quickly traveled to Oslo with his troops.

The final battle between Haakon and Skule was fought in the streets of Oslo, near St. Hallvard's Church. Skule escaped north to Trondheim, but was killed at the Elgesaeter Abbey in Trondheim in 1240.

This ended Norway's disastrous 110-year Civil War. Skule was about sixty years old at the time of his death.

Norway's Golden Years

1240–1405 AD

The Civil War was not considered over until about 1240. However, by this time, Haakon IV the Old (#43), Sverre's son, had been king for over twenty years, and had begun to bring about a period of peace which was comparable to the time before the start of the war. It was Sverre's genealogical line that ruled in Norway up until almost the end of the 14th century. The Viking age was long over, and no major wars took place during this time. The rulers considered themselves as kings by "the grace of God." They were powerful but not absolute and had a high respect for the law. This century and a half is noted for the development of many cities, the increase in the flow of goods into the market places, and heavy trading during the Hanseatic period. The 14th century ends with Queen Margrete (#52), the Danish wife of Haakon VI (#50), taking over the rule of Norway and putting it under the reign of Denmark where it remained for the next 400 years.

Magnus VI the Lawmender 46

Magnus Lagabøte, Magnus VI Haakonsson

Son of Haakon IV the Old (#43) and Queen Margrete, daughter of Skule Baardsson (#44)

b.3 May 1238 in Tønsberg, d.9 May 1280 (42 yrs.)
R.1263–1280
m.Ingeborg Eiriksdatter in 1261, b.1244 d.1287, daughter of the Danish King
Erik Plovpenny and Jutte, Princess of Saxony
Children:
Olav, b.1262 d.1267 (5 yrs.)
Magnus, b.1264 d.1264, died in infancy
Erik II (#47), b.1268 d.1299 (31 yrs.) R.1280–1299
Haakon V (#48), b.1270 d.1319 (49 yrs.) R.1299–1319

Haakon IV the Old (#43) made his son, Magnus VI (#46) a joint king with him in 1261, the same year Magnus was married. Evidently Haakon VI wanted to be sure the crown remained in his family. Magnus didn't take over the reign of Norway until 1963 when Haakon died, but it was customary in those days for the heir apparent to be crowned in anticipation of his succession.

In preparation for the wedding, the Danish Princess Ingeborg, set sail for Bergen. The voyage was stormy and took over three weeks. Once there, she was escorted to Munkeliv Abbey where she stayed until the great event took place. She was strong-willed and able, and also fabulously wealthy. Elaborate preparations were made in the three halls of the Royal Palace. The wedding took place on a Sunday, the 11th of September, 1261, with Archbishop Einar Smorbak officiating. Then the feasting began in Haakonshallen, the magnificent stone cathedral Haakon VI erected. There were 1600 guests, and never before had there been such a grand feast in Norway.

The feasting lasted for three days, after which the coronation took place. Fourteen years earlier, King Haakon IV had been coronated, but this was the first time for a queen. First a crown was placed on Magnus' head. Then the Archbishop led Ingeborg to the throne, and she was crowned. It is said that it was such a moving event that many tears were shed. Magnus wore his crown for the rest of the day, and there is little doubt that Queen Ingeborg did the same.

King Magnus VI and Ingeborg traveled to Stavanger after their wedding and coronation in Bergen. They spent three months there on their honeymoon and continued to make their home there.

Magnus was a kind person, a very earnest man, and wanted peace. He was pious and excessively serious and conscientious, and the crown was as a heavy burden. He was a disciple of the gentle St. Francis and founded many hospitals, one of which was in Stavanger. At a meeting of the council in 1273 he issued a law regulating the succession to the throne. Twelve heirs were mentioned in order of succession, and it was provided that if none of these were to be found, the nearest male heir according to the general law of inheritance was to succeed. At the same time, his oldest son Erik, although just a child, was given the title of king but did not rule until his father's death.

The great work of Magnus VI was the collecting, recoding and unification of all the old laws of Norway to form one common law for the whole kingdom. Henceforth he was known as Magnus the Lawmender.

Many of the white stone churches with Gothic portals to be found in the valleys and fjords of Norway were also erected at the time Magnus reigned. At the monastery of St. Olav's in Bergen he erected a church which he intended as a burial place for himself, and although the church is now much changed, the porch remains as a beautiful piece of architecture.

Magnus VI and Ingeborg had four sons. Olav was the first son, but died at about age five. Magnus, the next son, died as an infant. When King Magnus died in 1280, his oldest surviving son, Erik, was made king. He was only twelve years of age, and ruled under a regency, but his mother, Queen Ingeborg was very influential in decisions. Haakon, age 10, was made Duke and was assigned East Norway as his kingdom. When Erik died in 1299, Haakon became King Haakon V Magnusson (#48) and ruled all of Norway.

After Magnus died, in about 1280, the Germans and Norwegians came to an agreement that looked as if it would lead to peace. However, Queen Mother Ingeborg was still alive, and had appointed a young fellow named Alv Erlingsson, as Duke. He turned pirate, gathered together a band of ruffians and plundered the coasts of Denmark. His activities were not curbed until Ingeborg died in 1287. He lost her support, felt his position was in danger so marched his motley crew into Oslo and burned it to the ground. At the time, both Erik and Haakon were at their mother's funeral. They quickly rushed to Oslo, but Alv had already retreated to Sweden. Alv was eventually captured in Skane in 1290 and executed. Many folk tales are told about *mindre Alv* (little Alv)—so called because he did so many exiting things, even though he was small.

Magnus ruled Norway for seventeen years. He died in his "sick-bed," and is buried in *Fransiskanarklosteret* in Bergen.

Erik II Magnusson
47

Erik the Priest-Hater

> Son of Magnus the Lawmender (#46) and Queen Ingeborg Eriksdatter from Denmark
>
> b.1268 d.1299 (31 yrs.)
> R.1280–1299
> m1)Margrete Alexandersdatter, the daughter of King Alexander III the Glorious of Scotland and Margrete of England. The marriage took place in 1281 when Erik was 13 and Margrete was 20. Margrete died in childbirth when her daughter was born.
>> Children:
>>> Margrete, b1283 d.1290, heiress to the Scottish throne. She was also called "The Maid of Norway" or "The Maid of Scandinavia."
> m2)Isabella Bruce in 1293, a sister of Robert I Bruce of Scotland
>> Children:
>>> Ingeborg, b.1300 d.1357. At age four she was betrothed to Orken's Jarlen Jon, who was 30 years older than she, but he died before they were married. At age 10 she was betrothed to King Valdemar Magnusson of Sweden, and married him in 1312. They had one son, Erik, who died young.

When Magnus the Lawmender (#46) died in 1280, he left two sons, Erik (#47) and Haakon V (#48), to inherit his throne. They were twelve and ten years old at the time and not yet of age. Their mother, Queen Ingeborg, a very able and determined woman, had great influence with the regents and managed to have Erik made ruler in East Norway and Haakon the ruler in the west. On July 1, 1280, Erik was crowned in Bergen Cathedral. This was the last coronation to be held in the great city of Bergen.

There had been friction between Norway and Scotland for many years, and when Erik took over, his first act was to make peace with Scotland with the Treaty of

Perth in 1266. However, the relationship between the two countries remained strained. In order to help restore peace, a marriage was arranged between King Erik of Norway and Margrete, the daughter of King Alexander III of Scotland. It had been carefully planned. A marriage contract was signed stipulating the amount of Margrete's dowry, and also stating that if her father, King Alexander III had no legitimate heirs, Margrete and her offspring would be the Scottish heirs also.

Princess Margrete left Scotland for Norway in August of 1281, accompanied by a large group of high-ranking officials and aristocrats. The next year, in the autumn of 1281, Eric, at age thirteen, married twenty-year-old Margrete. The grand wedding took place in the Cathedral in Bergen. These were the last royal events to be held in Bergen in the Cathedral.

King Erik and Queen Margrete resided in Bergen for the next few years. Margrete was a good influence on her young husband, and taught him to speak French and English. She was a popular queen, admired and respected by the people. However, in 1283, she died (she was in her early twenties) after their first child, also named Margrete, was born.

When little Margrete was about three years of age, her Scottish grandfather, Alexander III, died. Margrete, according to the previously signed marriage contract, was next in line for the royal throne of Scotland.

Representatives from Norway, Scotland and England gathered and elected the little Norwegian princess as the rightful heir to the Scottish throne. It was also agreed that she should marry the son of Edward I of England, also named Edward. Little Margrete was only three years of age at the time, and Edward was two years of age, and consequently Margrete was to continue to live in Norway for a few years. However, before he died, England's King Alexander III had taken as his second wife, Princess Yolanda of France. This worried King Edward I, as any children from the marriage would give France more power. In order to hasten the marriage between his son and little Margrete, he loaned King Erik 200 pounds of sterling silver, in order to alleviate Norway's financial problems.

Further complications developed when the church decided little Margaret's marriage would be illegal because they were too closely related. Margrete's mother was Edward's niece, therefore little Margrete would be marrying her uncle. However, Pope Nicholas IV was finally persuaded to give his permission. (This is an example of how the countries vied for power by the intermarriage of their children, which eventually led to the "royal disease," hemophilia.)

When little Margrete was seven years of age, she set sail for Scotland, to marry young Edward. She was accompanied by many people of importance. However, the sea was stormy, and the ship stopped at the Orkney islands, which was owned by

Norway at the time. She became ill and died, under suspicious circumstances. She had been called "The Maid of Norway" *(Pigen fra Norge)*, and it was hoped that she would have been influential in forming a "Union of North Sea Powers." However, with her death this hope was dashed. Margrete never set foot on Scottish soil, but is the theme of many mournful Scottish ballads. There can be a great deal of speculation as to the course history would have taken if this marriage had been consummated.

Erik was a weak king. He was well-meaning, but sickly, unfortunately crippled and unable to assert himself. His reign became a rule of the aristocracy with abuse of power and much wrangling. Erik was blamed for the quarrel between Church and State which became bitter and lasted for many years. He wanted peace with the church, but was undeservedly nicknamed "Priesthater." Erik's headstrong mother, Ingeborg, could be blamed for many of these problems. After her death in 1287, King Erik took it upon himself to develop an amiable relationship with the church, and an agreement was reached whereby there was to be peace between the state and the church. His brother, Haakon (#48), who followed him as king, also wanted peace.

After both his Scottish wife and daughter had died, King Erik, as an heir, laid claim to the Crown of Scotland. In 1293 he married Isabella, a sister of Robert Bruce I of Scotland, a famous Scottish national hero, who later became king of Scotland. They had one daughter, Ingeborg, who married King Valdemar Magnusson of Sweden. Isabelle lived to a ripe old age in Norway, as pious and gentle as her brother was warlike and courageous.

Perhaps influenced by his Scottish queens and their aspirations, Erik sided with France against England and thereby incurred the wrath of the great King Edward I of England—which caused untold harm to Norwegian overseas trade and shipping.

King Erik's reign was troubled by a continued war with Denmark. He died in Bergen in 1299 at age thirty-one, and is buried in Christ Church in Bergen.

Haakon V Magnusson
48

Håkon Magnusson, Duke Haakon, Magnus V Langbein

Son of Magnus IV the Lawmender (#46) and Queen Ingeborg, from Denmark

b.1270 d.8 May 1319 (49 yrs.)
R.1299–1319
Before he married Queen Eufemia, Haakon had an illegitimate daughter,
      Agnes, b.c1292, who married Hafthor Jonsson Roos. Had children.
m1)Queen Eufemia in 1299, granddaughter of Prince Vislav of Rugen, d.1312
    Children: (No male heirs)
        Ingeborg, Princess Ingeborg, b.1301 d.c1361 (60 yrs.), m.Duke Erik
        (Wryneck) Magnusson of Sweden. They had two children, Magnus
        VII (#49) and Eufemia, who married Albrect of Sweden and had a
        son, Duke Albrect of Mecklenburg. Ingeborg[1] later married Knut
        Porse. Erik Wyneck also had two illegitimate children who died in
        the Black Death.
m2)Isabella Joiny. Marriage arranged, but may not have taken place.
    No children.

After Erik's death, Haakon succeeded him as King Haakon V Magnusson (#48) of Norway. Haakon was then twenty-nine years of age. The same year he married Eufemia, the granddaughter of his friend and adviser, Prince Vislav of Rugen. From then on the sympathies of the royal family began to turn towards Russia and the east rather than the British Isles.

Before Haakon married Eufemia, he became infatuated with another woman. In about 1395 (Haakon did not marry Eufemia until 1399), Haakon apparently asked bishop Audfinn of Bergen to approach Prince de Joigny of France and asked him, on Haakon's behalf, for the hand of his daughter, Isabella Joiny, in marriage. Bishop

Audfinn made the arrangements, but it was rumored that during the process he seduced the princess, which roused Haakon's violent anger. This was possibly the reason Haakon had Audfinn imprisoned. It is not known whether the marriage between Haakon and Isabella ever took place, but it is listed by some historians.

During the trend to move eastward, King Haakon made Oslo the capital in 1286, and he was crowned there in 1299. At about the same time, he built Akerhus, Oslo's ancient royal fortress in the Oslo harbor. It was the largest and strongest castle in the Scandinavian countries. In time it became in need of repair, and in 1963 restoration work was completed, and today Akerhus stands as a magnificent Renaissance Palace.

Haakon was a good king, loved by his people. He was concerned with the welfare of the peasants, and had issued decrees for regulating the conditions of their employment. During this time forests were cleared and numerous farms were beginning to flourish. He was also concerned about commerce, and made regulations regarding trade.

His German Queen, Eufemia, was more the romantic type, and was fascinated by the sentimental literature of chivalry which was the fashion of the day, and she encouraged it in Norway. Although her literary functions may not have been considered intellectual, she did provide Norway with a taste of European customs and culture.

The king's interests were more serious. He was quite learned, had read many classics, and could make speeches in Latin. He established schools for the clergy, whom he felt were ignorant and lacked proper education. He ordered the translations of many sagas of chivalry, including the stories of Roland, Charlemagne, Thidrik (Theodoric), Tristan and Isolde, and many others. They were called sagas, though quite different from the old sagas in content and style. It was a literature that was meant to be read rather than recited. Under Haakon V, the court became the center of considerable intellectual life.

During this time, dancing was also introduced into the country, probably from France. The Norwegians loved it, and it swept the country from small *gaards* to palaces. They danced to the tunes of folk songs with the leader singing the stanzas and the people joining in for the refrains. To this day, dancing is a favorite pasttime of Norwegians.

In 1313 Haakon also put into effect new laws in respect to the Lapps, stating that the Norwegians were to take care of them and no longer subject them to extortions. He also introduced Christianity for the Lapps by cleverly and wisely exempting those who accepted the faith from taxation for twenty years.

King Haakon and Queen Euphemia had a daughter, Ingeborg, in 1301. The next year King Haakon promised the hand of his one-year-old baby daughter to Duke

Erik (Wryneck), the brother of King Birger of Sweden. It was a custom during this time to betroth (engage) their daughters at a very early age as they wished to secure for their royal children a marriage that would augment their family's wealth and power. Soon afterwards, King Haakon broke the engagement, apparently because of a conflict with Erik's brother, King Birger in Sweden. Haakon then betrothed his daughter to nine-year-old Magnus, the heir to the Swedish throne, and had it confirmed and blessed by the church. Again, the political situation reversed and Haakon allowed Ingeborg to be betrothed to Erik. Then Erik changed his mind and chose another princess to be his future wife. For the third time, Erik decided he wished to marry Ingeborg. (Did he suddenly remember that she was heir to the throne in Norway?) Poor Ingeborg. One must wonder what was on her mind. To make matters even worse, Haakon's Queen Eufemia fell in love with Erik! An agreement was also reached that Erik's brother, Valdemar was to be betrothed to Haakon's niece, also named Ingeborg.

The climax of this affair was a Scandinavian royal wedding which included all the pomp and circumstances of the time. Both Ingeborgs were to be married on the same day and the wedding celebration was held in Oslo at Michaelmas in 1312. Haakon's daughter, Ingeborg, was only eleven years old, and his niece, Ingeborg, was fifteen. Queen Eufemia died several months before her "lover" married her daughter, but Queen Isabella traveled from Bergen to attend the marriage of her fifteen-year-old daughter. About twelve months after the wedding, the two child-brides were sent to live with their respected husbands.[2] Four years later both of the Ingeborg's had sons. Duke Erik's son was named Magnus and he was to become King Magnus VII the Good (#49). Ingeborg and Valdemar's son was named Erik, after Queen Isabella's husband, Erik II Magnusson (#47). This Erik died at a very young age and does not enter into future affairs of the state.

Both of the husbands of the Ingeborgs met horrible deaths in Sweden where they were both incarcerated and murdered by their brother's followers.[3]

After the death of Haakon V, in 1319, the old royal house of King Harald I Fairhair (#1), in the direct male line, was extinct, after ruling for 450 years. However, his family continued to reign for sixty-eight more years, through his daughter Ingeborg, as three successive descendants of Haakon occupied the throne.

Haakon was a conscientious national leader and took his responsibilities seriously. He was a vigorous man and had a great desire to work things out. In the sixteenth century, the Danish king of Norway, Christian II, petitioned the Pope to canonize King Haakon V, but was not successful in this attempt. King Haakon V had made Oslo his residence in 1299 and it became the main military capitol, taking over from Tønsberg, and it was to Tønsberg that King Haakon returned to spend his last winter.

After much suffering, King Haakon V died on May 8, 1319. His body was taken to Oslo, where he is buried in the Royal Chapel of Maria. He was forty-nine years of age at the time of his death.

1. See Chapter 49 for more information on Ingeborg.
2. If the bride was very young when her wedding took place, she usually stayed with her parents for a period of time.
3. Check Vilhelm Moberg's book for more information on the capture and murder of the two brothers.

Magnus VII the Good
49

Magnus VII, Magnus Smek, Magnus II Eriksson of Sweden

Son of Duke Erik (Wryneck) Magnusson of Sweden, brother of King Birgir Magnusson of Sweden, and Ingeborg, daughter of Haakon V Magnusson (#48)

b.1316 d.1 Dec 1374 at sea (58 yrs.)
R.1319–1374, became king of Norway and Sweden at age three
R.1319–1350, King of Norway
R.1319–1363, King of Norway, and King of Sweden as Magnus II Eriksson
m.Blanca from Namur (Flandern). b. d.c1363, daughter of Count Hohn of
    Namur (Sweden). On her maternal side, related to the royal family of France
    and Edward IV of England.
    Children:
        Erik, (became King Eric III of Sweden), b.1339 d.1359; in 1344 was
            elected heir to the Swedish throne
        Haakon, became King Haakon VI of Norway (#50) b.1340 d.1380
            R.1350–1380, m.Margarete (#52) in 1363, daughter of king
            Valdemar and Queen Helvig of Denmark. One son, Olav IV (#51).
    Magnus also had two illegitimate sons who died in the Black Death.

Magnus' grandfather, Haakon V. (#48) died in 1319. Ingeborg, Haakon's eighteen-year-old daughter, had become a widow at age sixteen, and now she quickly claimed the Norwegian throne for her son, three-year-old Magnus. As the son of Duke Erik of Sweden, he also became the king of Sweden. The sagas state that three-year-old Magnus was present at his own election in Sweden. One of his advisors placed him on his shoulder and swore the oath of office on his behalf. Both countries now had Magnus, a three-year-old, as king, and needed leaders in each country to rule in his behalf. The Swedes traveled to Oslo and met with the Royal Council. It was decided that Magnus should spend half his time in Norway and half in Sweden. Each country was to be governed by its own council, and if necessary, each was to give military aid to the other.

After he became king, Magnus VII continued to live in Tønsberg with his mother, Ingeborg for another year. However, it was not long before the Swedes demanded that their king be brought to Sweden. From then on he spent almost all of his time in Sweden, where he also received his education.

As soon as Magnus became king, at age three, the regency in Norway was dominated by his powerful mother, Ingeborg. She had a great deal of control over both Norway and Sweden. She was not popular and, furthermore, the Norwegians did not appreciate being ruled by a woman. Ingeborg also used national funds extravagantly for herself and her lover, Knut Porse. She later married him and when she left Norway there was not a single mark (dollar) left in the treasury!

In 1323, with Ingeborg gone, the Norwegians gathered at a National Meeting in Oslo. Magnus was about seven at the time, and they chose a leading figure in Norway, Erling Vidkunnson, then about thirty years of age, to be Viceroy and Lord High Constable for Magnus. Erling was given royal power, and Norway was very fortunate to have someone with his outstanding qualities to lead the government at this crucial time.

King Magnus came of age (16) in 1332, and took over the great Seal of Norway himself but Erling Vidhunnson continued as a leading advisor until he died in 1355.

Magnus' personal life during the first years was quite happy. When he was eighteen years of age, he went to Namur, Sweden, and took as his wife, Countess Blanca, the beautiful and lovable daughter of Count Hohn of Namur, related to the royal families in France and England. The wedding festivities were held at Tønsberg, because its buildings were more "cosmopolitan and European" than Oslo. However, due to financial problems, it was necessary to borrow table linens and services from a nunnery at Oslo. Blanca was popular and loved by the common people, and Magnus gave her a desirable piece of property, Vestfold, including Tønsberg, as a "morning-gift."[1]

Magnus and Blanca had the misfortune of having in their household a somewhat "crazed" Swedish woman, Birgitte,[2] who served as Blanca's "Mistress of the Robes," a sort of "lady-in-waiting" or personal maid. She apparently had a great influence over both Magnus and Blanca. She spread gossip and scandal about their personal lives and gave them damaging advice. She also intervened in their marital relationship. Magnus decided to discontinue having sexual intercourse with his wife, and even though Blanca agreed to this arrangement, Birgitte claimed that this was responsible for Magnus becoming a homosexual. There was no proof of this, but it helped to lead to his downfall, and historians often refer to him as *Smek* or "little girl."

An unfortunate event took place during his reign. In 1328, on Easter Monday, the nearly completed Nidaros Cathedral at Trondheim was burned to the ground. It was many years later before it was restored to its present grandeur.

Sweden enjoyed a couple of decades of peaceful development and progress during Magnus' reign. Among his achievements, Magnus introduced a code of laws for the whole country, including the abolishment of bondage, and established the Swedish constitution. A common code of laws, the *Magna Carta*, stating a king's duties to his people was also instituted. Many cultural literary events were also developed during this time.

In 1343 an agreement was reached to sever the dynastic union with Sweden. King Magnus and Blanca had two sons, Erik and Haakon. Although the older, Erik, was heir to the throne, the king and council legally set aside the law, and agreed that the younger Haakon should be king of Norway and begin the rule when he came of age. Swedish leaders promised to choose Erik as successor to the throne in Sweden, and both parties agreed that neither brother should have any claim to the throne of the other.

However, in time, political problems also arose and Magnus ran into trouble in Sweden when he raised taxes in order to purchase Skane, a region in the southern part of modern Sweden. He also curbed the economic power of both the church and the landed nobility, thus causing more opposition.

His own son, Erik, also chose to oppose him, and received support from King Valdemar IV of Denmark. Magnus finally gave Erik about half of his Swedish kingdom. He began to make further concessions to the nobility and to make peace with Valdemar IV by arranging the marriage of his son, Haakon VI (#50) to Margrete, Valdemar's daughter.

At about the same time, the Black Death also occurred. An Icelandic report states: "A ship arrived from England with a large crew and anchored at Vaagen in Bergen. Only a small part of the cargo had been unloaded when everybody on board died, and when the goods that had been landed reached the city many inhabitants perished immediately. Thence the infection spread all over Norway..."

In 1349 the population of both countries dropped by about one-half to almost two-thirds. Magnus survived, but his empire began to fall. Erik, who was born in 1339 took over as king of Sweden at age eleven. The same year, 1350, at a meeting in Bergen, attended by the whole royal family, the ten-year-old Haakon VI (#50) was placed on the royal throne, and he became ruler in Norway.

Erik died in 1359. Although it is rumored that he was poisoned by his mother, Blanca,[3] it is most likely that he died in the second wave of the Black Death.[4]

Magnus was later captured (c1265) by his nephew, Duke Albrecht of

Mecklenberg, and imprisoned in Sweden. In 1371, for a large ransom, Haakon freed his father.

Magnus lived to the age of fifty-eight, which was quite old for that period of time. Even though there were many changes and much upheaval during his reign, he was preferred by the common peasants, and was sometimes called "Magnus the Good." He was probably too good. People took advantage of his trusting nature. It was Magnus' good qualities that brought him to his evil end. He differed from the three preceding generations of his family who treacherously took the lives of their political opponents, but Magnus did not participate in this kind of cruelty.

To summarize the life of King Magnus VII, he became king of two countries at about age three. After ruling for almost half a century, he was imprisoned for six years, driven out of his country, and died as a king without a kingdom at age fifty-eight.[5] He was a typical loser, a poor administrator, and was consequently also called "Magnus the Simple Minded."

He died on December 1, 1374, when a great storm struck in the fjord and he was shipwrecked. He jumped overboard and swam ashore, but he suffered severe cramps, and died. His bad luck followed him to the end. However, he was the only person to reach shore, and therefore it was considered a miracle. Consequently he was called "holy" and was buried on hallowed ground. Was Magnus vindicated in the end?

1. It was customary for kings to give their brides gifts on the day after their marriage and these were called "morning gifts."
2. She was later canonized in Sweden as St. Birgitte.
3. Blanca's motive? Perhaps revenge for Erik breaking off from his father.
4. The Black Death hit Norway and Sweden in 1350, and the second wave hit in 1359 and another in 1371.
5. Magnus turned over the thrones of both Norway and Sweden at an earlier date, but was titular (existing in title only) king until he died in 1374.

Haakon VI
50

Haakon Magnusson the Younger, Haakon Magnusson, Håkon VI

Son of Magnus Erickson VII (#49) and Queen Blanca (from Flanders)

b.1340 d.1380 (40 yrs.)
R.1350–1380
m.Margrete, daughter of King Valdemar of Denmark. Haakon was betrothed to
  Margaret in 1363 when she was 10 years old. Married Margrete 5 years
  later.
  Children:
      Olav IV (#51), b.1 Dec 1370 d.1387

Haakon VI was the second son of Magnus VII (#46). Magnus was also king of Sweden. Although his eldest son, Erik, was the rightful heir to the throne, Magnus made Haakon king of Norway and Erik the king of Sweden. Neither was to make any claim on the others kingdom. Haakon was ten years old at the time, but did not take over as ruler of Norway until 1355 when he was fifteen.

Erik, however, was not satisfied with the arrangements they had made, and went on a warpath against his father, which created a three-way division of Sweden and Norway. Erik died in 1359, but hostilities did not stop. Margrete's father, Valdemar Atterdag of Denmark, also stepped into the picture and marched into southern Sweden. This made it necessary for Haakon and Magnus to unite, and go to war against Denmark. Valdemar had a brief victory, and convinced Magnus and Haakon that all three should unite, and Valdemar gave his ten-year-old daughter, Margrete, to Haakon for a bride. The wedding took place on April 9, 1363. Haakon was twenty-three years old. Margrete was thirteen. Margrete was later to become one of the greatest queens of all time.

Haakon's troubles did not cease. He and his father, Magnus, were temporarily deposed after a battle with Magnus' Swedish nephew, Albrect of Mecklenburg, and Magnus was made a prisoner for six years. Haakon managed to gain enough control to stay in power. Many more problems occurred, but Haakon eventually received help from the Swedes, and his father was released. Haakon staunchly stood by his father during the time he was imprisoned and they ruled together quite amicably until Magnus drowned in 1374.

Haakon was brought up in Norway, and was guided by some of the best men in the land and had the support of the people. He was an able man, respected and loved by high and low. "People called him a good man" says an Icelandic saga. Another stated, "He is said to have been a splendid man, wonderfully loved and obeyed by his subjects."

Magnus made Haakon king in 1350. One of the greatest calamities in Europe, the Black Death, occurred that year. The worst fire in Oslo's history also happened during Haakon's reign. The economy of Norway suffered extensively, and poverty also evidently affected royalty. Margrete was residing in Akerhus, and wrote a letter to Haakon begging him to send her money so her servants would not leave.

A pestilence also raged in Oslo in 1370, probably the second wave of the Black Death, which only made matters worse. It was during the midst of this that Queen Margrete gave birth to a son, Olav, at Akerhus on December 1, 1370.

Not much is noted in the history books about Haakon's reign during the 1370s, but he continued to hold on to certain portions of Sweden as well as Norway.

King Haakon died in 1380, and is buried in the beautiful Maria Church in Oslo.

Olav IV
51

Olav IV Haakonsson, Olav Hakonsson

Son of King Haakon VI (#50) and Margrete Valdemarsdatter (#52) of Denmark

b.1 Dec 1370 d.3 Aug 1387 (17 yrs.)
R.1380–1387 as King Olav IV of Norway
R.1376–1387 as King Olav III of Denmark

Olav was named after Saint Olav.

King Valdemar had agreed earlier that the Danish throne should pass to the son of Margrete's elder sister, Ingeborg. However, when her father died in 1375, Margrete shrewdly managed to get her own five-year-old son, Olav, elected as king of Denmark. She also tried, unsuccessfully, to have Olav acclaimed king of Sweden. In 1380, when her husband died, Olav also inherited the throne of Norway at age ten.

Norway's government was largely conducted by a state council, but Margrete managed to have considerable power, and had plans to unite Norway, Sweden and Denmark. At age fifteen, Olav attained majority, but died suddenly, allegedly from poison,[1] two years later, at age seventeen. He is buried at Sorø, Denmark. The inscription (in Latin) on his gravestone reads: "Here rests Olav, son of Queen Margrete, whom she bore to Norway's King Haakon."

1. Although rumors were that Olav was poisoned by his ambitious mother, it is inconceivable for this to be true. Olav was her only child and we will feverishly hope that this is a false rumor and can be put to rest.

Margrete

The greatest Scandinavian monarch of all time.

Margrete
52

Margrete Valdemarsdatter, Margrethe

Daughter of King Valdemar Atterdag IV of Denmark and Queen Helvig also from Denmark

b.1353 d.Oct 1412 (59 yrs.)
R.1388–1412
m.King Haakon (#50). Betrothed to Haakon in 1363 when she was 10 years old. Married at age 15.
   Children:
      Olav IV (#51), b.1370 d.1387 at age seventeen

Winston Churchill called Margrete the greatest Scandinavian monarch of all time. She was the daughter of Danish King Valdemar IV, but had a Swedish education. She also inherited her father's best qualities: his strength of character, his inventiveness, his enormous energy and power of endurance. Her father said of Margrete that she was "an error of nature"—she should have been created a man! Moberg writes that Margrete showed the world that she was one of the greatest leaders of her time.

At age five, Margrete was promised as a future bride to King Haakon V (#50) of Norway. At about ten years of age, she was betrothed (engaged), but it wasn't until five years later, in 1368, that the marriage was consummated. Before the marriage, she was sent to live with a Swedish noblewoman, Margrete Ulfsdatter who became her foster mother. Margrete Ulfsdatter was the daughter of Saint Birgitte[1] and her father was a Swedish nobleman. They had a daughter, Ingegard, who became Margrete Valdemarsdatter's foster sister. Both girls were brought up in severe discipline and "fear of the Lord." It is stated that they often "both tasted the same birch." Margrete also became familiar with current politics and her environment doubtless shaped her opinion about women in society.

In 1370 Margrete gave birth to her only child, a son, Olav IV (#51), who was an heir to the Norwegian throne, and as a grandchild of King Magnus (#49) was also heir to the Swedish throne.

When Valdemar IV died, Margrete acted quickly, and after many negotiations, the Danes elected Olav to be king of Denmark in May of 1376. A problem arose with the Swedish Mecklenburgs, but Duke Albrect Mecklenburg died 1379. Margrete's next problem was with King Albrecht, also known as Albrecht of Mecklenburg. He was arrogant and ruthless and could not even speak the Swedish language. The people hated him. Bo Johnson, a gifted and ruthless climber of power, was soon at odds with King Albrect and Sweden was in turmoil.

Margrete's husband, Haakon died in 1380, and the next summer, ten-year-old Olav was acclaimed king with all rights as king of Norway.

In the meantime, King Albrecht of Sweden gradually lost his control. In Norway, King Olav died suddenly on August 3, 1387, at the young age of seventeen. Norway was now without a king and again Margrete had to work quickly. On August 10, 1387, she established herself as "authorized lady and husband and guardian of all of the realm of Denmark," until a new king could be elected according to her proposal. The following year she was able to pull off the same deal in Norway, and quickly managed a similar recognition from some of the Swedish nobles. This however, resulted in a war with King Albrecht of Sweden, with a victory for Margrete on February 24, 1389. King Albrecht was captured, and Margrete obtained Sweden, but was unable to keep Stockholm.

The same year, 1389, Margrete adopted her sister's maternal grandson, Erik (Erik of Pomeroy), and made him king of all three countries. Then another war broke out with the Mecklenburgs, but peace was reached in 1395 and King Albrecht was released, with Stockholm as a pledge for the release sum. The pledge was not paid, so in 1398, Stockholm finally fell into the hands of Margrete.

The year before, 1397, Margrete had instituted her celebrated Act of Union or Treaty of Kalmar, which united the three countries. The union between Denmark and Norway lasted until 1814, and with Sweden, until the 1520s.

Margrete died in 1412. She was a remarkable queen.

1. Additional information about Birgitte under King Magnus (#48). Many books have been written about her.

Union with Denmark
1405–1814

Norway entered a long period of foreign rule upon the death of Olav IV in 1387 and with the signing of the Union of Kalmar in 1397. The Norwegians themselves chose Margrete as their ruler at a meeting on February 2, 1388. They elected "the highborn princess, our beloved lady, Lady Margrete, by the grace of God, Queen of Norway and Sweden and rightful heir and regent of the kingdom of Denmark." Margrete is the only woman who has been raised to the position of a "king," with full royal power in Norway. Denmark continued to rule over Norway for the next 400 years. Henrick Ibsen, a staunch Norwegian, writes in *Peer Gynt*:

"Twice two hundred years of darkness."

DANISH RULERS
(Ruled from about 1400 to 1814)

Erik III: 1389–1442
Christopher of Bavaria: 1442–1448
Karl Knutson of Sweden: 1449–1450
Christian I: 1449–1481
Hans: 1483–1513
Christian II: 1513–1523
Frederik I: 1524–1533

REFORMATION: 1536

Christian III: 1537–1559
Frederik II: 1559–1588
Christian IV: 1588–1648
Frederik III: 1648–1670
Christian V: 1670–1699
Frederik IV: 1699–1730
Christian VI: 1730–1746
Frederik V: 1746–1766
Christian VII: 1766–1808
Frederik VI: 1808–1814

Union with Sweden
1814–1905

In 1814, at the close of the Napoleonic Wars, the 400-year union with Denmark was brought to a close by the Treaty of Kiel, whereby Norway was united with Sweden. Although under the jurisdiction of Sweden, on May 17th of that year, 1814, a national assembly meeting at Eidsvold signed the Norwegian Constitution, and thereafter the Norwegians celebrate this date as their Independence Day.

SWEDISH RULERS
(Ruled from 1812 to 1905)

Carl XIII: 1814–1818
Carl XIV (Bernadotte): 1818–1844
Oscar I: 1844–1859
Carl XV: 1859–1872
Oscar II: 1872–1905

Independence
1905–Present

The union with Sweden was dissolved in 1905, without bloodshed, after an extended political struggle. The Norwegians unanimously elected Prince Carl of Denmark as their king and he was crowned, taking the Viking name of Haakon VII, a continuation of the Viking names after Haakon VI who died in 1380. Norway has had three kings since that time. The country managed to stay out of World War I, but after the Germans invaded Norway on April 9, 1940, they spend the next five years under German siege. Norway put up an unusually strong military resistance, but was not free from the Nazis until the country was liberated on May 8, 1945.

Haakon VII[1]

He was originally named:
Christian Frederik Carl George Valdemar Axel

Second son of King Frederick VIII of Denmark and Louis Josephine, daughter
of King Charles XV (Bernadotte) of Sweden

b.3 Aug 1872 d.21 Sep 1957 (85 yrs)
R.1905–1957
m.Maud Charlotte Mary Victoria, the youngest daughter of King Edward VII of
    England and Princess Alexandra of Denmark
  Children:
        Olav V, Olav Alexander Edward Christian Frederik, reigned after
        Haakon VII

Haakon was elected king by the Norwegian parliament on November 18, 1905, and was crowned on June 22, 1906, after the union between Norway and Sweden was dissolved. He agreed to accept it only if he were approved by the Norwegian *Storting* (Parliament) and they overwhelmingly voted their approval.

Haakon was Danish, and was originally called Prince Charles (Carl) of Denmark. He adopted the old Norse name, Haakon VII, before he was crowned. He married Maud in 1896 and they had one son, Olav V, who succeeded him to the throne.

Haakon refused to accept the puppet regime of Vidkun Quisling, when Hitler invaded Norway in 1940. The Storting, pressured by the Germans, asked Haakon to abdicate. He refused and made a thrilling escape to England and set up a government in exile. This inspired the Norwegians to put up an extremely heavy resistance during WWII. He returned to Norway in 1945 after the end of the war, and was jubilantly received.

Haakon was a champion of democracy, and ruled during two world wars. He was a popular king, noted for his simple, democratic lifestyle.

King Haakon died at age eighty-five, and at the time of his death, was the oldest reigning monarch in the world. His son, Olav V, succeeded him.

1. The continuation of names from the Viking days. The last Haakon was Haakon VI (#50) who ruled in Norway from 1350-1380.

Olav V[1]

Olav Alexander Edward Christian Frederik (Glücksburg)

Son of King Haakon VII of Norway and Queen Maud (from Victories, England). Grandson of England's King Edward VII. Great grandson of Queen Victoria

b.2 Jul 1903 at Appleton House, near Sandringham, Norfolk, England.
d.17 Jan 1991 in Oslo (at age 87)
R.1957–1991 (Became king on 22 Jun 1958)
m.Princess Martha of Sweden, Martha Sofia Louisa Dagmar Thyra (Bernadotte),
    b.1901 d.1954, daughter of the Swedish Prince Carl (1861–1951) and
    Princess Ingeborg of Denmark (1878–1958)
     Children:
       Ragnhild Alexandra, b.9 Jun 1930, m.Erling Sven Lorentzen,
       Astrid Maud Ingeborg, b.12 Feb 1932, m.Johan Martin Ferner
       Harald (King of Norway, R.1991–   ), b.21 Feb 1937, m.Sonja in 1968

Olav V. was born at Appleton House in England. When he was two years old, in the arms of his father, he took the Norwegian name of Olav V.

In 1957, after the death of his father, King Haakon VII, he became king of Norway.

Olav was educated at Oxford University in England and at the Norwegian Military Academy. He was a celebrated athlete and sportsman, and excelled in ski jumping and yachting. He is often referred to as the "Sports King" and also the "People's King."

He married Princess Martha of Sweden in 1929 and they had three children.

During the invasion of the Nazis in 1940, Olav fled to England, where his father set up his government. In 1944, he was named head of the Norwegian armed forces. In 1945, after the war ended, he returned to Norway.

Olav was loved by all of his constituents.

1. A continuation of names from the Viking period. The last Olav was Olav IV (#51) who was king in Norway from 1380–1387.

King Harald V[1]

Son of King Olav V Glücksburg of Norway and Crown Princess Martha
(Bernadotte) of Sweden

b.23 Feb 1937
R.17 Jan 1991–present
m.Sonja Haraldsen, b.4 Jul 1937, in August of 1968, daughter of Charles
Augustus Haraldsen
    Children:
        Martha Louise, b.22 Sept 1971
        Prince Haakon Magnus, b.20 Jul 1973

When King Olav V died on January 17, 1991, King Harald V became ruler of
Norway. He adopted the motto "All for Norway," as his father and grandfather
had done.

King Harald was the first prince to be born in Norway for over half a century.
(The last prince born in Norway was King Olav IV who was born in 1370.) King
Harald's birth in 1937 ensured the Norwegian people the line of succession of the
newly (since 1905) established Norwegian Royal Family. The constitution of 1814
stated that only a male heir could inherit the throne. That provision has been
amended and now, the first child (male or female) can become king.

Prince Harald was born at Skaugum, near Oslo, the estate that is still used by the
Royal Family. He was only three years of age when Hitler's troops invaded Norway
in the early hours of April 9, 1940. The Royal Family and government were one of
Hitler's primary targets. Just hours before the Nazis invaded Oslo, they were forced
to flee, by train, in great haste. At Hamar, about seventy-five miles north of Oslo,

they separated. Crown Princess Martha took her three children, and under cover of darkness crossed over to Sweden to her family. King Haakon and part of the government traveled secretly to Trondheim and in June escaped to London where they set up a government in exile

Shortly thereafter, Princess Martha and her children left for the USA and lived just outside of Washington, D.C. until Norway was liberated in 1945. While in the United States, Prince Harald and his sisters learned to speak excellent English.

On May 23, 1945, after the war was over, Crown Prince Olav returned to Norway from England and was joined by King Haakon. Princess Martha and their children arrived in June and were greeted by jubilant crowds. Norway was extremely happy to have them back home.

The Royal Family returned to Skaugum, and Prince Harald and his sisters attended public elementary school, along with other children. Aside from the police guard in the corridor, his schooling did not differ from that of the other children. He took part in a wide variety of sports. At the age of ten he had his own boat, and became an avid yachtsman, winning numerous Norwegian and international championships. In 1964 he represented Norway in the Olympics and placed in the 5.5 meter class, and the following year won the U.S. Open Championship.

Harald received his upper secondary diploma in science in 1955 and matriculated at the University of Oslo that same year. Immediately after, he began his military career by attending the Officer's Candidate School, and then the Military Academy, from which he graduated in 1959. When his grandfather, King Haakon, died in 1957, Harald became Crown Prince. He began a two-year study of economics, political science, and history at Balliol College at Oxford in England. He achieved numerous ranks while in the military service and, in 1977, was promoted to General of the Army, Admiral of the Navy, and General of the Air Force; ranks he still holds.

Harald broke with tradition by marrying a commoner, Sonja Haraldsen. The wedding took place on August 20, 1968, after a ten-year courtship and the Norwegian people looked favorably upon the marriage.

Queen Sonja grew up in Oslo, and after completing secondary school, received a diploma in dress-making and tailoring, and also a diploma in dress-making from the Ecole Professionelle des Jeunes Filles in Lausanne, Switzerland. She continued with her education to receive a Bachelor of Arts degree in English, French, and art history from the University of Oslo. Besides her interest in art and culture, she is also involved in humanitarian work, particularly the Norwegian Red Cross.

Skaugum continues to be the residence of the Royal Family. It was a wedding gift from King Olav, and consists of about 325 acres with livestock and cultivated fields. There are plans to move the Royal Palace at a later date.

The Royal Family is a symbol of social stability and political continuity and unity. This proved extremely important during the Second World War. In Norway today, the monarchy continues to be in a strong position, due in part to the deep commitment shown by King Harald V and Queen Sonja.

1. A continuation of Viking names. The last Harald in Norway was King Harald IV (#23) who ruled from 1136–1155.

Glossary

Additional information about people, and also Scandinavian words, and phrases that have a specific meaning that may differ from customary usage.

Aarmenn. See Lendmenn.

Baglers. From the Latin word *bacula*, meaning a bishop's crosier, a crosier being a Bishop's staff. Also called the Crosier party. This was a clerical party, who were enemies of the Birchleg party.

Bailiffs. See Lendmenn.

Beserker. A company of picked fighters in Viking kings courts. They were often used as bodyguards on whom the king particularly relied. They were sometimes known as "bearskins" or "wolfskins," and often fought naked or with clothes made of animal skins. They were devotees of Odin, according to legend.

Birchlegs. A band of rebels made up of the poor peasants who were tired of being ruled by the upper class group of clerics called the Baglers. King Eystein Moyla (#32) was probably the originator of the Birchlegs in about 1174. Their name derived from the fact that they were so poor that they had to use birch bark to wrap around their legs to keep out the cold. Norway's beloved Sverre (#33) later took over this group.

Bonde. (plural bonder) The bonde was a free land-owning farmer. He generally had considerable property and prestige. The bonde was prominent in the rural areas.

Concubine. A mistress. More than a "one night" stand.

Crofter. See husman.

Crosier. See Baglers.

Danegold. Also Danegeld. A bribe, usually silver or gold. Often used to pay off the Vikings to get them to retreat.

Eric the Red. Eric was a Norwegian navigator in the tenth century AD. He was banished from Norway and Iceland for his violent deeds. From 982–985 he explored the southwest cost of Greenland, and gave it that name to attract colonists. Eric is commemorated in the Icelandic *Saga of Eric the Red*. He was the father of Leif Ericson, now recognized as the discoveror of North America.

Fostered. A custom used during this time in history whereby a child was sent to live with another family where he was taught "wisdom and learning" that was not always available at home.

Free farmer. An independent farmer. He may not have been better off economically, but he was free. From the poetic Edda: "Better a house, though a hut it be, A man is master at home; A pair of goats and a patch of roof, Are better far than begging."

Frey. The lustful pagan goddess of peace and fertility. One of the three major heathen gods, along with Thor and Odin. The sagas state that Frey possessed a collapsible boat that could be folded to fit into a small pouch and when she commanded, could expand into a ship large enough to carry all the gods.

Fylki. Sometime called the *Fylkis Thing*. It was made up primarily as an assembly of the free odal-born peasants/proprietors. These were leading men and each fylki had one or more chiefs. If they agreed upon one chief, he was called Jarl. He was a ruler under the king, and supported himself with his estates.

Gaard. Farm.

Hanseatic. A confederacy of German merchants set up to control the shipping and commerce in the Baltic area, causing considerable trouble for Norway.

Herse. A title even higher than that of Jarl.

Hird. A large band of warriors. These were young men who eagerly agreed to the service of the king, "the wise dispenser of gold." Often referred to as Royal Guards of the Kings' Men. They had beautiful weapons and lived lavishly in the king's court.

Hov. A place of worship—a church.

Husman. Often called crofter. He had a small place on the outskirts of a large farm and paid his rent in service and kind.

Jarl. (Earl in English) A title. Usually conferred on someone by the king. A jarl was generally at the head of a district. He might however, be a chief with no state to rule, but gathered around him a group of followers who accompanied him on expeditions. A jarl was a highly esteemed individual. One report states: "The Jarl had yellow hair, his cheeks were rosy and his eyes were as keen as a young serpent's. He occupied himself shaping shields, shooting with bow and arrow, hurling the javelin, riding horses, throwing dice, fencing and swimming. He waged war, reddening the battlefield with blood and killing the damned."

Jernbyrd. See ordeal by fire.

Kark. The *kark* (yeoman farmer) was red and ruddy with rolling eyes and took up breaking oxen, making ploughs, building houses and making carts.

King. (As related specifically to Norway.) Before a man could become king, it was necessary to have: (1) hereditary rights and (2) recognition by the people assembled in *Things*. All the sons of a king, legitimate or illegitimate, had an equal right to the throne. Any heir could present his claims at a thing and ask to be accepted as king. He would then have to be approved by the local *thing*. Consequently, there would sometimes be two or more heirs claiming a right to reign. This was usually not a peaceful affair, as will be noted by the many kings or would-be kings who ruled during that time.

Konung. King.

Lendmenn or Thanes. Local officials who represented the royal power and interests of the king. These were of two classes. The highest were the lendmenn or thanes, who were leading men in the community, often land owners. Then there were the "bailiffs" of *aarmenn* who did the real work for the king.

Leif Ericsson. (Also Eriksen; Erikson; Erikson) Norse mariner and adventurer. He was the son of Eric the Red, and at the beginning of the 11th century discovered a transatlantic country, which he called Vinland, from the vines which abounded there. Here an Icelandic settlement was established. Leif is now recognized as the discoveror or North America.

Longships. The Viking vessels were called longships. They could be rowed anywhere the water was waist-deep.

Mead. An alcoholic beverage made of fermented honey.

Odal Farmer. The odal farmers were not only important in the social and economic life, but they were a significant factor in the political development, particularly in the movement for unification when their support or resistance would often determine the issue. They became more elevated above the common freemen as the aristocracy of powerful landowners and chieftains became stronger and stronger in every district.

Odin. One of the three major heathen gods, along with Thor and Frey. Snorri calls him "the chief of all gods, creator of manking, ruler of heaven and earth, who, when the end of the world draws near, will lead a band of chosen heroes to war against the forces of evil, and will die heroically in combat with a monstrous world." He is also the pagan god of death and also of wisdom.

Ordeal by fire. A ceremony whereby a person claiming to be the descendant of a king was required to walk in his bare feet across nine red-hot iron plow shares. If he came out unscathed, he had royal blood. The DNA test of the Viking period!

Ore. A small Norwegian coin. From the Latin word *aureus*, a Roman gold coin.

Ribbungers. A band of about 150 barbarian/archers whom Sverre had recruited.

Rollo. Rollo was noted for being so tall that he was unable to ride a horse because his feet dragged on the ground. Therefore he walked and became known as "Rollo the Walker." The spelling of his name varies; in Norway it is *Hrolf*, in Norman it is *Roll, Harotel, Rauoul* or *Rou*, in Latin *Rollus* and in French *Rollon*. He was the son of a powerful Jarl whose wealth and ambition was of mounting concern to Harold I Fairhair (#1), King of Norway. The sagas state that Rollo was the black sheep of the family, but made a name for himself when he founded Normandy.

Skalds. Court poets. Skalds won royal favor and costly gifts by poems written as eulogies of their master.

Slaves. The slaves, who were at the bottom of the social scale, were either born unfree or lost their freedom through capture in war, bankruptcy or crime. They were employed as household servants or farmhands.

Slittungers. A rebel band who rallied round a priest named Bene *Skinnkniv*, a reputed son of Magnus IV. Many reputable peasants later joined them, for it was a class movement directed just as much against the "bagler" as "birchlegs." They were known as cutthroats, and both the Baglers and Birchlegs opposed them.

Snorri Sturluson. A renouned Icelandic scholar and historian. The most widely read book in Norway, next to the Bible, is Snorri Sturluson's *Saga of the Kings, Heimskringla* (The Earth Is Round). It is a narrative of Norway's kings during the Viking era to 1177 AD. It is an exciting and fascinating novel. Although critical scholars have found details in *Heimskringla* that may not be reliable, it is, nevertheless, noted as a great literary source of Norwegian history. Snorri Sturluson was born in western Iceland in ca.1179 and died in 1241. He was a wealthy chieftain, a polititian, and poet. Iceland was a Norwegian colony at this time and writing sagas about Norwegian kings was one way of getting ahead in the world. The *Heimskringla* manuscript was rediscovered in the 16th century and was translated into a modern Scandinavian language. It has since been translated into many languages, the best and most complete, is the work of the eminent scholar Lee M. Hollander, and was originally published in 1963 by the American-Scandinavian Foundation at Texas University Press.

Sysselman. A royal official or district governor in Norway.

Thing. A gathering of local people which served as a judicial body.

Thor. One of the three major heathen gods, along with Frey and Odin. Thor was a sky-god, more particularly a storm-god, wielding a hammer which symbolized a thunderbolt. In myths he appears as a great fighter, of huge size and strength.

Thralls. Worked as servants or tenants for the chieftains or for the wealthier farmers.

Valhalla. After his heroic death in battles, a Viking hero would be sent to the great hall of Valhalla where they could feast and continue fighting forever!

Bibliography

Aarflot, Andreas. *Norsk Kirke i Tusen År.*. Universitetsforlaget: Oslo, 1978.

Allstrom, Carl Magnus. *Dictionary of Royal Lineage of Europe and Other Countries.* Vol. 2, 1904.

Armann, Øivind Berntzen. *Borgerskringen's Fyrster of Deres Familietilknytning.*

Baden, Gustav Ludvig, 1764-1840. "The History of Norway From the Earliest Times-1817." From *The Union of Calmar,* by Baron Holberg. Translated from the Danish, and continued to the present time by A. Andersen Feldborg. London: Hmblin and Seyfang.

Bakken, Russ. "A Viking Fortress in England." *The Viking Magazine,* Sons of Norway, April 1987.

Brent, Peter. *The Viking Saga.* Putnam: NY, 1975.

Brĭgger, Waldemar, ed., *Gyldendals Navne Leksikon.* Gyldendal Norsk Forlag A/S 1958. Aas and Wahls Boktrykkeri: Oslo, 1975.

Butler, Ewan. *Scandinavia.* American Heritage: NY, 1973.

Call, Michel L. *Royal Ancestors of Some American Families.* Volume 1, 1989, Chart No. 11703.

Clayman, Charles B., MD., Medical Editor. *Home Medical Encyclopedia.* Random House: NY, 1989.

Clough, Ethlyn T. (Ed. and Arr.). *Norwegian Life, An Account of Past and Contemporary Conditions and Progress In Norway and Sweden.* Bay View Reading Club: Detroit, 1909.

Cohar, Yves. *The Vikings, Lords of the Seas.* Harry N. Abrams: NY, 1981.

Derry, Tik. *The History of Scandinavia, Norway, Sweden, Denmark, Finland, and Iceland.* University of Minnesota: Minneapolis, 1979.

Ganeri, Anita. *Focus on Vikings.* Gloucester Press: NY, 1992.

Gibb, Christopher. *A Viking Sailor.* Rourke Enterprises:Vero Beach, FL, 1986.

Haywood, John. *Historical Atlas of the Vikings.* Penquin: London, 1995.

Hopp, Zinken. *Norwegian History Simplified.* Bergen, Norway, John Griegs Boktrykkeri, 1961. John Griegs Forlag. Tr. 1905. University of Minnesota: Minneapolis.

Gibson, Michael. *The Vikings.* Wayland: London, 1981.

Graham Campbell, James; Kidd, Dafydd. *The Vikings.* The British Museum: London; The Metropolitan Museum of Art: New York. Distributed by William Morrow: New York. 1980.

Henriksen, Vera; Rian, Øystein; Hjort, Johan; Greve, Tim. *Norges Konger Fra Sagatid Til Samtid.* Hovedredaktor: Nyquist, Finn P., 1987, Grondahl & Son Forlag: Oslo.

Hintz, Martin. *Enchantment of the World, Norway.* Children's Press: Chicago, 1982.

Hollander, Lee M., Tr., *The Saga of the Jomsvikings,* University of Texas Press: Austin, 1955.

Jones, Gwyn. *A History of the Vikings.* Oxford University Press: Oxford, 1984.

La Fay, Howard. *The Vikings.* National Geographic Society: Washington, DC. (Out of print.)

Larsen, Karen. *A History of Norway.* Princeton University: Princeton NJ. (Out of print.)

Maclagan, Michael. *Lines of Succession, Heraldry of the Royal Families of Europe.* Tables by Jiri Louda. Orbis: London, 1981.

Madsen, O., Tr. David Macrae. *The Work of the Vikings.* 1976.

Magnusson, Magnus. *Viking Expansion Westward.* Drawings by Rosemar. Henry Z. Walck: NY, 1973.

Margesen, Susan M., Photographs by Peter Anderson. *Vikings.* Knopf: NY, 1982.

Martell, Hazel. *The Vikings.* Warwick Press: New York, 1986.

Midgaard, John. *A Brief History of Norway*, 3rd Ed. Johan Grundt Tanum Forlag: Oslo, 1966.

Moriarity, George Andrews. The Planegenet Ancestry. Generation 3, FHL Film No. 441438. About 1950.'

Norberg, Svein Nic. Trondheim, *Aune Forlag As Trondheim*, Norway. 1997.

Nyquist, R.B. *Sons of the Vikings.* Hutchinson: London.

Oxenstierna, Count Eric. *The Norsemen.* New York Graphic Society: NY, 1959.

Parin, Ingri and Edgar. *Leif the Lucky.* Doubleday: NY, 1941.

Pluckrose, Henry, Ed. *Small World.* Gloucester Press: NY.

Poertner, Rudolf. *The Vikings, Rise and Fall of the Norse Sea Kings*, English Version. St. James Press: London,1975.

Popperwell, Ronald G. *Norway.* Praeger: NY, 1972.

Roesdahl, Else., Tr. Susan M. Margeson and Kirsten Williams. *The Vikings.* Penguin:London, 1987.

Sawyer, P.H. *Kings and Vikings.* Methuen: London, 1982.

Schwennicke, Detlev. *Europaische Stammtafeln.* Volume II, Table 104, Generation 1.

Schiller, Barbara. *Eric the Red and Leif the Lucky.* Troll Associates: Mahwah, NJ, 1979.

Simon, Charnan. *Leif Eriksson and the Vikings.* Childrens' Press: Chicago, 1991.

Simpson, Jacqueline. *The Everyday Life In the Viking Village.* Putnam: NY, 1967.

Stagg, Frank Noel. *The Heart of Norway.* Ruskin House: London, 1953.

Stagg, Frank Noel. *South Norway.* Ruskin House: London, 1953.

Stagg, Frank Noel. *North Norway.* Ruskin House: London, 1952.

Stagg, Frank Noel. *West Norway and Its Fjords.* Ruskin House: London, 1954.

Stagg, Frank Noel. *East Norway and Its Frontier.* Ruskin House: London, 1956.

Sturluson, Snorri., Tr. Lee M. Hollander. *Heimskringla.* University of Texas Press: Austin, 1964.

Tapsell, R.F. (Compiled by). *Monarchs, Rulers, Dynasties, and Kingdoms of the World.* Facts on File Publication: NY, 1993.

Turton, W.H. *The Plantagenet Ancestry.* Generation 1; Generation 2; Generation 3; Generation 4. FHL Film No. 87859. 1928.

Wise, L.F.; E.W. Egan. *Kings, Rulers and Statesmen.* Sterling Publishing: NY, 1967.

Windrow, Martin. *The Viking Warrior.* Franklin Watts Limited, NY, 1984.

Wisniewski, David. *Elfwyn's Saga.* Lothrop, Lee & Shepard: NY, 1990.

Wright, Rachel. *Viking Craft Projects.* Franklin Watts: NY, 1992.

ENCYCLOPEDIAS:

Medieval Scandinavia. Ed. Phillip Pulsiano. Garland: NY, 1993

The World Book Encyclopedia. "Leif Ericson." Vol. 6. 1990.

Scandinavia. Library of Nations. Time-Life Books: Amsterdam, 1985.

Dictionary of Saints. Delaney, Doubleday: NY, 1980.

Index of Personal Names

The sequence used is that of the Latin Alphabet. The three Norwegian letters – Æ, æ, Ø, o, Å, å – are with their nearest equivalent.

KEY

ca. – circa/about
b. – birth date   e.g. b.c1172 or b.21 Jan 1072
d. – death date   e.g. d.21 Jan 1072
R. – time of reign
illeg. – illegitimate
dau. – daughter
legit. – legitimate
mar. – married
m1) – First marriage
m2) – Second marriage, etc.
* – petty king (small king)

"It is difficult, if not impossible, to achieve consistency in the rendering of Old Norse names." (Translator's note from *The Saga of the Jomsvikings*.) And I agree.

ABEL KING OF DENMARK. Son of Valdemar II (#41) and Queen Berengaria of Poland. Married Mathilde, Countess of Holstein. 121.

ADELBERT. Archbishop of Bremen and Vicar of the Scandinavian countries. 68.

AELFHILD. See Alvhild.

ÆLGIFU. See Emma, Princess of Normandy.

AENEAS SYLVIUS. Pope Pius II.

AGNAR. King of Vestfold. Grandfather of Hild, the wife of Eystein Halfdansson (#-4). Eystein was Harald Fairhair's (#1) great-great grandfather. 4.

AGNES. b.c1292. Illeg. daughter of Haakon V Magnusson (#48). Mother unknown. Mar. Hafthor Jonsson Roos. 139.

ALBRECT. King Albrect of Sweden. Father of Albrect of Mecklenburg. 152.

ALBRECT OF MECKLENBURG. Son of Eufemia, the granddaughter of Haakon V Magnusson (#48) and King Albrect of Sweden. 145, 147, 152.

ALEXANDER. King Alexander III of Scotland. Father of Margrete, the first wife of Erik II Magnusson (#47). 136, 137.

ALEXANDRA. Princess Alexandra of Denmark. Mother of King Haakon VII's (R. 1905–1959) wife Maud. 158.

ALFAR. King Alfar. Father of Alvhild, the first wife of Guthroth the Hunting King (#-2). 6.

ALFRED. Son of King Ethelred of England and Emma. 52, 53.

ALFHILD. See Alvhild.

ALFIVA. Mistress or common law wife of Knut the Great (#10) of Denmark. Knut also ruled England. Alfiva was mother of Svein Alfivasson (#11) and Harald Harfot. 51, 52, 54, 55.

ALOF ARBOT. Oldest daughter and first child of Harald Fairhair (#1) and Gyda. Alof married Jarl Thorir the Silent of Rognvald. Mother of Bergljot. 15, 19.

ALV ERLINGSSON. Appointed Duke by Queen Mother Ingeborg, the wife of Magnus VI (#46). 135.

ALVHILD. Daughter of Hring Dagsson of Ringeriki. Wife of Harald Fairhair (#1). 15, 20.

ALVHILD. Daughter of King Alfar of Alfheim. First wife of Guthroth the Hunting King (#-2). 6.

ALVHILD. "The little English girl." St. Olav's (#9) mistress. Mother of Magnus I the Good (#12). 47, 57.

ANDREAS SIMONSSON. Son of Simon Thorbergsson and Gunnhild. Foster brother of Haakon Broadsholder (#28). 95, 99.

ARNE ARNESSON OF STOTHREIM. Called King's Stepfather. A Lendsmann. Husband of Ingerid, the widow of Harald Gilchrist (#23). They became parents of the famous Nicholas Arnesson (1150–1225) and Margrete, who had a son, Filippus Simonsson (#38). Also parents of Inge and Filippus of Herthla. 88, 117.

ARNFINN. Son of Thorfinn Hausakljuf, a prominent Jarl in Denmark. Husband of Ragnhild, the daughter of Erik Bloodaxe (#2). A good friend of King Gorm of Denmark. 26.

ASA. Also called "Asa the Fair." Mistress of Erling Skakke. Mother of Finn and Sigurth.

Asa. Wife of Halfdan the White, the son of Haakon I Fairhair (#1) and Asa. 19.

ASA EYSTEINSDATTER. Daughter of Eystein the Hardruler and Solveig Halfdansdatter. First wife of Halfdan Whiteleg (#-5). Great-great-great grandmother of Harald I Fairhair (#1). 3, 4.

ASA HAAKONSDATTER. Daughter of Jarl Haakon Grjotgarthsson. First wife of Harald I Fairhair (#1). 15, 16, 19.

ASA HARALDSDATTER. Second wife of King Guthroth the Hunting King (#-2). Grandmother of Harald I Fairhair (#1). 6, 7, 8, 9.

ASHILD. See Alvhild

ASLAK ERLINGSSON. Married to Sigrid, the daughter of Jarl Svein (#8) and Holmfrid. 44.

ASTA. Wife of Erik, son of Sigurd the Mouth (#26). Eric, Asta and their two sons were poisoned when living at St. Olav's Abby in Tønsberg. 94.

ASTA GUDBRANDSDATTER. Was first married to Harald Grenski and they were the parents of St. Olav (#9). After Grenske's death married Sigurd Syr, and with him had Harald III the Hard (#13), and Guthorm, Gunnhild, Halfdan and Ingerid. 47, 60.

ASTRID. Daughter of Tryggve. Sister of Olav Trygvasson. Great granddaughter of Harald I Fairhair (#1) and Svanhild.

ASTRID. Queen Astrid. Daughter and love child of King Olav Stotkonung of Sweden and Edla. Wife of Saint Olav (#9). 47, 50, 57, 58.

ASTRID ERIKSDATTER FROM JAREN. Wife of Tryggve Olavsson. Mother of Olav Trygvasson (#6). Later married Lodin and had three children. 37, 38.

ASTRID MAUD INGEBORG. b.1932. Sister of the present King Harald V of Norway. Married to Johan Martin Ferner. 160.

ASTRID ROESDATTER OF SWEDEN. Wife of Sverre Sigurdsson (#33). Mother of Cecelia and Ingeborg. Sister of Knut Eriksson of Sweden. 109.

ATHALBRIKT. A priest. Married to Thora Saxeasdatter. While Thora was married to Athalbrikt, she had a son, Sigrid II Slembe (#24) with Sigurd the Mouth (#26). Snorri lists Athelbrikt as Sigurd Slembe's father. 89.

ATHELSTAN. Athelstan the Victorious, Athelstan the True Believer. King of England. Foster father of Haakon the Good (#3). 18, 25, 28, 29.

AUGUSTINE MAGNUSSON. See Eystein I Magnusson (#20).

BAARD GUTTORMSSON. A lendsmann from Rein in Trondelag. Son of Guthorm from Rein in Trondelag. Married Cecelia Sigurdsdatter, the illeg. daughter of Sigurd the Mouth (#26). Father of Haakon Galen and Inge II Baardsson (#39) with Cecelia. Later married Ragnhild Erlingsdatter from Valdres and their son was Skule Baardson (#45). 94, 119, 130.

BATAAN. King Bataan of Sweden. Father of Svein Forkbeard and Thyre. 37.

BEATHACK. b.c1110. Mother of Eystein II Haraldsson (#27). Irish mistress of Harald Gilchrist (#23). 86, 97.

BERGENGARIA, PRINCESS OF PORTUGAL. b.c1270. Fourth wife of Valdemar II of Denmark (#41). Four children. 121.

BERGLJOT THORESDATTER. Daughter of Alof Arbot and Thorir the silent. Granddaughter of Harald Fairhair (#1). Wife of Jarl Sigurd Grjotgarthsson, and they had one son, Haakon of Lade (#5). 19, 22, 34.

BERGLJOT HAAKONSDATTER. Daughter of Jarl Haakon of Lade (#5) and Thora Skagesdatter. Married to Einar Tambarskelfir. They had a son, Eindrithi. Both Einar and Eindrithi were killed by King Harald III the Hard's (#13) hird. 34.

BIADMUIN. Princess Biadmuin. From Ireland. b.c1093. Mistress of Sigurd the Crusader (#21). Daughter of Muikertach, King of Ireland. 79, 80.

BIRGIR. King Birgir of Sweden. 141, 143.

BIRGIR BROSA. Jarl. Swedish. b.c1130. Fourth husband of Brigitha, the daughter of Harald Gilchrist (#23). Father of Kristin. 106.

BIRGITTE OF SWEDEN. Was "lady-in-waiting" to Blanca, wife of Mangus VII the Good (#49). Later canonized as Saint Birgitte. 144, 151.

BJATHMYNJA. See Biadmuin.

BJATHOK. See Beathack.

BJORN THE CHAPMAN. Son of Harald I Fairhair (#1) and Svanhild Eysteinsdatter. 15, 18, 20, 25.

BJORN FARMANN. See Bjorn the Chapman.

BJORN KAUPMANN. See Bjorn the Chapman.

BLAATAN. King Blaatan of Denmark. Father of Olav Trygvasson's (#6) fourth wife, Queen of Thyre.

BLANCA FROM NAMUR. b.c1363. Daughter of Count Hohn of Namur (Flanders). Wife of Magnus the Good (#49), On her maternal side was related to the royal family of France and Edward IV of England. 143, 144, 145, 147.

BLANCH. See Blanca of Namur.

BORGHILD OLAVSDATTER FROM SKJEBERG. b.c1094. Daughter of Olav-in-the-Dale. Mistress of Sigurd the Crusader (#21), and with him had Magnus IV the Blind (#22). 79, 80, 84.

BOTHVAR THORTHARSON. Snorri's maternal grandfather.

BRIDGET. See Birgitte.

BRIGIDA. See Birgitte.

BRIGITHA HARALDSDATTER. Princess of Norway. b.c1130. Had 4 marriages and many children. Daughter of Harald Gilchrist (#23) and Ingerid. M1)King Ingi Hallsteinson of Sweden, m2)Jarl Karl Sonason, m3)Magnus Henriksson, King of Sweden, m4)Jarl Birgir Brosa. Had many children. 86, 88, 106.

BURIZLAF. King of Vendland (Germany). Married to Thyre Haraldsdatter. 40, 41.

CANUTE II THE GREAT. See Knut the Great (#10). 51.

CARL. Prince Carl of Sweden (1861–1951). Married to Princess Ingeborg (1878–1958). Their daughter was Princess Martha, who married Olav V of Norway (R.1957–1991). Three children: Ragnhild Alexandra, Astrid Maud Ingeborg and Harald, who became king of Norway in 1991. 160.

CARL XIII. Swedish ruler of Norway. R.1814–1818. 155.

CARL XIV (BERNADOTTE). Swedish ruler of Norway. R.1818–1844. 155.

CARL XV. Swedish ruler of Norway. R.1859–1872. 155.

CECELIA. Wife of Guthroth, the grandson of Harald I Fairhair (#1) and Svanhild. The grandmother of St. Olav (#9).

CECELIA. b.c.1103. Wife or mistress of Sigurd the Crusader (#21). An act of bigamy by Sigurd as he was already married. She deserted him on his deathbed. 79, 80, 81.

CECILIA. Mother of Inge II Baardsson (#39). 119.

CECELIA HAAKONSDATTER. Illeg. daughter of Haakon IV (#43) and Kanga the Young. Married to Harald Olavsson, King of Isle of Mann. 125, 127.

CECELIA SIGURDSDATTER. Illeg. daughter of Sigurd the Mouth (#26) and unknown mistress. M1)Folkvid Lagmann, m2)Baard Guttormsson. Cecelia's children: Haakin Galen and Inge II Baardsson (#39). Skule Baardsson (#45), was evidently not her child, but son of Baard's second wife. 94, 119.

CECELIA SVERRESDATTER. b.c1177. Daughter of Sverre Sigurdsson (#33) and Astrid Roesdatter of Sweden. M1)Kik Gregorius, and m2)Einar Prest. 109.

CHARLEMAGNE. (Old Norse Karlamagnus). King of the Franks and Emperor of the West. Where St. Olav's (#9) son, Magnus (#12), got his name. 57.

CHRISTIAN I. R.1449–1481. Danish ruler of Norway. 154.

CHRISTIAN II. R.1513–1523. Also called Christian the Cruel. Danish ruler of Norway. 141, 154.

CHRISTIAN III. R.1537–1559. Danish ruler of Norway. 154.

CHRISTIAN IV. R.1588–1648. Danish ruler of Norway. 154.

CHRISTIAN V. R.1670–1699. Danish ruler of Norway. 154.

CHRISTIAN VI. R.1730–1746. Danish ruler of Norway. 154.

CHRISTIAN VII. R.1766–1808. Danish ruler of Norway. 154.

CHRISTIAN FREDERIK CARL GEORGE VALDEMAR AXEL. Second son of Frederik VIII of Denmark and Queen Louis, daughter of Carl of Sweden. 158.

CHRISTIN. See Kristin.

CHRISTINA. See Kristin.

CHRISTINE BJORNSDATTER of Jernside, Sweden. Wife of Swedish King Erik IX Jedvardsson. Mother of Margrete Eriksdatter, one of Sverre's (#33) wives. 109.

CHRISTOFFER. King Christoffer. Son of Valdemar II (#41). 121.

CHRISTOPHER OF BAVARIA. Conrad II Emperor of Rome. Ruled Norway from 1442–1448. 154.

CNUT. See Knut.

CONRAD II. Emperor of Rome. His son, Henry III, married Gunnhild, daughter of Knut the Great (#10). 51, 52.

DAG. King Dag. King of Vestfold. Father of Liv Dagsdatter, the wife of Halvdan the Gentle (#-3). 5.

DAG. Son of Harald I Fairhair (#1) and Alvhild. 15, 20.

DAGMAR (Margrete). Princess of Bohemia. b.c1174 d.24 May 1212. Second wife of Valdemar II (#41). 121.

DEACON MAGNUSSON. See Sigurd II Slembe (#24).

DON PHILIP (Spanish). Married Kristin Haakonsdatter, daughter of Haakon IV the Old (#43) and Margrete. 125, 127.

DUKE SKULE. See Skule Baardsson (#45).

EDWARD. Son of Edward I of England. Proposed husband of Margrete of Scotland. 137.

EDWARD THE CONFESSOR. A King in Enland. Son of King Ethelred and Emma. 52, 53.

EDWARD I. King of England. Father of Edward. 137.

EDWARD VII of England. Father of Maud, wife of King Haakon VII (R.1905–1957). 158, 160.

EDLA WENDS. Mistress of King Olav Stotkonung of Sweden. Mother of Astrid, the wife of Saint Olav (#9). 47.

EINAR KONGSMAAG. See Einar Prest.

EINAR PREST. Second husband of Cecelia, Sverre's (#33) daughter. Fostered Guttorm Sigurdsson (#40). A Birchleg. Also known as Einar Kongsmaag. 109, 120.

EINAR SKULASON. A *skald*. 98.

EINAR SMORBAK. Archbishop. Officiated at the coronation of King Magnus VI the Lawmender (#46) and Ingeborg. 134.

EINAR TAMBARSKELFIR. The most powerful landed-man in the Trondheim District. Had a son named Eindrith. Married to Bergljot, the daughter of Jarl Haakon of Lade (#5) and Thora Skagesdatter. He was counselor and advisor for 11-year-old King Magnus I (#13), the son of St.Olav (#9). 34, 43, 45, 58.

EIRIK. See Erik.

EIRIK BLODOKS. See Erik I Bloodaxe (#2).

ELDRID BJARNESDATTER. Wife of Magnus V. Erlingsson (#29). No children from this marriage. 101.

ELIZABET. See Illisif.

ELLISIF. See Illisif.

EMMA. Princess of Normandy. First wife of Knut the Great (#10) of Denmark). She was the widow of King Ethelred of England. Mother of Hardeknut and Gunnhild. She changed her name to Ælgifu when she married King Ethelred. 51, 52, 53.

ERIC. See Erik.

ERIK. King Erik of Jutland (Denmark). Father of Ragnhild, wife of Harald I Fairhair (#1). 21.

ERIK THE PRIEST-HATER. See Erik II Magnusson (#47).

ERIK OF POMEROY. Grandson of Ingeborg, Margrete's (#52) sister. Great grandson of King Valdemar of Denmark. 152.

ERIK. Son of Agnar, King of Vestfold. Father of Hild, the wife of Eystein Halfdansson (#-4), the great-great grandfather of Harald Fairhair (#1). 4.

ERIK. Son of King Valdemar Magnusson of Sweden and Ingeborg, the daughter of Erik II Magnusson (#47) and Isabella Bruce. Died young. 136, 141.

ERIK BJOTHASKALLI. Father of Astrid, the mother of Olav Trygvasson (#6). 37.

ERIK BLOODYAXE. See Erik I Bloodaxe (#2).

ERIK HAAKONARSON. See Erik, Jarl (#7). 42.

ERIK, JARL (#7). Jarl Erik. (Eric Haakonarson). Illeg. son of Haakon of Lade, Jarl (#5), and an attractive mistress from Oppland. Half-brother of Jarl Svein (#8). Married Gyda, daughter of King Svein Forkbeard of Denmark. 34, 42, 43, 44, 49.

ERIK. Jarl Erik. Illeg. son of Sigurd II the Mouth (#26). Married Asta. 94.

ERIK KONGSSON. Swedish. See Folkvid Lagmann.

ERIK MAGNUSSON. Erik Wryneck of Sweden. Married Haakon V Magnusson's (#48) daughter, Princess Ingeborg and with her had two children. He was brother of King Birgir of Sweden and Valdemar of Sweden. Erik had two illeg. sons who died of the Black Death. 139.

ERIK "SEGERSALL" VII. King of Sweden. Father of Holmfrid, who was the wife of Jarl Svein (#8). 44.

ERIK SIGURDSSON. Prince of Norway. Illeg. son of Sigurd II the Mouth (#26). He was half brother of Sverre Sigurdsson (#33) and was Sverre's Jarl. Eric married Asta. Eric, Asta and two sons were poisoned when living at St. Olav's Abbey in Tønsberg. 94.

ERIK I BLOODAXE (#2). (Eirik Blodoks, Erik Bloodyaxe). Son of Harald I Fairhair (#1) and Princess Ragnhild Eriksdatter. Many children. 16, 17, 20, 21, 22, 23-27, 28, 29, 31, 47.

ERIK II MAGNUSSON (#47). (Erik the Priest-Hater). Son of Magnus the Lawmender (#46) and Queen Ingeborg Eriksdatter from Denmark. Erik was first married to Margrete Alexandersdatter, Princess of Scotland. Then married Isabella Bruce. 134, 135, 136, 137, 139, 141.

ERIK II "EMUN." King of Denmark. Married to Princess Malmfrida before she married Sigurd the Crusader (#21). 79, 80.

ERIK III. Became King of Sweden from 1389–1442. Son of Magnus VII the Good (#49) and Blanca from Namur. 143, 145, 147, 154.

ERIK IV PLOVPENNY. King of Denmark. Son of Valdemar II (#41) and Berengaria, Princess of Portugal. Married Jutte I, Princess of Saxony. One of their children was Ingeborg, who married King Magnus the Lawmender (#46). 121, 125.

ERIK IX JEDVARDSSON. King of Sweden. Father of Margrete Eriksdatter the second wife of Sverre (#33). Erik's wife was Christine Bjornsdatter of Jernside, Sweden. 109.

ERLAND. Son of Jarl Haakon of lade (#5). Unknown mother. 34.

ERLING KROKKRYGG "crooked neck." See Erling Skakke.

ERLING HAAKONSSON. Illeg. son of Jarl Haakon of Lade (#5). 34.

ERLING, JARL OF NORWAY. b.c1125. Killed Sept. 19, 1179.

ERLING. Son of King Erik Bloodaxe (#2) and Gunnhild. 23, 26, 27.

ERLING SKAKKE "WRYNECK." b.c1126 d.1178. Married Kristin, the daughter of Sigurd the Crusader (#21) and Malfrida and with her was the father of Magnus V Erlingson (#29) and Ragnhild. Erling had four or more illegitimate sons. 79, 80, 93, 94, 95, 99, 100, 101, 103, 104, 105, 106.

ERLING SKJALGSSON. Father of Ragnhild, the wife of Thorberg Arneson. Married sister of Olav Trygvasson (#9).

ERLING STEINVEGG. See Erling Stonewall (#42).

ERLING STONEWALL (#42) (Erling Steinvegg) Claimed to be son of Magnus V Erlingsson (#29)and unknown mother. Father of a son, Magnus, and also father of Sigurd Ribung. Buried in famous round church in Slesvig (Vestfold) in 1207. 101, 118, 122, 123.

ERLING SVEN LORENTZEN. Married to Ragnhild, the sister of present King Harald V of Norway (R.1991–present). 160.

ERLING SVERRESSON. b.1186. Son of Sverre Sigurdsson and Margrete, the Princess of Sweden. Died young. 109, 115.

ERLING VIDKUNNSON. b.1292. Advisor to King Magnus VII (#49). 144.

ERLING WRYNECK. See Erling Skakke.

ESTRID. Sister of Knut the Great. Mother of Svein Estridsson. 51.

ETHELRED. King Ethelred II of England. "Ethelred the Unready." 51.

EUFEMIA. Queen Eufemia. Granddaughter of Prince Vislav of Rugen. Wife of King Haakon V Magnusson (#48). One daughter, Ingeborg, married to Duke Erik (*Wryneck*) Magnusson of Sweden, the brother of Swedish King Birgir. 139, 141.

EUFEMIA. Granddaughter of Haakon V Magnusson (#48) and Ingeborg. Married Albrect of Sweden. Had one son, Duke Albrect of Mecklenburg. 139.

EYSTEIN. Archbishop Eystein. He crowned Margus V Erlingsson (#29). 103.

EYSTEIN. Bishop Eystein. Archbishop of Bergen. 103.

EYSTEIN THE *FART.* See Eystein Halfdansson (#-4).

EYSTEIN THE HARDRULER. King of the Upplands and Jarl of Trondheim. Married to Solveig Halfdansdatter. Father of Asa Eysteinsdatter, the wife of Halfdan Whiteleg (#-5). 3.

EYSTEIN HALFDANSSON (#-4). (Øystein, Eystein the *Fart*, Eystein II). Son of Halfdan Whiteleg (#-5) and Asa Eysteinsdatter. Great-great grandfather of Harald I Fairhair (#1). Married Hild Eriksdatter. Father of Halfdan the Gentle (#-3). 3, 4, 5.

EYSTEIN, JARL. Father of Svanhild, one of Harald I Fairhair's (#1) wives. 19.

EYSTEIN MAGNUSSON. See Eystein I Magnusson (#20).

EYSTEIN MEYLA. See Eystein Moyla (#32).

EYSTEIN MOYLA (#32). (Oystein Moyla, Eystein Meyla). Illeg. son of King Eystein II Haraldsson (#27). Mother of Eystein Moyla, unknown. 97, 103, 106-107.

EYSTEIN I MAGNUSSON (#20). (Eystein Magnusson, Øystein I Magnusson, Augustine Magnusson). Illeg. son of Magnus III Barelegs (#17) and unknown mistress, who was said to be of low birth, but a "fine, distinguished woman." Married Ingeborg, daughter of Guthorm, the son of Steigar-Thorir. 71, 75, 76, 77-78, 79, 80.

EYSTEIN II. See Eystein Halfdannson (#-4).

EYSTEIN II HARALDSSON (#27). (Oystein II Haraldsson). b.c1125 d.21 Aug 1157. Illegitimate son of Harald Gilchrist (#23) and Beathack (from Ireland). Married Ragna Nikolsdatter. No children from this marriage. Illegitimate children listed for Eystein are Eystein Moyla (#32), Torliev Breiskjegg, and a daughter. 86, 91, 95, 96, 97-98, 103, 106.

EYVIND KELDA. Grandson of Rognvald Rettilbeini. Great grandson of Harald I Fairhair (#1) and Svanhild.

EYVIND SKALDASPILLIR. A renounded Islandic skald and son of Gunnhild, the granddaughter of Harald I Fairhair Fairhair (#1). 22.

FILIPPUS. Son of Birgir Brosa and Brigitha, daughter of Harald Gilchrist (#23).

FILIPPUS OF HETHLA. Son of Arne of Stothreim.

FILIPPUS SIMONSSON (#38). (Fillip(pus) Simonsson, Philip Simonsson). b.c1182 d.1217. Son of Simon Karlsson and Margrete, the daughter of Harald Gilchrist's (#23) Queen, Ingerid Ragnvaldsdatter, in her marriage with Arne Arnesson. Filippus married Kristin, daughter of Sverre Sigurdsson (#33) in 1209. She died in childbirth. 88, 109, 117-118, 123, 126.

FILIP(PUS) SIMONSSON. See Filippus Simonsson(#38).

FINN. Illeg. son of Erling Skakke. His mother was Asa the Fair.

FINN ARNESON. Brother of Thorberg Arneson and Arne Arnesson.

FOLKI. Son of Harald Gilchrist's (#23) dau., Brigitha and Birgir Brosa.

FOLKVID LAGMANN. Swedish. Married to Cecelia, the daughter of Sigurd II the Mouth (#26). He is the same as Erik Kongsson. 94.

FREDERIK I. R.1524–1533. Danish ruler of Norway. 154.

FREDERIK II. R.1559–1588. Danish ruler of Norway. 154.

FREDERIK. III. R.1648–1670. Danish ruler of Norway. 154.

FREDERIK. IV. R.1699–1730. Danish ruler of Norway. 154.

FREDERIK V. R.1746–1766. Danish ruler of Norway. 154.

FREDERIK VI. R.1808–1814. Danish ruler of Norway. 154.

FREDERIK VII. Father of Haakon VII, King of Norway from 1905-1957. 158.

FREDKULLA. See Margrete Fredkulla.

FREY. One of the three major heathen gods, along with Thor and Odin.

FRITHKOLLA. See Margrete Fredkulla.

FRODE. Son of Harald I Fairhair and Gyda. 15, 19.

FROTHI. See Frode.

GADABOUT DEACON. See Sigurd II Slembe (#24).

GAMLI ERIKSSON. Son of King Erik Bloodaxe (#2) and Gunnhild. Named after his grandfather, Gorm the Old, of Denmark. Killed. 23, 25, 30.

GAUTHILD ALGAUTSDATTER. Wife of King Ingjald of Sweden. Mother of Olav Tree-Hewer (#-6), and Ingjald, Prince of Vestfold. 2.

GEIRA. From Germany. First wife of Olav Trygvasson (#6). 37, 39.

GILLE. See Harald Gilchrist (#23).

GILLI. See Harald Gilchrist (#23)

GORM. King Gorm the Old, King of Denmark. Father of Harald Bluetooth and Gunnhild, wife of Erik I Bloodaxe (#2). 23.

GREGORIUS DAGSSON. Considered the greatest chieftain among the landed men of Norway. Son of Dag Elifsson and Ragnhild, the daughter of Skopti Ogmundarson. A staunch supporter of King Inge (#23). 98.

GREGORY VII. Pope Gregory. Archbishop of Bremen. 68.

GRIM RUSLI. Kristin, daughter of Sigurd the Crusader (#21), left Norway with him.

GRJOTGARTH. Father of Haakon Grjotgarthsson. A great chieftain who supported Harald I Fairhair (#1). 16.

GRJOTGARTHSSON. Son of Grjotgarth. See Jarl Haakon Grjotarthsson.

GUDROD VEIDEKONGE. See Guthroth the Hunting King (#-2).

GUDRUN. Gudrun Skeggesdatter. Third wife of Olav Trygvasson (#9). 37, 40.

GUNHILD. See Gunnhild.

GUNNHILD. Gunnhild Kingsmother. Daughter of King Gorm of Denmark and Thyre, Queen of England. Wife of Erik Bloodaxe (#2). Fostered by Ozur Toti from Halogaland. Gunnhild acquired supernatural power from the Lapps. 18, 19, 23, 25, 26, 27, 31, 32, 34, 38.

GUNNHILD. Princess Gunnhild. Daughter of Earl Erland of the Orkneys and a sister of Magnus.

GUNNHILD. Wife of Simon Thorbergsson. Simon and Gunnhild fostered Haakon Broadshoulder (#28). Svein and Gunnhild had two sons, Onund and Andreas. 99.

GUNNHILD. Daughter of Ingeborg, Harald I Fairhair's (#1) daughter. Gunnhild was the mother of Eyvind Skaldaspiler. 22.

GUNNHILD from Poland. Mother of Knut II the Great (#10) of Denmark. Married to Svein Forkbeard of Denmark. 51, 52.

GUNNHILD. Daughter of Knut II the Great (#10) of England, and Emma of Normandy. She married the future Roman Emperor, Henry III, son of Roman Emperor, Conrad II. 51.

GUNNHILD . Wife of Unas, a combmaker in Bergen. While married to him was also mistress of Sigurd the Mouth (#26), and with him had a son, Sverre Sigurdsson (#33). 95, 109, 110.

GUNNHILD. Second child and oldest daughter of Asta Gudbrandsdatter and Sigurd Syr. Sister of Harald III the Hard (#13). 60.

GUNNHILD SVEINSDATTER. Daughter of Jarl Svein (#8) and Holmfrid. She married Svend (Svein) II Estridsson, king of Denmark). She later married King Anund (Jacob) Olavsson of Sweden. 44.

GUNNHILD VYRTGOERNSDATTER. Wife of Haakon, the son of Jarl Erik (#7). 42.

GUTHBRAND SKAFHOGGSSON. Married Maria, the daughter of Eystein I Magnusson (#20) and Ingeborg Guthormsdatter. They had a son, Olav Ill-Luck. 70, 77.

GUTHNY. Snorri's mother.

GUTHORM. Son of Steiger-Thoris. Father of Ingeborg, the wife of Eystein I Magnusson (#20). 77.

GUTHROM. See Guttorm.

GUTHROTH. Son of Asa Eysteinsdatter and Halfdan Whiteleg (#-5). 3.

GUTHROTH. Son of King Erik I Bloodaxe (#2) and Gunnhild. 23, 27.

GUTHROTH THE HUNTING KING (#-2) (Guthroth the Generous, Gudrød Veidekonge). Son of Halfdan the Gentle (#-3) and Liv Dagsdatter. Grandfather of Harald I Fairhair (#-1). M1)Alvhild, daughter of King Alfar of Alfheim. They had one son, Olav Geirstatha Alf I. M2)Asa Haraldsdatter. They had one son, Halfdan the Black (#-1). 5, 6, 7, 9.

GUTHROTH THE GENEROUS. See Guthroth the Hunting King (#-2).

GUTHROTH BJARNARSON. Son of Bjorn the Chapman and grandson of Harald I Fairhair (#1). His son was Harald Grenski, the Grenlander. 20, 47.

GUTHROTH BJORNSSON. Son of Bjorn the Chapman, and grandfather of St. Olav (#9). 18, 20, 25, 31, 32.

GUTHROTH LJOMI "THE RADIANT." Son of Harald I. Fairhair (#1) and Snafrid. Thjotholf of Hvinir was his foster father. 15, 17, 21.

GUTHROTH SKIRJA. Son of Harald Fairhair (#1) and Alvhild. He was fostered by Olav Geirstatha-Alf II. 15, 20.

GUTTORM. Son of Inge II Baardsson (#39) and Cecelia, daughter of Sigurd the Mouth (#26). 119.

GUTTORM HARALDSSON. Oldest son of Harald I Fairhair (#1) and Asa Haakonsdatter. 15, 18, 19.

GUTTORM. Maternal uncle of Harald I Fairhair (#1). Brother of Ragnhild, Harald I Fairhair's (#1) mother. 16.

GUTTORM. Third son of King Erik I Bloodaxe (#2) and Gunnhild. 23, 26, 30, 35.

GUTTORM GRAYBEARD. Father of Thora, mother of Sigurd II the Mouth (#26). 86, 94.

GUTTORM SIGURDSSON (#40). Son of Sigard Lavard, the oldest son of King Sverre Sigurdsson (#33) and an unknown mother from the Faroe Islands where Guttorm was born. He was fostered by Einar Prest and Peter Styper. 109, 117, 119, 120, 122.

GYDA SVEINSDATTER. Princess of Denmark. Daughter of King Svein Forkbeard of Denmark. Wife of Jarl Erik I (#7). One son, Haakon. 34, 42.

GYDA. A Dublin princess. Second wife of Olav Trygvasson (#9) and with him had a son, Tryggve Olavsson. Gyda was a sister of Olav Kvaan who was king of Ireland. 37, 39.

GYDA ERIKSDATTER. Daughter of King Erik of Horthaland. A young princess who married Harald I Fairhair (#1) after the Battle of Hafrsfjord. She was fostered in Valdres. 15, 16, 17, 18, 19.

GYRD BAARDSSON. Foster father of Sigurd the Mouth (#26). 95.

GYRID. Wife of Inge Baardsson II (#39). Mother of Guttorm. 119.

HAAKON I THE GOOD (#3). (Hakon I, Hakon den Gode, Haakon Adalsteinfostre, Haakon Haraldsson). Son of Harald Fairhair (#1) and Thora Mosterstang. 16, 18, 20, 22, 25, 26, 28-30, 31.

HAKON I. See Haakon I the Good (#3).

Hakon den Gode. See Haakon I the Good (#3).

HAAKON ADALSTEINFOSTRE. See Haakon I the Good (#3).

HAAKON HARALDSSON. See Haakon I the Good (#3).

HAAKON TORESFOSTRE (#16). ((Haakon Magnusson) Son of King Magnus II Haraldsson (#14) and unknown mistress. 66, 70, 73, 75.

HAAKON MAGNUSSON. See Haakon Toresfostre (#16).

HAAKON BROADSHOULDER (#28). (Haakon II Sigurdsson, Haakon *Herdebreid*). Illeg. son of Sigurd the Mouth (#26) and Thora, a servant girl of a powerful ruler in Vik. A grandson of Harald Gilchrist (#23). Probably never married. He was fostered by Simon Thorsbergsson. 93, 95, 99, 100, 101, 104, 105.

HAAKON II SIGURDSSON. See Haakon Broadshoulder (#28).

HAAKON *HERDEBREID*. See Haakon Broadshoulder (#28).

HAAKON III (#37). (Haakon the Younger, Haakon Sverresson). Son of Sverre Sigurdsson (#33) and Margrete, Princess of Sweden. Never married, but with Inga of Varteig had a son, Haakon IV (#43). 109, 115, 116, 117, 120, 125.

HAAKON THE YOUNGER. See Haakon III (#37).

HAAKON SVERRESSON. See Haakon III (#37).

HAAKON IV THE OLD (#43). (Haakon the Old, Haakon Haakonsson, Håkon IV, Håkonarsonar). Illeg. son of Haakon III Sverresson (#37) and Inga from Varteig. Married Margrete, daughter of Skule Baardsson, when she was seventeen. 109, 115, 116, 124-128, 129, 130, 133, 134.

HAAKON THE OLD. See Haakon IV the Old (#43).

HAAKON HAAKONSSON. See Haakon IV the Old (#43).

HÅKON IV. See Haakon IV the Old (#43).

HÅKONARSONAR. See Haakon IV the Old.

HAAKON HAAKONSSON. Son of Haakon IV the Old (#43) and Margrete Skulesdatter. Married Richiza Birgirsdatter (Swedish). 125, 127.

HAAAKON MAGNUSSON. See Haakon Toresfostre (#16).

HAAKON V MAGNUSSON (#48). (Håkon Magnusson, Duke Haakon, Magnus *Langbein*). Son of Magnus IV the Lawmender (#46) and Queen Ingeborg from Denmark. Married Queen Eufemia of Ruppin and then Isabella Joigny. Had one legit. daughter, Ingeborg Haakonsdatter, with Eufemia. Also had an illeg. daughter: Agnes. Father, with Eufemia, of Albrect and Magnus VII (#49). 134, 135, 136, 138, 139, 143.

HÅKON MAGNUSSON. See Haakon V Magnusson (#48).

HAAKIN VI MAGNUSSON (#50). (Haakon Magnusson the Younger, Håkon VI). Son of King Magnus VII Erickson (#48) and Queen Blanca from Flanders. Married Margrete Valdemarsdatter of Denmark. Had one son, Olav IV (#51). 133, 143, 145, 147, 148, 149, 151, 152, 157, 159, 160.

HAAKON MAGNUSSON THE YOUNGER. See Haakon VI (#50).

HAAKON VII. R.1905–1957. Christian Frederik Carl George Valdemar Axel. Danish. Was unanimously chosen king of Norway when Norway gained its independence in 1905. Married to Maud, daughter of King Edward VII of England. Had one son, Olav V, who reigned after him. 157, 158, 159, 160, 161, 162.

HAAKON MAGNUS. Crown Prince of Norway. Son of King Harald V and Queen Sonja. Haakon was born in 1973. 161.

HAAKONSDATTER. Daughter of Haakon of Lade (#5) and unknown mistress. 34.

HAAKON GALEN, JARL. Son of Cecelia Sigurdsdatter, who was the daughter of Sigurd the Mouth (#26). Haakon was the father of Junker Knut (#44). Guttorm Sigurdsson (#40) was guided by Haakon Galen. Haakon Galen is Sverre Sigurdsson's (#33) half-Swedish nephew. Married Kristin Nikolasdatter. 94, 116, 117, 118, 119, 120, 121, 122, 129.

HAAKON, JARL. Haakon Eriksson. Son of Jarl Erik (#7) and Gyda Sveinsdatter. Married Gunnhild Vyrtgoernsdatter. 42, 43, 45, 49.

HAAKON IVARSSON, JARL OF DENMARK. Son of Ivar the White (Haakon Ivarsson of Denmark). Married Ragnhild Magnusdatter, the illeg. daughter of Magnus I the Good (#13). 57.

HAAKON GRJOTGARTHSSON. Jarl Haakon the Mighty. Jarl of Hlathir. Son of Grjotgarth. Sometimes referred to as Haakon the Mighty. He had under him the government of all disticts of Trondheim whenever King Harald I Fairhair (#1) was gone, and enjoyed the highest confidence of the king. 16, 19.

HAAKON OF LADE, JARL (#5) (Haakon Jarl [Ladejarl], Jarl the Mighty, Haakon Sigurdsson, Haakon the Great). The exiled son of the murdered Jarl Sigurth and Bergljot Toresdatter. Grandson of Haakon Grjotgarthsson. Haakon married Thora Skagesdatter. Their children were Svein (#8), Heming and Bergljot. He was father with unknown mothers of Erik (#7) and Ragnhild. Murdered at age 60. He was from the "mighty Norwegian family of the Jarls of More from Trondelag." No royal blood from the male side. Later became an enemy of Harald Fairhair. 26, 27, 32, 33-35, 38, 42, 44.

HAAKON JARL [Ladejarl]. See Haakon of Lade (#5).

HAAKON SIGURDSSON. See Haakon of Lade (#5).

HAAKON THE GREAT. See Haakon of Lade (#5).

HAAKON HAAKONSSON. Son of Haakon IV the Old (#43) and Margrete Skulesdatter. Married Richiza Birgirsdatter (Swedish). Haakon may be illeg. His body is buried in St. Hallvard's church. 125.

HAFTHOR JONSSON ROOS. Married to Agnes, the illeg. daughter of Haakon V Magnusson (#48). 139.

HAKI. An enamy of Halfdan the Black (#-1) A beserker. 10.

HALFDAN THE BLACK (#-1) (Halvdan *Svart*) Son of Guthroth the Hunting King (#-2) and Asa. Father of Harald Fairhair (#1). 6, 7, 8, 9, 10, 11, 15.

HALVDAN *SVART*. See Halfdan the Black (#-1).

HALFDAN THE BLACK. Son of Harald I Fairhair (#1) and Asa Haakonsdatter. Twin of Halfdan the White. 15, 17, 18, 19.

HALFDAN THE WHITE. Son of Harald Fairhair (#1) and Asa Haakonsdatter. Twin of Halfdan the Black. 15, 17, 18, 19.

HALFDAN THE GENTLE (#-3). (Halfdan The Generous and Stingy of Food, Halfdan the Mild, Halfdan II King of Vestfold). Son of Eystein Halfdansson (#-4) and Hild Eriksdatter. Married Liv Dagsdatter. Father of Sigurd and Guthroth the Hunting King (#-2). 4, 5, 6.

HALFDAN THE GENEROUS AND STINGY OF FOOD. See Halfdan the Gentle (#-3).

HALFDAN THE MILD. See Halfdan the Gentle (#-3).

HALFDAN II KING OF VESTFOLD. See Halfdan the Gentle (#-3).

HALFDAN GOLDTOOTH OF SOLEYAR. Father of Solveig, wife of Olav Tree-Hewer (#-6). 2, 3.

HALFDAN HALEGG "LONGSHANK." Son of Harald I Fairhair (#1) and Snafrid. 15, 21.

HALFDAN, JARL. Husband of Harald Fairhair's (#1) daughter Ingeborg. Had a daughter, Gunnhild. 22.

HALFDAN SIGURDSSON. Son of Sigurd Syr and Asta Gudbrandsdtr. Brother of Harald III the Hard (#13).

HALFDAN WHITELEG (#-5). (Halvdan *Hvitbein*, Halfdan Olavsson of Vestfold). Son of Olav Tree-Hewer (#-6) and Solveig. Was first king of the Upplanders and first king of Vestfold. Great-great-great grandfather of Harald I Fairhair (#1). Married Asa Eysteinsdatter. Two children: Eystein Halfdansson (#-4) and Guthroth. 1, 2, 3, 4.

HALFDAN *HVITBEIN*. See Halfdan Whiteleg (#-5).

HALFDAN OLAVSSON OF VESTFOLD. See Halfdan Whiteleg (#-5).

HALFDAN. Son of Sigurd Hrisi "The Bastard." Grandson of Harald I Fairhair (#1) and Snafrid. 21.

HALLKEL HUK. Father of Simon Skalp and Hafthor Jonsson Roos. 86.

HALLVEIG. Snorri's wife.

HARALD. Son of Halfdan the Black (#-1) and his first wife, Ragnhild. Harald died at age ten. 9, 10.

HARALD. King Harald of the Isle of Man. Married Cecelia, Daughter of Haakon IV (#43) and Kanga the Young. 125, 127.

HARALD BLAATAND. (Harald I Bluetooth). Danish king. Son of King Gorm the Old of Denmark. Father of Svein Forkbeard, who succeeded him to the throne. He was Harald II Grayskin's (#4) uncle, who adopted him, and accepted him as his foster son. 26, 31, 33, 34, 35.

HARALD BLUETOOTH. See Harald Blaatand. 20.

HARALD HARFAGR. See Harald I Fairhair (#1).

HARALD FINEHAIR. See Harald I Fairhair (#1).

HARALD FLETTIR. Danish father of Svein Haraldson (#18). 75.

HARALD *HAARDRAADE*. See Harald III the Hard (#13).

HARALD THE HARD. See Harald III the Hard (#13).

HARALD *HARDRÅDE*. See Harald III the Hard (#13).

HARALD *HARFAGRE*. See Harald I Fairhair (#1).

HARALD *HARFAGRI*. See Harald I Fairhair (#1).

HARALD *HARFOT*. (Harald "Hasenfuss.") Son of Knut the Great (#10) of Denmark. His mother was Alfiva. Ruled England for a period of time. 51, 52, 58.

HARALD *"HASENFUSS."* See Harald Harfot.

HARALD GILCHRIST (#23). (Harald IV Gilchrist, Harald Gilli, Harald IV Magnusson, Gille, Gilli). Claimed to be the son of Magnus Barelegs (#17) and an Irish mistress, Irin. Married Ingerid Ragnvaldsdatter, a Swedish Princess. They had two children: Brigitha and Inge I Hunchback (#25). With an Irish mistress, Beathack, had one son, Eystein II (#27). With Thora Guttormsdatter he had Sigurd the Mouth (#26). With unknown mistress or mistresses, he had Magnus, Maria and Margrete. 73, 81, 84, 85, 86-88, 89, 90, 91, 94, 97, 99, 117.

HARALD GILLI. See Harald Gilchrist (#23).

HARALD GOLDENBEARD. King of Sogn, and father of Ragnhild, the first wife of Halfdan the Black (#-1). 9, 10.

HARALD GOLDTOOTH. Petty king of Soleyar. Father of Solva, Olav Tree Hewer's (#-6) wife. 2.

HARALD GORMSON. See Harald Blaatand.

HARALD *GRAFELDR*. See Harald II Graycloak (#4).

HARALD GRENSKI. Also called Sigurd Syr. Formerly called Harald Guthrothsson. Great grandson of Harald I Fairhair (#1) and Svanhild. Grandson of Bjorn the Chapman and son of Guthroth. Married Asta Gudbrandsdatter. They were the parents of St. Olav (#9). 20, 47, 60.

HARALD GREYPELT. See Harald II Graycloak (#4).

HARALD *GRAFELL*. See Harald II Graycloak (#4).

HARALD GRAY-SKIN. See Harald II Graycloak (#4).

HARALD GREYCLOAK. See Harald II Graycloak (#4)

HARALD GUTHROTHSSON. Harald Grenske's former name. See Harald Grenske. 47.

HARALD KESJA of Denmark. Married Ragnhild Magnusdatter, the daughter of Magnus III Barelegs (#17). 71.

HARALD KONGSSON. Illeg. son of Inge I Hunchback (#25). 86, 91.

HARALD *LUFA*. See Harald I Fairhair (#1).

HARALD MOP-HAIR. See Harald I Fairhair (#1).

HARALD OLAVSSON. llleg. son of Haakon IV the Old (#43) and Kanga the Young. Married to Cecelia Haakonsdatter.

HARALD OLAVSSON. Prince of Norway. Son of Olav Trygvasson (#6) and Thyre of Denmark. 37.

HARALD REDBEARD. King Harald Redbeard of Agthir. Father of Asa, the second wife of King Guthroth the Hunting King (#-2). 6.

HARALD THE RUTHLESS. See Harald III the Hard (#13).

HARALD SIGURDSSON. See Harald III the Hard (#13).

HARALD SIGURDSSON. Love-child of Kristin Sigurdsdatter, daughter of Sigurd the Crusader (#21) with Sigurd the Mouth (#26), before she married Erling Skakke. 94, 95, 101.

HARALD SIGURTHARSON. See Harald III the Hard (#13).

HARALD THE STERN. See Harald III the Hard (#13).

HARALD TRYGVASSON. Prince of Norway. Son of Olav Trygvasson (#6) and Queen Thyre of Denmark. Died at age one.

HARALD I FAIRHAIR (#1). (Harald *Harfagr*, Harald *Lufa*, Harald Finehair, Harald Mop-Hair, Harald *Harfagri*, Harald I *Harfagre*). Son of Halfdan the Balck and his second wife Ragnhild. xi, xv, xvi, 1, 2, 3, 4, 5, 6, 7, 9, 10, 11, 13, 15-22, 23, 24, 25, 28, 30, 34, 37, 38, 39, 44, 45, 47, 60, 96, 141.

HARALD II GRAYCLOAK (#4). (Harald *Grafeldr*, Harald Greypelt, Harald *Grafell*, Harald Gray-Skin, Harald Greycloak) Fourth son of King Erik Bloodaxe (#2) and Gunnhild. 20, 23, 25, 26, 27, 30-33, 34, 37, 38.

HARALD III THE HARD (#13). (Harald Sigurdsson, Harald III, Harald the Hard, Harald *Haardraade*, Harald Sigurtharson, Harald the Stern, Harald *Hardråde*, Harald the Ruthless). Son of Sigurd Syr and Asta Gulbrandsdatter. Father of Olav III Kyrre (#15), and Magnus II Haraldsson (#14) with Thora Thorbergsdatter. Harald was also the father of Maria and Ingegerd. 13, 48, 50, 58, 60-63, 66, 67, 75.

HARALD III. See Harald III the Hard (#13).

HARALD IV GILCHRIST. See Harald Gilchrist (#23).

HARALD IV MAGNUSSON. See Harald Gilchrist (#23).

HARALD V. King Harald V. Present king of Norway. (Since 1991). Married to Sonja Haraldsen. 160, 161, 162, 163.

HARDEKNUT. See Knut III Magnusson.

HAVARD "SEASON PROSPEROUS." Earl of Okney. Brother of Thorfinn Hausakljuf. Married Ragnhild, daughter of Erik Bloodaxe (#2) and Gunnhild after Thorfinn's death. 26.

HEINRICH HEINKEL. The step-son of Svein Sveinsson, King of Denmark. Married to Ingigerth.

HELEN. Mother of Margrete Fredkulla. 71.

HELEN GUTTORMSDATTER. First wife of Valdemar II (#41), the king of Denmark. No Children. 121.

HELLIG OLAV. See Olav II, St. Olav (#9).

HELVIG. Queen Helvig of Denmark. Mother of Margrete (#52). Queen Helvig was married to King Valdemar Atterdag of Denmark. 143, 151.

HEMING HAAKONSSON. Son of Jarl Haakon (#5) and Thora Skagesdatter. 34.

HENRY III. Son of the Roman Emperor, Conrad II. Married Gunnhild, daughter of Knut the Great (#10) and Emma of Normandy. 51, 52.

HERDIS. Snorri's wife.

HERSIR KLYPP. Hersir is a title. See Klypp.

HERSIR THORIR. Hersir is a title. See Thorir. 21.

HERTHLA. Son of Ingerid, widow of Harald Gilchrist (#23) and Arne Arnesson.

HILD ERIKSDATTER. (Also Hilda). Wife of Eystein Halfdansson (#-4), 4, 5.

HILDA. See Hild

HOHN. Count Hohn of Namur (Flandern). His daughter, Blanca, was married to Magnus the Good (#49). 143, 144.

HOLLANDER, LEE M. A prominent translator of Norwegian sagas. Translated *Heimskringla*.

HOLMFRID. Princess of Sweden. daughter of King Erik "Segersall" of Sweden. Married Jarl Svein (#8), and had two daughters, Sigrid and Gunnhild. Snorri's story of St. Olav (#9) states that Holmfrid is the daughter of Olav Stotkonung of Sweden, but she is probably his sister. 34, 44, 50.

HORTHA KARI. (Hortha Kri). A kin of Thora, one of Harald Fairhair's (#1) wives.

HRANI THE WIDELY-TRAVELED. Son of Hroi the White. Hrani was Harald Grenski's foster father. 47.

HREITHAR. Illeg. son of Erking Skakke.

HRING. Son of Harald Fairhair and Alvhild. Named after his grandfather, Hring Dagsson. Also called Ring and Kring. 15, 20.

HRING DAGSSON OF RINGERIKI. Father of Alvhild, one of Harald Fairhair's wives. 20.

HROI THE WHITE. A king's steward. Harald Grenski fostered Harald, the son of Guthroth. He also had a son who was about the same age as Harald. 47.

HROREK. See Rorek.

ILLISIF. Queen Illisif. Also called Elizabet or Ellisif. Wife of Harald the Hard (#13) and with him had Ingegerd and Maria. 60, 63, 67.

ILL-LUCK OLAV. See Olav Guthbrandsson.

INGA OF VARTEIG. "The Peace Maiden." A mistress of Hakon III (#37) and with him had Haakon IV the Old (#43). Inga died in 1234. 109, 115, 116, 125.

INGE. King Inge Hallsteinsson of Sweden. Husband of Brigitha, Harald Gilchrist's (#23) daughter. Father of Ragnvald Ingersson. Grandfather of Ingerid Ragnvaldsdatter. 88.

INGE. King Inge Steinkelsson of Sweden. Grandfather of Ingerid, the wife of Harald Gilchrist (#23). Father of Margrete Fredkulla, "The Peace Maiden," who became the wife of Magnes II Barelegs (#17). 71, 73, 79.

INGE ARNESSON. Son of Arne Arnesson and Ingerid, the widow of Harald Gilchrist (#23).

INGE HARALDSSON. See Inge I Hunchback (#25).

INGE KROKRYGG. (Krykrygg—crooked neck). See Inge I Hunchback (#25).

INGE MAGNUSSON (#36). Claimed to be the son of Magnus V Erlingsson (#29). He was from Bagler party. 101, 111, 114.

INGE Magnusson. Illegitimate son of Erling Skakke.

INGE I HUNCHBACK (#25) (Inge Krokrygg, Inge Haraldsson, Ingi). Killed. The only legitimate son of Harald Gilchrist (#23) and Queen Ingerid from Sweden. Father of Jon Kuvlung (#34) with mistress. Also father of Harald Kongsson. Inge also had a sister Brigitha. 85, 86, 87, 88, 90, 91-93, 95, 96, 97, 98, 99, 112, 117.

INGE II BAARDSSON (#39) (Inge II, Inge II Bårdsson). Son of Lendman Baard Guttormsson from Rein and Cecilia Sigurdsdatter, daughter of Sigurd the Mouth (#26). His half-brother was Jarl Skule Baardsson. 94, 118, 119, 125, 126.

INGE II. See Inge II Baardsson (#39).

INGE II BÅRDSSON. See Inge II Baardsson (#39).

INGEBORG. Daughter of Tryggve. Sister of Olav Tryggvasson (#6). Great granddaughter of Harald I Fairhair (#1) and Svanhild.

INGEBORG. Daughter of Sigurd II the Mouth (#26). Mother of Roar Kongsfrende.

INGEBORG. Princess of Kiev (now Russia). Married to Knut the Great (Knut Lavard) of Denmark. Mother of Kristin Knutesdatter, the wife of Magnus IV the Blind (#22). No children. 84.

INGEBORG ERIKSDATTER. Princess of Saxony. Only daughter of King Erik Plovpenning of Denmark and Jutte, Princess of Saxony. Married Magnus VI the Lawmender (#46). Four children: Olav, died at age five; Magnus, died as an infant; Erik II (#47); Haakon V. Magnusson (#48). 121, 125, 128, 134, 135, 136, 139.

INGEBORG ERIKSDATTER. Daughter of Erik II Magnusson (#47) and second wife, Isabella Bruce. Niece of Haakon V Magnusson (#48). Married King Valdemar Magnusson of Sweden in 1312. Had one son, Erik. 136, 137, 138, 141.

INGEBORG HARALDSDATTER. Daughter of Harald Fairhair (#1). Mother: Unknown. Married Jarl Halfdan. 16, 22.

INGEBORG HAAKONSDATTER, DUCHESS. Daughter of Haakon V Magnusson (#48) and Queen Eufemia. Married Duke Erik Magnusson of Sweden. 139, 141, 143, 144.

INGEBORG GUTHORMSDATTER. Daughter of Guthorm, the son of Steiger Thoris. Wife of Eystein I Magnusson (#20). Had one daughter, Maria, who married Guthbrand Skofhoggson. 71, 77.

INGEBORG MAGNUSDATTER. daughter of Magnus V Erlingsson (#29). Mother unknown. Married to Peter Steyper. 101.

INGEBORG SVERRESDATTER. daughter of Sverre Sigurdsson (#33) and Astrid Roesdatter. Wife of Karl Sverkersson of Sweden. 109.

INGEBORG VALDESMARSDATTER. Daughter of King Valdesmar of Denmark. Sister of Margrete (#52). 149.

INGEGERD. Granddaughter of St. Birgitte of Sweden. Margarete's (#52) foster sister. 151.

INGEGERD. Daughter of Astrid Eriksdatter and Lodin.

INGEGERD. Wife of Olav III Kyrre (#15), and daughter of King Svein Estridsson of Sweden. No children. 44.

INGEGERD BIRGIRSDATTER. Illeg. daughter of Harald Gilchrist's (#23) daughter Brigitta and Birgir Brosa. Married King Sorkvir of Sweden.

INGEGERD HARALDSDATTER. Princess of Norway. Daughter of Harald III the Hard (#13) and Queen Illisif. Married Olav Sveinsson of Denmark. Then married King Phillip Hallstensson of Sweden. Half-sister of Olav Kyrre (#15) and Magnus II (#14). 60, 63.

INGEGERD HARALDSDATTER. Daughter of Harald Fairhair (#1) and Alvhild. 15, 20.

INGEGERD (ANNA) OLAVSDATTER. Daughter of King Olav Stotkonung of Sweden. Married Yaroslav I the Wise, the Grand Prince of Kiev. Mother of Illisif and Maria. 50, 60.

INGEGERD SIGURDSDATTER. Daughter of Sigurd Syr and Asta. Sister of Harald III the Hard (#13). 60.

INGEGERD SVEINSDATTER. Princess Ingegerd. Daughter of Svein Estridsson, King of Denmark. Married Olav III Kyrre (#15) in about 1070. 67.

INGERID RAGNVALDSDATTER. A Swedish Princess. Daughter of Ragnvald Ingersson of Sweden, and granddaughter of King Inge Steinkelsson. Wife of Harald Gilchrist (#23). Married several times: m1)A Danish Prince, and had several sons; m2)Harald Gilchrist, and with him had Inge I Hunchback (#25) and Brigitha; m3)Ivar Sneus, and had one son, Orm Kongsbror; and m4)Arne Arnesson, and with him had Margrete Arnesdatter, Nikolas Arnesson, Inge Arnesson and Herthla. 86, 87, 91, 117.

INGERID SKULESDATTER. Daughter of Jarl Skule Baardsson (#45). Married Junker Knut (#44). 129, 130, 131.

INGERITH. See Ingerid.

INGI. See Inge I Hunchback (#25).

INGJALD. King Ingjald of the Yngling royal family of Varmaland,Sweden. Also called King Ingjald the Wicked. Son of Halfdan Guldand of Solver. Father of Olav Tree-Hewer (#-6) and the last Yngling King of Sweden. 2.

INGJALD OLAVSSON. Prince of Vestfold. Son of Olav Tree-Hewer (#-6) and Gauthild Algautsdatter. Brother of Halfdan Whiteleg (#-5). 2, 3.

IRIN. Irish mistress of Magnus Barelegs (#17), and with him had Harald Gilchrist (#23). 73, 86.

ISABELLA BRUCE. Daughter of Robert Earl. Second wife of Erik II Magnusson (#47), and with him had Ingeborg who married King Valdemar of Sweden. Sister of Robert Bruce of Scotland. 136, 137.

ISABELLA JOIGNY. Second wife of Haakon V Magnusson the Younger (#48). No children. 139.

IVAR. King Ivar. A Viking king in Dublin.

IVAR THE BONELESS. Son of Ivar the Widefathomer, of the Swedish Yngling royalty. Father of Ivar the Boneless.

IVAR THE WIDEFATHOMER of the Swedish Yngling royalty.

IVAR SNEIS. A lover of Ingerid, the widow of Harald Gilchrist (#23). They had a son, Orm Kongsbror. 88.

JARIZLEIF. King Jarizleif. King of Kiev. See Yaroslav I the Wise.

JARL EIRIK I. See Erik, Jarl (#7).

JARL ERIK. See Erik, Jarl (#7).

JARL THE MIGHTY. See Haakon of Lade (#5).

JARL SKULE. See Skule Baardsson (#45).

JARLEN JON. He was betrothed to Ingeborg, daughter of Erik II Magnusson (#47). 136.

JARNSKEGGE. (Ironbeard). A powerful chieftain in Trondheim area. 39.

JOHAN MARTIN FERNER. Married to Astrid, the sister of King Harald V of Norway. 160.

JOHANNE I MARGRAVE. Married Sofia, Princess of Denmark. Had 1 daughter, Kristin. 121.

JON. Nephew of Sverre (#33). Killed in Trondheim.

JON, KING JON OF SWEDEN. Grandson of Harald Gilchrist's (#23) daughter, Ingegerd.

JON HALLKELSSON. Son of Hallkel Huk. Married to Margrete, daughter of Harald Gilchrist (#23). Brother of Simon Skalp. 86.

JON KUVLUNG (#34). A monk from the Abbey of Hovedoy at Oslo. Son of Inge I Hunchback (#25) mistress. Murdered. 86, 91, 111, 112.

JON LOPTSSON. The most powerful chieftain in Iceland. He fostered Snorri. His father was Lopt Saemundarsson. 71.

JON THORBERGSSON. Married to Ragnhild Erlingsdatter, the daughter of Kristin Sigurdsdatter, great-great granddaughter of Sigurth the Crusader (#21) and daughter of Erling Skakke.

JUNKER KNUT (#44). See Knut, Junker.

JUTTE. Princess of Saxony. Daughter of Danish King Erik IV Plovpenney. Mother of Ingeborg, the wife of Magnus the Lawmender (#46). 121, 134.

KALF ARNESSON. Brother of Thorberg, Finn and Arne.

KANGA THE YOUNG. Mistress of Haakon the Old (#43), and with him had Sigurd and Cecelia. 125, 127.

KANUTE II. See Knut the Great (#10).

KARK. The thrall that murdered Haakon of Lade (#5). 35, 39.

KARL KNUTSON OF SWEDEN. R.1449-1450.

KARL SONASSON, JARL. Married. to Brigitha, Harald Gilchrist's (#23) daughter.

KARL SVERKERSSON OF SWEDEN. Married to Ingeborg, daughter of Sverre Sigurdsson (#33) and Astrid Roesdatter. 109.

KARLAMAGNUS. See Charlamayne.

KIK GREGORIUS. First husband of Cecilia Sverresdatter, the daughter of Sverre (#33). 109.

KLERK. Olav Tryggvasson (#6) was sold to Klerk. 38.

KLYPP. Hersir Klypp. Hersir is a title. He killed Sigurd Slefa. 27.

KNUD. See Knut the Great (#10).

KNUT ERIKSSON. King of Sweden. Brother of Astrid Roesdatter, the wife of Sverre Sigurdsson (#33). 109.

KNUT THE GREAT (#10). (Knut II, Knut den Mektige, Canute II the Great, Kanute II, Knud, Cnut, Canute). Son of King Svein Forkbeard of Denmark and Gunnhild from Poland. Alfiva was his wife or mistress, and they had two sons, Svein, and Harald Harfot. Knut then married Emma of Normandy and had two children, Hardeknut (Knut III) and Gunnhild. 43, 48, 49, 51-53, 54, 58.

KNUT, JARL. Son of Harald Gilchrist's (#23) daughter Brigitha, and Birgir Brosa.

KNUT, JUNKER (#44). Son of Haakon Galen. Married Ingerid Skulesdatter, daughter of Skule Baardsson (#45). 126, 129, 130, 121.

KNUT LAVARD. See Knut III Magnusson of Denmark.

KNUT. King Knut Eriksson of Sweden. Brother of Astrid Roesdatter, wife of Sverre (#33). 122.

KNUT DEN MEKTIGE. See Knut the Great (#10).

KNUT PORSE. Second husband of Ingeborg, daughter of Haakon V Magnusson (#48). 144.

KNUT II. See Knut the Great (#10).

KNUT III. See Hardeknut.

KNUT III MAGNUSSON of Denmark. Father of Valdemar the Great (#31). 51, 52, 58, 105.

KNUT VI. King of Denmark. Son of Valdemar the Great (#31) and succeeded him as king. 105.

KRING. See Hring Dagsson.

KRISTIN (Christin). Wife or mistress of Sigurd the Mouth (#26). 95.

KRISTIN. (Christine). Princess Kristin of Denmark. Married to Magnus the Blind (#22). 79.

KRISTIN. Daughter of Sofia, the daughter of Valdemar II (#41) and Johanne I Margrave. Married Magnus the Blind (#22). 120.

KRISTIN. m1)Kik Gregorius. m2)Einar Prest.

KRISTIN BIRGIRSDATTER. Daughter of Birgir Broso and Ingerid.

KRISTIN BJORNSDATTER. (Also called Christine) Daughter of Prince Bjorn Haraldsson of Denmark and Katerina Ingesdatter. Married King Erik Jedvardsson of Sweden. Had five children: 1)King Knut Eriksson of Sweden, 2)Philipp, 3)Katharina, 4)Margrete and 5)a son. Margrete married Sverre Sigurdsson (#33), and had 3 children 1)Haakon III (#37), 2)Ingeborg, 3)a son.

KRISTIN HAAKONSDATTER. Daughter of Haakon IV the Old (#43) and Margrete, the daughter of Skule Baardsson (#45). Married Don Phillip (Spaniard). 125, 126.

KRISTIN INGESDATTER. Daughter of Inge Steinkelsson. Mother of Malmfrida, wife of Sigurd the Crusader (#21)). Kristin is the grandmother of Kristin, the wife of Erling Skakkee. 79.

KRISTIN KNUTSDATTER. Princess of Denmark. Daughter of Knut the Great (who was also called Knut Lavard) and Ingeborg. Princess of Kiev (now Russia). She was also sister of Valdemar, King of Denmark. Wife of Magnus the Blind (#22). No children. 84.

KRISTIN MAGNUSDATTER. daughter of Magnus V. Erlingsson (#29). Mother unknown. Married Reidar Sendemann. 101.

KRISTIN NIKOLASDATTER. Haakon Galen's Swedish wife. Probably mother of Junker Knut. 117, 121.

KRISTIN SIGURDSDATTER. b.1126 d.1178. Daughter of Sigurd the Crusader (#21) and Malmfrida. Wife of Erling Skakke and with him had Magnus V Erlingsson (#29), and Ragnhild. Mistress (or lover) of Sigurd the Mouth (#26) and had one son, Harald. Later married Grim Rusli and left Norway. 71, 79, 80, 91, 94, 95, 100, 101.

KRISTIN SVERRESDATTER. Princess of Norway. b.c1185 d.1213/1215. Daughter of Sverre (#33), and Princess Margrete Eriksdatter of Sweden. Married Filippus Simonsson (#38), King of the Baglers. Died in childbirth. On chart twice, once as daughter of Sverre (#33), and once as wife of Filippus. 109, 115, 117, 118.

LADEJARLER. See Earl Haakon Grjotgardsson.

LEIF ERIKSSON. Son of Eric the Red. Discovered America. See glossary.

LEIV ERIKSSON. See Leif Eriksson.

LIF. See Liv.

LIFA. See Liv.

LIV DAGSDATTER. (Also called Lif, and Lifa.) Daughter of King Dag of Vestfold. Wife of Halfdan the Gentle (#-3). Mother of Guthroth the Hunting King (#-2) and Sigurd. 5, 6.

LJOT. Jarl Ljot. Third husband of Ragnhild, the daughter of Erik Bloodaxe(#2) and Gunnhild. 26.

LODIN. Married Astrid, the widow of Olav Tryvasson (#6).

LOPT SAEMUNDARSSON. Jon Loptsson's father from Iceland. Lopt was Snorri's foster father. 71.

Louis Josephine. Daughter of King Charles XV (Bernadotte) of Sweden. Mother of KIng Haakon VII, Norway's king from 1905–1957. 158.

MAGNUS. Son of Erling Stonewall. 101, 122, 123.

MAGNUS *BERREFOTT.* See Magnus III Barelegs (#17).

MAGNUS BAREFOOT. See Magnus III Barelegs (#17).

MAGNUS *BARFOT.* See Magnus III Barelegs (#17).

MAGNUS *DEN BLINDE.* See Magnus IV the Blind (#22).

MAGNUS THE BLIND. See Magnus IV the Blind (#22).

MAGNUS OF BRUNSWICK, DUKE. Son of Ulfhild, the daughter of St. Olav (#9).

MAGNUS ERICKSSON. See Magnus VII the Good (#49).

MAGNUS ERLINGSSON. See Magnus V Erlingsson (#29).

MAGNUS *DEN GODE.* See Magnus I the Good (#12).

MAGNUS HARALDSSON. b.1125. d.1145. Illeg. son of Harald Gilchrist (#23) He died young. Mother unknown. 86.

MAGNUS HARALDSSON. See Magnus II Haraldsson (#14).

MAGNUS HENRIKSSON. King Magnus of Sweden. Third husband of Brigitha, the daughter of Harald Gilchrist (#23).

MAGNUS *LAGABØTE*. See Magnus VI the Lawmender (#46).

MAGNUS *LANGBEIN*. See Haakon V Magnusson (#48).

MAGNUS MAGNUSSON. Son of Magnus VI the Lawmender (#46) and Ingeborg. Died as an infant. 134, 135.

MAGNUS OLAVSSON. See Magnus I the Good (#12).

MAGNUS PALSSON THE PRIEST. Icelandic Priest. Son of Pal Solveson.

MAGNUS SIGURDSSON. See Magnus IV the Blind (#22).

MAGNUS SIGURTHARSON. See Magnus II Haraldsson (#14).

MAGNUS *SLITTUNG*. (*Bøne Skinnknive*). Ill son of Erling Skakke.

MAGNUS *SMEK*. See Magnus VII the Good (#49).

MAGNUS *STYRJALDER*. See Magnus III Barelegs (#17).

MAGNUS THE TALL. See Magnus III Barelegs (#17).

MAGNUS I THE GOOD (#12) (Magnus I Olavsson, Magnus den Gode, Magnus Olavsson). Illeg. son of St. Olav (#9) and mistress, Alvhild. Later became king of Norway. 47, 49, 52, 53, 55, 56-59, 62, 69, 78.

MAGNUS I OLAVSSON. See Magnus I the Good (#12).

MAGNUS II HARALDSSON (#14). (Magnus II, Magnus Haraldsson, Magnus Sigurtharson). Son of Harald III the Hard (#13) and Thora Torbergsdatter. Probably not married. Father of Haakon Toresfostre with unknown mother. 60, 63, 66, 67, 70.

MAGNUS II. See Magnus II Haraldsson (#14).

MAGNUS II ERIKSSON OF SWEDEN. See Magnus VII the Good (#49). 143.

MAGNUS III BARELEGS (#17). (Magnus Berrefott, Magnus Barefoot, Magnus Barfot, Magnus Styrjalder, Magnus the Tall. Magnus III Olavsson). Illeg. Son of Olav Kyrre (#15) and Thora Jonsdatter, a mistress. Many children. 67, 70, 71-74, 75, 76, 77, 79, 86, 89.

MAGNUS III OLAVSSON. See Magnus III Barelegs (#17).

MAGNUS IV THE BLIND (#22). (Magnus den Blinde, Magnus the Blind, Magnus Sigurdsson) Son of Sigurd the Crusader (#21) and Borghild Olavsdatter. Magnus married Kristin Knutsdatter, Princess of Denmark. 71, 79, 80, 84, 85, 86, 90, 91, 120.

MAGNUS V ERLINGSSON (#29). (Magnus Erlingsson). Son of Erling Skakke and Kristin, the daughter of Sigurd the Crusader (#21). Married Eldrid Bjarnesdatter (from Rein). No children from this marriage. Illeg. children: Kristin; Ingeborg; Sigurd Magnusson (#35); Inge Magnusson (#36); Erling Stonewall (#42); and Margrete. 94, 95, 100, 101-103, 105, 106, 107, 110, 113, 114, 122.

MAGNUS VI THE LAWMENDER (#46). (Magnus *Lagabøte*, Magnus VI Haakonsson) Son of Hakon IV the Old (#43) and Queen Margrete, daughter of Skule Baardsson (#44). Married Ingeborg, daughter of King Erik of Denmark. Four children: Olav; Magnus; Erik II (#47); and Haakon V (#48). 121, 125, 127, 128, 131, 134, 135, 136, 139.

MAGNUS VI HAAKONSSON. See Magnus VI the Lawmender (#46).

MAGNUS VII THE GOOD (#49). (Magnus VII, Magnus Smek, Magnus II Ericksson of Sweden) King of both Norway and Sweden. Son of Duke Erik of Sweden and Ingebjorg, the daughter of Haakon V Magnusson (#48). Married Blanca. Two sons: Erik III, became king of Sweden, and Haakon VI (#50), who succeeded Magnus as king of Norway. 141, 143-146, 147, 148.

MAGNUS VII. See Magnus VII the Good (#49).

MAID OF NORWAY. Or Maid of Scandinavia. See Margrete Eriksdatter of Norway.

MALMFRIDA. Grandaughter of King Inge Sveinkelsson of Sweden. Great-great granddaughter of the King of England (maternal). Malfrida was the sister of the mother of King Valdemar of Denmark. 79, 80.

MARCUS. Foster father of Sigurd Markusfostre (#30), 104.

MARGRETE (#52). Margrete Valdemarsdatter, Queen Margrete of Norway. Daughter of Valdemar Atterdag of and Queen Helvig of Denmark. One son, Olav (#51), 133, 143, 145, 147, 149, 150, 151, 152, 154.

MARGRETE. Margrete of Sweden. Wife of Magnus Barelegs (#17). 71.

MARGRETE. Wife of King Christofer of Denmark.

MARGRETE. Daughter of Brigitha, daughter of Harald Gilchrist (#23) and Birgir Brosa. Grand daughter of Harald Gilchrist.

MARGRETE. Daughter of Ingerid, Harald Gilchrist's (#23) widow, and Arne of Stothreim. 88.

MARGRETE. Princess of Bohemia. See Dagmar.

MARGRETE ALEXANDERSDATTER OF SCOTLAND. Queen of Scotland. Daughter of King Alexander III of Scotland and Margrete of England. First wife of Erik II Magnusson (#47). Had one daughter, also called Margrete who was called "Maid of Scandinavia" or "Maid of Norway." 136, 137

MARGRETE ARNESDATTER. Daughter of Arne Arnesson and Ingerid, the widow of Harald Gilchrist (#23). Married Simon Karlsson. Mother of Filippus Simonsson. 117.

MARGRETE OF ENGLAND. Married to King Alexander III. Grandmother of Margrete "Maid of Norway" or "Maid of Scandinavia." 136

MARGRETE ERIKSDATTER. Princess of Scotland. b.c1283. Daughter of Erik II Magnusson (#47) and Margrete Alexandersdatter of Scotland. Also called "Maid of Norway" or "Maid of Scandinavia." Died young. 136, 137, 138.

MARGRETE ERIKSDATTER. Daughter of Erik IX Jedvardsson, King of Sweden and Christine Bjornsdatter of Jernside, Sweden. Wife of Sverre (#33) and with Sverre had two children: Kristin, Princess of Norway, and Erling, Prince of Norway (died young). Margrete died in 1204, a few days after her daughter married Filippus Simonsson (#38). 109, 115, 116, 118.

MARGRETE FREDKULLA OF SWEDEN. Also known as "The Peace Maiden." Daughter of King Inge of Sweden. Married (in 1101) Magnus III Barelegs at age fourteen. Also called Frithkolla. 71, 73.

MARGRETE HARALDSDATTER. Daughter of Harald Gilchrist (#23). Mother unknown. Married Jon Hallkelsson. 86.

MARGRETE MAGNUSDATTER. Daughter of Magnus V Erlingsson (#29). 101.

MARGRETE SKULESDATTER. Daughter of Skulle Baardsson and Ragnhild. Married Haakon IV the Old (#43). Mother of Magnus VI, the Lawmender (#46). Sister of Ingerid, who married Junker Knut (#44). 125, 126, 128, 129, 130, 131, 134.

MARGRETE ULFSDATTER. Margrete's (#52) foster mother. Daughter of St. Birgitte. 151.

MARIA. Daughter of Harald III the Hard (#13) and Queen Illisif. Died at age 17. 60, 63.

MARIA. Daughter of Eystein I Magnusson (#20) and Ingeborg. Wife of Guthbrand Skafhoggson. Mother of Olav Ill-Luck. 71, 77.

MARIA. Daughter of Queen Zoe's brother. 62.

MARIA HARALDSDATTER. Illeg. daughter of Harald Gilchrist (#23). Mother unknown. Married Simon Skalp, the son of Hallkel Huk. One son, Nikolas. 86.

MARTHA LOUISE. Princess of Norway. daughter of present King Harald of Norway and Sonja. 161.

MARTHA. Queen Martha of Sweden. Martha Sofia Louisa Dagmar Thyra. Wife of King Olav V of Norway who reigned from 1957–1991. Had three children. 160, 161, 162.

MATHILDA. Countess of Holstein. Married King Abel of Denmark. 121.

MAUD. Queen Maud. Daughter of Edward VII of England and Princess Alexandra of Denmark. Wife of Haakon VII of Norway who reigned from 1905–1957. Had one son, Olav I who ruled from 1957–1991. 158, 160.

MUIKERTACH. King of Ireland. Father of Sigurd the Crusader's (#21) wife, Biadmuin. 79, 80.

NIKOLAS. Son of Maria Haraldsdatter and Simon Skalp. Grandson of Harald Gilchrist (#23). 86.

NIKOLAS ARNESSON. Bishop. b.1150 d.1225. Son of Arne Arnesson and Ingerid, the widow of Harald Gilchrist (#23). 88, 114, 117, 118, 122.

NIKOLAS MASA. Father of Ragna, wife of Eystein II Haraldsson(#27). 97.

OLAF. An often used spelling of Olav.

OLAV BIG-MOUTH. See Olav II (#9).

OLAV BONDE. See Olav III Kyrre (#15).

OLAV-IN-THE-DALE. A powerful and wealthy farmer. Father of Sigurth the Crusader's (#21) mistress, Borghild Olavsdatter from Skjeberg. 79.

OLAV *DIGERBEIN*. See Olav Geirstatha Alf II.

OLAV THE FARMER. See Olav II (#9).

OLAV THE FAT. See Olav II (#9).

OLAV GEIRSTATHA-ALF I . Son of King Guthroth (#-2) and Alvhild, the daughter of King Alfar. Ruled in Viken and Romerike. 6, 7, 8, 9.

OLAV GEIRSTATHA-ALF II (Olav *Digerbein*). Son of Harald I Fairhair (#1) and Svanhild Eysteinsdatter. Olav and Tryggve (the son of Olav Trygvasson and Gyda) were foster brothers. Olav fostered Guthroth Skirja, his brother's son. 15, 18, 19, 25, 37.

OLAV GUTHBRANDSSON. Son of Guthbrand Skafhoggsson, and Maria, the daughter of Eystein I Magnusson (#20). Grandson of Eystein I Magnusson (#20). 71, 77.

OLAV HAAKONSSON. b.c1227 d.1240 at age 13. Illeg. son of Haakon IV (#43) and unknown mother. 125, 127.

OLAV ILL-LUCK. See Olav Guthbrandsson.

OLAV KVAAN. King of Ireland from 938–980. 39.

OLAV MAGNUSSON. See Olav (IV) (#19).

OLAV MAGNUSSON. b.c1262 d.c1267. Son of Magnus VI the Lawmender (#46) and Ingeborg Eriksdatter of Denmark. Died at age five. 134, 135.

OLAV MUNDUS. See Olav III Kyrre (#15).

OLAV THE PEACEFUL. See Olav III Kyrre (#15).

OLAV THE QUIET. See Olav III Kyrre (#15).

OLAV STOTKONUNG. King of Sweden. Father of Astrid, St. Olav's (#9) wife. Married Sigrid the Haughty. 41, 42, 45, 47.

OLAV THE STOUT. See Olav II (#9).

OLAV SVEINDSSON. (Olav I Hunger). King of Sweden. Married to Ingegerd, the daughter of Harald III the Hard (#13). 60.

OLAV TREE-HEWER (#-6). (Olav Tretelgja, Olof, Olav the Woodcutter, Olav, Olav I King of Vestfold) R.? 710. Son of the Yngling King Ingjald of Sweden and Gauthild Algautsdatter. Married Solveig. Father of Halfdan Whiteleg (#-5) and Ingjald. Great-great-great-great grandfather of King Harald I Fairhair (#1). 1, 2, 3.

OLAV TRETELGJA. See Olav Tree-Hewer (#-6).

OLAV UGJEVA. See Olav Guthbrandsson.

OLAV THE UNFORTUNATE. See Olav Guthbrandsson.

OLAV THE UNLUCKY. See Olav Guthbrandsson.

OLAV THE WOODCUTTER. See Olav Tree-Hewer (#-6).

OLAV I KING OF VESTFOLD. See Olav Tree Hewer (#-6).

OLAV I . See Olav I Trygvasson (#6).

OLAV I TRYGVASSON (#6). (Olav I Tryggvason I, Olav I). Son of Tryggve Olavsson from Vik and Astrid Eriksdtr. from Jaren. Grandson of Olav Geiristha Alf-II, and Great Grandson of Harald I Fairhair (#1) and Svanhild. 19, 20, 27, 36-41, 42, 43, 47, 54.

OLAV I TRYGGVASON. See Olav I Trygvasson (#6).

OLAV II HARALDSSON. See Olav II (#9).

OLAV II ST. OLAV (#9). (Olav, Olav II Haraldsson, Olav the Stout, Olav Big-Mouth, Olav the Farmer, *Hellig* Olav, Olav The Fat). Son of Harald Grenske from Vestfold and Asta Gudbrandsdatter. Married Princess Astrid from Sweden, and had one daughter, Ulfhild. With a mistress, Alvild, had one son, Magnus the Good (#12) who later became king of Norway xvi, 11, 20, 45, 46-50, 52, 53, 54, 55, 57, 59, 60, 61, 62, 63, 68, 69, 78.

OLAV III KYRRE (#15). (Olav III Haraldsson, Olav the Peaceful, Olav the Quiet, Olav Bonde, Olav Mundus). Son of Harald III the Hard (#13) and Thora Torbergsdatter. Married Princess Ingegerd of Denmark. No children. With a mistress, Thora Jonsdatter had Magnus III Barelegs (#17) and Sigrid Olavsdatter. 44, 60, 66, 67-69, 70, 71, 73, 75.

OLAV III HARALDSSON. See Olav III Kyrre (#15).

OLAV IV (#51). (Olav IV Haakonsson). Son of Haakon VI Magnusson (#50), and Margrete (#52), the daughter of King Valdemar of Denmark. Died at age 17. 73, 76, 77, 143, 147, 148, 149, 151, 152, 154, 161.

OLAV IV HAAKONSSON. See Olav IV (#51).

OLAV (IV) (#19). (Olav Magnusson). Son of Magnus IV Barelegs (#17) and Sigrid Saxeasdatter from Saksvik in Strinda. Did not marry. No children. Died young. 76.

OLAV V. King Olav. Olav Alexander Edward Christian Frederik, king of Norway from 1957–1991. Son of King Haakon VII and Queen Maud. Married Princess Martha of Sweden. Had three children. 158, 159, 160, 161.

OLOF. An often-used spelling of Olav.

ONUND SIMONSSON. Foster brother of Haakon Broadsholder. Son of Simon Thorstensson and Gunnhild. 95, 99.

ORDULD, DUKE OF SAXONY. Husband of Ulfhild, daughter of Saint Olav (#9). 47.

ORM KONGSBROR. Illegitimate son of Ivar Sneis and Ingerid, the widow of Harald Gilchrist (#23). Orm married Ragna Nikolsdatter after Eystein II (#27) died. Orm died in the Battle of Fimreite in 1184. 88, 97.

ORM. Son of Ingegerth and Heinrich Heinkel the Halt of Denmark.

OSCAR I. Swedish. R.1859–1872 in Norway. 155.

OSCAR II. Swedish. R.1872–1905 in Norway. 155.

OTTAR BIRTING. One of the husbands of Ingerid, widow of Harald Gilchrist (#23). 87, 88.

OYSTEIN II HARALDSSON. See Eystein II Haraldsson (#27).

OYSTEIN HALFDANSSON. See Eystein Halfdansson (# 4).

OYSTEIN I MAGNUSSON. See Eystein I Magnusson (#20).

OYSTEIN MOYLA. See Eystein Moyla (#32).

ØYSTEIN. See Eystein Halfdansson (#-4).

OZUR TOTI. Probably the foster father of Gunnhild, the wife of Erik Bloodaxe (#2), although Snorri states he is Gunnhild's father. 24.

PETER. b.c1210. Adopted Son of Skulle Baardsson and Ragnhild. Probably fostered, and not adopted. 130, 131.

PETER STEYPER. b.c1165. Illegitimate son of Kristin, the daughter of Sigurd the Mouth (##26). Fostered Guttorm Sigurdsson (#40). Married Ingeborg, daughter of Magnus Erlingsson (#29). 101, 120.

PHILIP. Prince Philip of Spain. Married to Kristin, daughter of Haakon IV (#43) and Margrete. 125.

PHILLIP HALLSTENSSON. King of Sweden. Nephew of Bishop Nikolos. Married to Ingegerd, daughter of Harald III the Hard (#13). 60.

PHILIPPS. See Filippus.

PHILIPPUS SIMONSSON. See Filippus Simonson (#38).

RAGNA NIKOLASDATTER. b.c1133 d.after 1161. Daughter of Nikolas Masa. Wife of Eystein II Haraldsson (#27).No children. After Eystein died she married Orm Kongsbror, the half brother of King Inge I Hunchback (#25). 86, 97.

RAGNAR RYKKIL. Son of Harald I Fairhair (#1) and Svanhild Eysteinsdatter. 15, 20.

RAGNFRED. Fifth son of King Erik Bloodaxe (#2) and Gunnhild. 23, 26.

RAGNFRID ERLINGSDATTER from Valdres. b.c1190. Probably second wife (after Cecelia) of Baard Guttormson and mother of Skule Baardson (#45). Therefore Skule had no royal blood.

RAGNFRID SKULESDATTER. Daughter of Skule Baardsson (#45) and Ragnhild. 130, 131.

RAGNHILD. Daughter of Erling Skakke (b.c1148). Married to Hallkel Jonsson. Was also wife of Jon Thorbergsson of Randeberg.

RAGNHILD. First and only daughter of Erik I Bloodaxe and Gunnhild. Married a Jarl of Orkney Islands. 23, 26.

RAGNHILD. b.c1190. Wife of Skule Baardsson (#45) in 1209. Mother of Margrete, Ingerid, and Ragnfrid. 130, 131.

RAGNHILD. Daughter of Erling Skjalgsson. Wife of Thorberg Arnesson. Had a son, Eystein and daughter, Thora. Eystein was twelve years older than Thora.

RAGNHILD. Queen Ragnhild the Powerful. b.c872. A Danish princess. Daughter of King Erik of Jutland (Denmark). Wife of Harald I Fairhair (#1). They had one son, Erik Bloodaxe (#2). 15, 21, 23.

RAGNHILD. Great grandson of Sigurd Jerusalfar (#21). Married to Jon Thorbergsson.

RAGNHILD. b.c1243. Illeg. daughter of Magnus I the Good (#12). Married Haakon Ivarsson, Jarl of Denmark, and had one daughter. 57.

RAGNHILD ALEXANDRA. Daughter of King Olav V and Princess Martha. b.1930. Married Erling Sven Lorentzen. 160.

RAGNHILD. A wife of Harald I Fairhair's (#1) son, Halfdan the Black. 19.

RAGNHILD. Another wife of Harald I Fairhair's (#1) son, Halfdan the Black. 19.

RAGNHILD ALEXANDRA. Daughter of Olav V of Norway (R.1957–1991) and Princess Martha of Sweden. Married Erling S. Lorentzen. 160.

RAGNHILD ERLINGSDATTER. Second wife of Baard Guttormson of Rein. Mother of Skule Baardsson (#45). 130.

RAGNHILD "INGEBORG" HAAKONSDATTER. Illeg. daughter of Jarl Haakon of Lade (#5). Married Skopti Skagason. 34.

RAGNHILD HARALDSDATTER. b.c830 d.c860. Daughter of King Harald Goldenbeard of Sogn. First wife of Halfdan the Black (#-1). One son, Harald, named after his grandfather. Harald was brought up at the estate of King Harald Goldenbeard. 9, 10.

RAGNHILD MAGNUSDATTER. b.c1096. Daughter of Magnus Barelegs (#17) and Thora Guttormsdatter. Ragnhild married Harald Kesja of Denmark and had eleven children: Magnus, Olav, Knud, Harald, Bjorn, Erik, Sivard, Sven, Niels, Benedict and Mistivint. 71.

RAGNHILD SIGURDSDATTER. Daughter of Sigurd Hart, king of Ringeriki (formerly called Hringariki). Second wife of Halfdan the Black (#1). Mother of Harald Fairhair (#1). Halfdan the Black (#-1) had two wives, both named Ragnhild. 9, 10, 15.

RAGNVALD. First son of Erik I Bloodaxe (#2) and Gunnhild. Died young. Probably murdered, 23, 25.

RAGNVALD. Son of Olav Geirstatha-Alf I. 6, 7, 8, 9.

RAGNVALD INGERSSON. Son of King Inge Steinkelsson of Sweden. Father of Ingerid, the wife of Harald Gilchrist (#23). 86.

RAGNVALD, JARL. Ragnvald of More. The barber who clipped Harald I Fairhair's (#1) hair after his victorious battle at Hafrsfjord. 17.

RAGNVALD RETTILBEIN. "The Straightlimbed." Son of Harald I Fairhair (#1) and Snafrid. 16, 21.

REAS. Olav Tryggvessen (#6) stayed with Reas and his family for six years. 38.

REKON. Wife of Reas. 38.

REKONI. Son of Reas and Rekoni. 38.

REIDAR SENDEMANN. b.c1160. A Bagler. Married to Magnus V. Erlingsson's (#29) daughter, Kristin in c1201. 101.

RICHSA. Princess of Saxony. b.1172 d.1202. Third wife of King Valdemar II (#41) of Denmark. 121.

RICHIZA BIRGIRSDATTER (Sweden). b.1234 d.1262. Daughter of Jarl Birgir of Sweden. Married Haakon, the son of Haakon IV the Old (#43), and Margrete. 125.

RING. See Hring.

ROAR KONGSFRENDE. Son of Ingeborg, the daughter of Sigurd II the Mouth (#26).

ROBERT BRUCE of Scotland. Brother of Isabella Bruce who married Eric II Magnusson (#47). 136.

ROBERT EARL. Father of Isabella Bruce, the second wife of Erik II Magnusson (#47). 136.

ROLLO. Norwegian conqueror of Normandy. 17. See glossary.

ROREK. Son of Harald I Fairhair (#1)and Gyda Eriksdatter,. 15, 19.

SAINT BIRGITTE. See Birgitte.

SAXI IN VIK. A chieftain in the Trondheim district. Had two daughters: Sigrid Saxeasdatter, the mistress of Sigurd the Crusader (#21); and Thora Saxeasdatter, wife of Sigurd Slembe (#24). Both daughters were mistresses of Magnus III Barelegs (#17). 89.

SIGRID OLAVSDATTER. Daughter of Olav III Kyrre (#15) and his mistress, Thora Jonsdatter. Married to Sigurd Ranesson. 67.

SIGRID. "Sigrid the Haughty." Queen Sigrid. Widow of the king of Sweden. Married King Svein Forkbeard, King of Denmark. 40, 41.

SIGRID SAXEASDATTER. From Saksvik in Strinda. Daughter of Saxi in Vik. Mistress of Magnus III Barelegs (#17), and with him became mother and Olav (IV) (#19). 71, 76.

SIGRID SKJALDVOR. Sister of Magnes Barelegs (#17).

SIGRID SVEINSDATTER. Daughter of Jarl Svein (#8) and Holmfrid. Princess of Sweden. Married Aslak Erlingsson. Had one son and two daughters. 44.

SIGROD. Fourth son of Harald I Fairhair (#1) and Asa Haakonsdatter. 15, 18, 19.

SIGTRYGG. Son of Harald I Fairhair (#1) and Gyda Eriksdatter. 15, 19.

SIGURD. Son of Harald Bluetooth of Denmark. Brother of Thyre, Olav Trygvasson's (#6) fourth wife.

SIGURD. Son of Erik Bjothaskalli. Brother of Astrid, Olav Trygvasson's (#6) mother.

SIGURD BRENNA. Son of Inge I Hunchback (#25).

SIGURD THE CRUSADER (#21) (Sigurd I Magnusson, Sigurd Jorsalafarer, Sigurd I) Illegitimate son of Magnus III Barelegs (#17) and Thora Guttormsdatter. 67, 71, 73, 76, 77, 78, 79, 80, 84, 86, 87, 93, 94, 100, 101, 114.

SIGURD EINERSON. Son of Einar Tambarskelfir and Bergljot Thoresdatter.

SIGURD ERLINGSSON. Illeg. son of Erling Skakke. His mother was Asa the Fair.

SIGURD HAAKONSSON. Illeg. son of Jarl Haakon of Lade (#5). 34.

SIGURD HAAKONSSON. b.c1222. Illegitimate son of Haakon IV the Old (#43) and Kanga the Young. 125, 127.

SIGURD HALFDANSSON. Son of Halfdan the Gentle (#-3) and Liv Dagsdatter. 5.

SIGURD HARALDSSON. See Sigurd II the Mouth (#26).

SIGURD HART. King of Ringeriki. Father of Ragnhild, the second wife of Halfdan the Black (#-1). 9, 10, 15.

SIGURD HRISI "The Bastard." Son of Harald Fairhair and Snafrid. Had a son called Halfdan. His genetic line brought forth many kings. 15, 21, 60.

SIGURD JARLSSON. b.c1148. In 1197 Sigurd arrived at Tønsberg where he killed Sverre's (#33) brother. Probably one of Erling's illegitimate sons.

SIGURD, JARL SIGURD HLATHAJARL. Son of Jarl Haakon Grjotgarthsson. Father of Jarl Haakon of Lade (#5). Married to Bergljot, Harald Fairhair's (#1) granddaughter. Murdered by Gunnhild and her son Erling. 22, 27, 28, 31, 32.

SIGURD JORSALAFARER. See Sigurd the Crusader (#21). 80.

SIGURD KONGSSON. See Sigurd Magnusson (#35).

SIGURD LAVARD. Prince of Norway. b.c1175 d.c1202. Illeg. son of Sverri Sigurdsson (#33). Father of Guttorm Sigurdsson (#40). 109, 120.

SIGURD MAGNUSSON (#35). (Sigurd Kongsson) A petty king. b.c1180. Son of Magnus V Erlingsson(#29) and unknown mother. 95, 101, 103, 111, 113, 114.

SIGURD MARKUSFOSTRE (#30). (Sigurd III Markusfostre). A petty king. Illeg. son of Sigurd II the Mouth (#26) and unknown mistress. 104.

SIGURD MUNN. See Sigurd II the Mouth (#26).

SIGURD RANESON. Married to Sigrid Olavsdatter, a half sister of Magnus Barelegs (#17). 67.

SIGURD RIBUNG. b.c1204 d.c1126. Son of Erling Stonewall (#42). 101, 122, 123, 126, 129.

SIGURD SLEFA. Son of Eric Bloodaxe (#2) and Gunnhild. 23, 27.

SIGURD SLEMBI. See Sigurd II Slembe (#24).

SIGURD SYR. Son of Halfdan Sigurdsson, grandson of Sigurd Hrisi, great grandson of Harald I Fairhair (#1) and Snafrid. Father of Harald III the Hard (#3). Married Asta, after Harald Grenske, her first husband, died she married Sigurd Syr. He is stepfather of Olav II the Saint (#9). Had five children: Guthorm, Gunnhild, Halvdan Sigurdsson, Ingerid, and Harald III the Hard (#14). 47, 60.

SIGURD I. See Sigurd the Crusader (#21).

SIGURD I MAGNUSSON. See Sigurd the Crusader (#21).

SIGURD II THE MOUTH (#26). b.c1133 d.10 Jun 1155. (Sigurd Munn, Sigurd II, Sigurd II Mund, Sigurd Haraldsson). Illeg. son of Harald Gilchrist (#23) and Thora Guttormsatter (daughter of Guttorm Graybeard). Sigurd's mistress was Gunnhild and while she was married to Unas, she had a son with Sigurd: Sverre Sigurdsson. 85, 86, 87, 90, 91, 94-96, 97, 98, 99, 101, 103, 104, 109, 110, 119.

SIGURD II . See Sigurd II the Mouth (#26).

SIGURD II MUND. See Sigurd II the Mouth (#26).

SIGURD II SLEMBE (#24) (Sigurth *Slembidjakn*, Gadabout Deacon, Sigurd Slembi, Deacon Magnusson). Claimed to be the son of Magnus Barelegs (#17) and Thora Saxeasdatter, the daughter of Saxi in Vik. Magnus was Thora's lover when she was married to Athride, a priest. Sigurd had no children. 73, 85, 87, 89, 90, 91, 95.

SIGURD III MARKUSFOSTRE. See Sigurd Markusfostre (#30).

SIGURTH *SLEMBIDJAKN*. See Sigurd II Slembe (#24).

SIGVAT. Snorri Sturluson's brother.

SIGVAT. The skald who "sprinkled with water," Saint Olav's (#9) son, Magnus (#12). 57.

SIMON KARLSSON. Married to Margrete Arnesdatter, the daughter of Arne Arnesson and Ingerid, the widow of Harald Gilchrist (#23). Father of Filippus Simonsson. 117.

SIMON THORBERGSSON. A wealthy man in Vik. Married to Gunnhild. two children: Onund and Andreas. They brought up and fostered Harald Broadshoulder (#28). 95, 99.

SIMON BONDE. See Simon Thorbergsson.

SIMON SKALP. Son of Hallkel Huk. Married to Harald Gilchrist's (#23) illeg. dau., Maria. He is the brother of Jon Hallkelsson. Simon was the father of Filippus Simonsson. Simon and Maria had a son, Nikolas. 86.

SKAGE SKOPTASON. A man of high rank. Father of Thora, the wife of Jarl I Haakon (#5). Also father of Skopti Skagasson, who was a favorite of Jarl Haakon (#5). 34.

SKJOLD. King Skjold. King of Varna. 4.

SKOPTI SKAGASON. Son of Skage Skoptason. Skopti married Bergljot, daughter of Haakon of Lade (#5). 34.

SKULE BAARDSSON (#45). (Skuli) Jarl. Son of Baard Guttormsson from Rein and Ragnfrid Erlingsdatter (his wife after Cecelia, so no royal blood) from Valdress. Married Ragnhild and had four children: Margrete, who married Haakon IV the Old (#43); Ingerid, who married Junker Knut (#44); Ragnfrid; and Peter. His father in law, Haakon IV, guided him from 1217–1223. 94, 118, 119, 125, 126, 129, 130, 131.

SKULI. See Skule Baardsson (#45).

SNAFRID. Daughter of Svasi of Finland. Wife of Harald Fairhair (#1). 15, 20, 21.

SNORRI THE PRIEST. Snorri's grandfather.

SNORRI STURLUSON. b.c1178 d.1241. Famous Islandic skald. Author of *Heimskringla*. xi, xv, xvi, 17, 22, 23, 28, 37, 40, 48, 58, 60, 62, 68, 69, 70, 73, 76, 78, 85, 100, 106, 131. Also see glossary.

SOFIA. Wife of Valdemar the Great (#31). Half sister of King Knut III of Denmark. Granddaughter of King Niels. 105, 120.

SOFIA. Princess of Denmark. Only daughter of Valdemar II (#41) and Berengaria, Princess of Portugal. Their daughter, Kristin, Married Magnus the Blind (#22) of Norway. 121.

SOLVA. See Solveig.

SOLVEIG. Wife of Olav the Tree-Hewer (#-6). Daughter of Halfdan Goldtooth of Soleyar. Also called Solva. 2, 3.

SOLVEIG HALFDANSDATTER. Mother of Asa, the wife of Halfdan Whiteleg (#-5). 3.

SOLVESON. An Icelandic priest.

SOLVI KLOFI. King in More. He killed Guttorm, son of Harald I Fairhair (#1) and Ase. 19.

SOLVI. The maternal uncle of Halfdan Whiteleg (#-5). Brother of Solveig, the wife of Olav Tree-Hewer (#-6). 3.

SONJA HARALDSEN. Queen Sonja. Wife of King Harald V, present king of Norway. 160, 161, 162, 163.

SOPHIA. Queen of Denmark. Wife of King Valdemar the Great (Valdemar I) (#31). Mother of the Danish king, Valdemar II (#41), and Knut VI. 105.

SOPHIA. Princess of Denmark. b.1217 d.1247. Daughter of Valdemar II (#41) and Queen Sophia. Married Johan I Margrave. Had one daughter, Kristin. 121.

SORKVIR. (Srkvir). King Sorkvir of Sweden. Married to Ingegerd, the daughter of Birgir Brosa and Birgitte. Granddaughter of Harald Gilchrist (#23).

ST. BIRGITTE. See Birgitte.

ST. OLAV. See Olav II Haraldsson (#9).

STEIGER THORIR. Foster father of Haakon Toresfostre (#16), son of Magnus II Haraldsson (#14). Father of Guthorm. Guthorm was the father of Ingeborg, Eystein I Magnusson's (#20) wife. 75.

STURLA THORTHARSON. Snorri's father.

SVANHILD. Daughter of Jarl Eystein. Wife of Harald I Fairhair (#1). 15, 19, 37, 38.

SVASI OF FINLAND. Father of Snafrid, one of Harald Fairhair's wives. 20.

SVEIN ALFIVASSON (#11). Son of Knute II the Great (#10) of Denmark and his mistress, Alfiva. Never married. He reigned for a few years after Knut. Brother of Harald Harfot. 51, 52, 54-55.

SVEIN FORKBEARD. King Svein Forkbeard of Denmark   Also called Svein Tjugeskjegg. Son of the Danish King, Harald Bluetooth. Married to Gunnhild of Poland. Father of Erik Haakonsson's (#7) wife, Gyda. Father of Knut II The Great of Denmark. Queen Thyre is Svein's sister. 35, 40, 41, 42, 43, 45, 51, 63, 66.

SVEIN HAAKONARSSON. See Svein, Jarl (#8).

SVEIN HARALDSSON of Denmark (#18). Son of Harald Flettir of Denmark. 73, 75.

SVEIN, JARL (#8). (Jarl Svein, Svein Haakonarsson, Svend Haakonsson). Son of Jarl Haakon I of Lade (#5) and Thora Skagesdatter. Half brother of Jarl Erik (#7). Married Holmfrid, Princess of Sweden. 34, 42, 43, 44, 45, 48, 50.

SVEIN SVEINSSON. King of Denmark. Had a son named Heinrick Heinkel the Halt.

SVEIN *TJUGESKJEGG*. See Svein Forkbeard.

SVEIN II. See Svein Forkbeard.

SVEIN II ESTRIDSSON OF DENMARK. Son of Knut the Great's sister, Estrid. Canute the Great's nephew. Married Gunnhild Sveinsdatter, the daughter of Jarl Svein (#8) and Holmfrid. Svein's daughter was Princess Ingegerd. 44, 58, 59, 67, 68.

SVEND HAAKONSSON. See Svein, Jarl (#8).

SVERRE SIGURDSSON (#33). (Sverre, Sverri). Son of Sigurd the Mouth (#26) and Gunnhild who was married to Unas, a combmaker in Bergen at the time. (Many historians doubt Sverre's "blue blood.") Married Astrid Roesdatterof Sweden and they had two sons: Kik Gregorius, and Einar Prest. Married Margrete Eriksdatter of Sweden and they had two children: Kristin, and Erling. Had two illeg. children with unknown mother: Sigurd Lavard and Haakon III (#37). 94, 95, 96, 103, 107, 108-111, 112, 113, 115, 117, 119, 120, 122, 126, 133.

SWAYNE FORKBEARD. See Svein Forkbeard.

SWEYN, JARL. One of the Danish Viceroys in Norway. He married Holmfrid, the daughter of King *Stotkunung* of Sweden.

THJOTHOLF OF HVINIR. Foster father of Guthroth Ljomi "The Radiant." 21.

THORA GUTTORMSDATTER. b.c1114. Daughter of Guttorm Graybeard. Mistress of Harald Gilchrist (#23), and with him had Sigurd the Mouth (#26). 87, 99.

THORA GUTTORMSDATTER. b.c1072. "She was of a good line but a hard hearted, unfeeling woman." Mistresse of Magnus Barleggs (#17), and with him had one son, Sigurd the Crusader (#21), and one daughter, Ragnhild. 71, 79, 86, 94.

THORA THORBERGSDATTER. b.c1015. Daughter of Thorberg Arnason and Ragnhild Erlingsdatter. Wife of Harald III the Hard (#13), and with him had two sons: Magnus II Haraldsson (#14), and Olav Kyrre (#15. 60, 63, 66, 67.

THORA HAAKONSDATTER. Illegitimate daughter and only child of King Haakon the Good (#3). 28.

THORA JONSDATTER. Mistress of Olav III Kyrre (#15). Mother of Magnus Barelegs (#17) and Sigrid Olavsdatter. 67, 71, 77.

THORA MAGNUSDATTER. Princess of Norway. b.c1099 d.1175. Illeg. daughter of Magnus Barelegs (#17) and unknown mother. Married Lopt Saemundarson, the most powerful, high born chieftian in Iceland. Lopt was the father of Jon Loptsson. 70.

THORA MORSTRSTONG. Thora "Mesterstrong" Karasdatter. Wife of Harald I Fairhair (#1). Mother of Haakon the Good (#3). 16, 22, 28.

THORA MOSTAFF . Mistress of Haakon the Good ((#3). One daughter, Thora. 28, 29.

THORA SAXEASDATTER. Daughter of a powerful ruler, Saxi in Vik. Mistress of Magnus Barelegs (#17) and with him had Sigurd II Slembe (#24). Thora is also the sister of Sigrid, the mother of King Olav (IV) Magnusson (#19). Thora was Magnus Bareleg's (#17) lover while she was married to a Priest, Athalbrikt. 73, 89.

THORA SIMONSDATTER. b.c1130. Servant girl. A working woman for a wealthy farmer, Simon Thorbergsson in Vik. Sigurd the Mouth (#26) "lay with her," and they had a son Haakon Broadsholder (#28). Haakon was raised by them. 95.

THORA SKAGESDATTER OF RIMA. Daughter of Skage Skoptason, a man of high rank. "She was an unusually beautiful woman." Wife or mistress of Jarl Haakon (#5)and with him had three children, Svein (#8), Heming and Bergljot. Thora had a brother, Skopti Skagason, who married Ragnhild, one of Jarl Haakon's daughter. 34, 44.

THORBERG ARNESON from Gizka (a small island NW of town of Alesund). Married to Ragnhild Erlingsdatter. Parents of Thora, the wife of Harald the Hard (#13), and Jorun and also two sons, Eystein and Ogmund. Thorberg had a brother named Finn Arneson and another named Arne Arneson. 60, 63.

THORD. Snorri Sturluson's brother.

THORE OF STEIG. A prominent man. Fostered Haakon Toresfostre (#16). 70.

THORFINN HAUSAKLJUF. A prominent Jarl in Denmark. Lived to be an old man. Father of Arnfinn, the husband of Erik and Gunnhild's daughter, Ragnhild. 26.

THORFINN SKULLCLEAVER. See Thorfinn Hausakljuf.

THORGILS. Son of Harald I Fairhair (#1) and Gyda Eriksdatter. 15, 19.

THORIR RAGNVALDSSON. Jarl of Ragnvald over More. He married Alof Arbot's daughter. They had a daughter, Bergljot. Thorir was foster father of Eric Bloodaxe (#2). 19.

THORIR THE SILENT. See Thorir Ragnvaldsson.

THORKEL NEFIA. Son of Astrid Eriksdatter and Lodin.

THORLEIF *BREISKJEGG*. b.c1150. Illeg. son of Eystein II Haraldsson (#27), and unknown mother. Brother or half brother of Eystein Moyla (#32). 97.

THORLEIF THE WISE. Counselor of Halfdan the Black (#-1), Harald I Fairhair's (#1) father. An interpreter of dreams. 11.

THOROLF LOUSEBEARD. Foster father to Astrid, Olav Trygvasson's (#6) mother. 37, 38.

TYRA. See Thyre.

THYRE HARALDSDATTER. Queen Thyre. Daughter of King Blaatan of Denmark. First married to Burizlaf. Fourth wife of Olav Trygvason (#6). A sister of Svein Forkbeard of Denmark. Mother of Harald, who died at age one. 37, 40, 41.

THYRE. Queen Thyre of England. Married to Gorm the Old of Denmark and and with him became the mother of Gunnhild, the wife of Eric Bloodaxe (#2). 23.

TRYGGVE OLAVSSON. Son of Olav Geirsiatha Alf II and father of Olav Trygvasson (#6). A grandson of Harald Fairhair. Married to Astrid Eriksdatter from Jaren. 18, 19, 20, 25, 31, 32, 33, 37, 47.

TRYGGVE OLAVSSON. Son of Olav Trygvasson (#6) and Gyda. Probably named after his grandfather. Tryggve and Olav Geristha Alf II were foster brothers. 37, 39, 54, 55.

ULFHILD. Daughter of Saint Olav (#9) and Queen Astrid. She married Orduld, Duke of Saxony. 47.

UNAS. A combmaker in Bergen. His wife, Gunnhild, had a son with Sigurd the Mouth (#26) while she was married to Unas. 95, 109.

VALDEMAR. THE GREAT of Russia.

VALDEMAR THE GREAT of Denmark (#31).(Valdemar d. Store, Valdemar I, Waldemar). Ruled in Norway for a short time in 1170. Son of King Knut III Magnusson (Knut Lavard) of Denmark. Married Sofia. 101, 105, 120, 123.

VALDEMAR IV. King Valdemar Atterdag (other day) of Denmark. Married to Queen Helvig. Their daughter was Margaret Valdemarsdatter (#52), who married Haakon VI (#50) and became Queen of Norway, Sweden and Denmark. 143, 145, 147, 151, 152.

VALDEMAR. D STORE. See Valdemar the Great (#31).

VALDEMAR MAGNUSSON OF SWEDEN. King Valdemar of Sweden. Brother of Eric Wryneck and King Birgir of Sweden. Valdemar was married to Erik II Magnusson's (#47) fifteen-year-old niece, also named Ingeborg. 136, 138, 141.

VALDEMAR THE VICTORIUS. See Valdemar II (#41).

VALDEMAR I. See Valdemar the Great (#31).

VALDEMAR II (#41). (Valdemar II Seier, Valdemar the Victorious). R. 1204–1204 in Norway. R.1202–1240 in Denmark. Son of Valdemar the Great (#31) of Denmark and Queen Sofia. M1) Helen Guttormsdatter; m2) Dagmar (Margrete) Princess of Bohemia; m3) Richsa, Princess of Saxony; m4)Berengaria, Princess of Portugal, and with her had four children: Eric IV, Sofie, Abel, and Christoffer. 105, 120, 121, 122, 123.

VALDEMAR II SEIER. See Valdemar II (#41).

VIDKUNN JONSON. Accompanied Magnus II Barelegs (#17) when he defeated the Normans in Ireland. 73, 74.

VIDKUN QUISLING. A Norwegian traitor who assisted the German Nazis in planning the invasion of Norway in 1940. 158.

VISLAV. Prince Vislav of Rugen. Friend and advisor of Hakon V Magnusson (#48). 139.

WALDEMAR I. See Valdemar I (#31).

WALDEMAR II. See Valdemar II (#41).

WILLIAM THE CONQUEROR. b.1028 d.1087. Of Norwegian descent. Immigrated to Normandy. Conquered England in Battle of 1066. King of England 1066–1087. Married Herleva (Arlette) and had ten children. 53.

YAROSLAV I THE WISE. Lord of Kiev and Novgorod. Grand Prince of Kiev. Father of Queen Illisif, wife of Harald III the Hard (#13). Married Ingegerd, the daughter of King Skotkonung of Sweden. Fostered Magnus, the son of Saint Olav (#9). Yaroslav was a shrewd and energetic statesman noted as one of the greatest princes of the Viking age,revered as a patron and founder of learning and literature in Russia during his 30-year reign,. 50, 58, 62.

YNGLING. The royal family of Sweden. From Uppsula in NE Sweden. 1, 2, 3.

Battles in Alphabetical Order
(Also see Battles in Chronological Order)

Agrifjord. BATTLE OF AGRIFJORD. 861. Harald I Fairhair's (#1) father, Halfdan the Black (#1) died in this battle.

Fimreite. BATTLE OF FIMREITE. 1184. Sverre (#33) won all of Norway with his defeat of Magnus V Erlingsson (#29) in this battle.

Fitjar. BATTLE OF FITJAR. 961. Haakon the Good (#3) was killed here.

Florevaag. BATTLE OF FLOREVAAG. 1194. Bergen. A victorious battle for Sverre. Sigurd Magnusson (#35) was slain in this battle.

Hafrsfjord. BATTLE OF HAFRSFJORD. 872. More recent scholars place this date as closer to 900. Harold I Fairhair (#1) won final victory over his enemies in this battle. It is considered as the battle which unified Norway. Hafrsfjord is near the modern Stavanger

Helgøya. BATTLE OF HELGØYA. 1199. Inge Magnusson (#36) was killed in this battle.

Holmengra. BATTLE OF HOLMENGRA. 1139. Magnus IV the Blind (#22), and Sigurd Slembe (#24) were killed in this battle. Sigurd had confined Magnus to a monastary. Slembe released him, but both lost their lives here.

Horundarfjord. BATTLE OF HORUNDARFJORD. 985. A victorious battle for Earl Haakon (#5). Although an old man, Skald Oyvind Skaldespiller served as his lieutenant.

Kalvskinnet. BATTLE OF KALVSKINNET. 1179. (Trondheim) This battle was won by Sverre (#33) and his "Birchlegs." After a long struggle, they re-established its decrees throughout the length and breadth of Norway. Nicholas' son, Sigurd, fell in this battle together with Erling Skakke.

Linisfarne. BATTLE OF LINISFARNE. 793. Listed in most text books as the start of the Viking Age.

Lyrskov. BATTLE OF LYRSKOV. 1042. Near Slesvig. Magnus I and his Norwegian f...s protected the Danes when they were invaded by the Wends, and put the Wends to flight.

Maldon. BATTLE OF MALDON. 991. In Essex, a county in SE England. Olav Trygvasson's (#6) greatest victory where he had assembled a fleet of 390 vessels.

Nesjar. PALM SUNDAY BATTLE OF NESJAR. 1016. St. Olav (#9) defeated Jarl Svein, Einar Tambarskjelver and Haarek of Tjotta at this battle, but all three succeeded in escaping

Nissa. BATTLE OF NISSA. 1062. Off the coast of Holland. Inge Magnusson (#36) was killed here.

Ramparts. BATTLE OF RAMPARTS. 1190. Nikolas Arnesson was with Jon Kuvlung in this battle near Trondheim.

Re. BATTLE OF RE. 1177. In this battle Eystein Moyla met his death. This is also the last event mentioned in Heimskringla. Re (Ramnes) is about 10 miles northwest of Tønsberg. Sigurd Slembe (#24) fell in the first battle of Re in 1163

Solkjel. BATTLE OF SOLKJEL. 866/867. Two of Earl Haakon's sons were killed in this battle fighting for Harald I Fairhair (#1).

Stainmore. BATTLE OF STAINMORE. 954. Where Erik I Bloodaxe died.

Stamford. BATTLE OF STAMFORD BRIDGE. 1066. The last Norwegian battle fought in England. Harald the Hard (#13) was killed by an arrow in this battle.

Stiklestad. BATTLE OF STIKLESTAD. July 29, 1030. Where St. Olaf lost his life in battle in northern Norway.

Svold. BATTLE OF SVOLD. 1000. Where King Olav Tryggvessen (#6) was killed. It is considered the most noteable battle in the history of Norway since Hafrsrfjord. This is the first date in Norwegian history which is generally accepted as accurate.

Ulster. BATTLE OF ULSTER. 1103. Magnus III Barelegs died in this battle.

Battles in Chronological Order

(See Battles in Alphabetical Order for descriptions)

AD

793	Battle of Linesfarne
861	Battle of Agrifjord
866/877	Battle of Solskjel
872	Battle of Hafrsfjord
954	Battle of Stainmore
985	Battle of Horundarfjord
961	Battle of Fitjar
991	Battle of Maldon
1000	Battle of Svold
1016	Palm Sunday Battle of Nesjar
1030	Battle of Stiklestad
1042	Battle of Lyrskov
1062	Battle of Nissa
1066	Battle of Stamford Bridge
1103	Battle of Ulster
1139	Battle of Holmengra
1062	Battle of Nissa
1177	Battle of Re
1179	Battle of Kalvskinnet
1184	Battle of Fimreite
1190	Battle of The Ramparts
1194	Battle of Florevaag
1199	Battle at Helgøya

Reference of Places

ABBEY OF HOVEDØYA. Oslo. Jon Kuvlung (#34) was a monk here.

AGIR. See Agthir.

AGTHIR. The neighboring kingdom south of Vestfold in southernmost part of Norway. Ruled by King Harald Redbeard in pre-Viking era.

AGRIFJORD. Battle of Agrifjord fought here. Where Halfdan the Black (#-1) lost his life.

AKERSHUS. Province in S. Norway. Towns: Oslo.

AKERSHUS *SLOTT*. Oslo's ancient royal fortress. Built by Haakon V Magnusson (#48) in about 1300 AD.

ALFHEIM. In Viking times the name of the district between the present day rivers of Glommen & Gota Elf, near Trondheim.

ANGLESEY. An island off the coast of Wales.

APOSTLE CHURCH. Bergen. Eystein's II Haraldsson's (#32) timber "Kongsgaard" burned to the ground here in 1207.

APPLETON HOUSE. In England. Olav V (King of Norway from 1957–1991) was born here.

AUST-AGDER. A Province in SE Norway. Towns: Risr, Arendal, Grimstad.

AUSTLANDET. "Ny Norsk" for Oeslandet. The area around Oslo in southern Norway.

BERGEN. A major seaport in Rogalnd Province in western Norway. Founded by Olav III Kyrre (#15) in about 1070/75. Second largest city in Norway. For many years the residence of Norwegian kings. Bergen suffered from several devastating fires. It was almost destroyed by a fire on July 4, 1248. Sverresborg and Bergenhus were located here. Also Haakonshallen, a great feasting hall of the Vikings.

BERGEN CATHEDRAL. In Bergen. Built by King Haakon the Old (#43). A magnificent stone structure; a splendid example of Gothic architecture. Dedicated to St. Olav (#9). Partially destroyed by fire in 1702 but later rebuilt. Erik II Magnusson (#47) was the last king to be crowned in this city on July 2, 1280.

BJARKY. An island off the coast of NW Norway. See Magnus Barelegs (#17).

BOKN ISLANDS. *Bøkn*. A group of small islands west of Rogaland in W. Norway. Battle between Tryggve Olavsson & Svein Alfivasson (#11) took place here.

BORRE. In Vestfold, near Horton on western shore of Oslo Fjord. Halfdan Whiteleg (#-5) and his son, Eystein Halfdansson (#-4) are buried at Skiringsal, which is in Borre. Halfdan the Gentle (#-3) is also buried here.

BUSKERUD. A Province in S. Central Norway. Towns: Ringeriki, Drammen, Kongsberg.

CATHEDRAL OF BERGEN. See Bergen Cathedral.

CHRIST CHURCH. Bergen. See Great Christ Church.

CHRIST CHURCH. Old Christ Church. Trondheim. The forerunner of the Great Nidares Cathedral at Trondheim. See Nidares Cathedral.

DOVREFJELL. The Dovre mountain range between Oslo and Trondheim. Harald I Fairhair (#1) led his *bird* over Dovrefjell in about 872. Also two Vikings, on skiis, took Haakon IV (#43), across these mountains when he was two years old.

EASTFOLD. On the eastern side of Oslofjord.

EIDSVOLL. Also called Firdafylke. Between Lake Mjose and Oslo. Erik Bloodaxe(#2) was brought up here.

ELGESAETER ABBEY. In Trondheim. Skulle Baardsson (#45) was killed here.

ESSEX. A county in SE England.

ESTONIA. A small country on the NE Baltic area of Europe.

FIMREITE. On shore of Sognfjord. Famous Battle of Fimreite between Magnus V. Erlingsson (#29) and Sverre (#33) fought here in 1184. Magnus lost his life here.

FINNLAND. The territory constituting the modern province of Finnmark.

FINNMARK. A Province in N. Norway. Towns: Hammerfest, Vard, Bodo.

FIRDAFYLKE. See Eidsvoll.

FITJAR. An island off SW Norway. Olav the Good (#15) was slain here. Also Haakon the Good (#3).

FOLDENFJORD. The former name of Oslofjord.

FORS CHURCH. In the Ranriki district. Eystein II Haraldsson (#27) is buried here.

FRANCISCAN ABBEY. Now the Bergen Cathedral in Bergen

GLOMMER. See Alfheim.

GOKSTAD. In the Vestfold region. Olav Geirstatha-Alf is buried here.

GOTLAND. The province of Sweden.

GREAT CHRIST CHURCH. Bergen. Following people buried here: Haakon Galen; Sverre (#33), d.1202; Cecelia Sigurdsdatter, d.1185; Harald Gilchrist (#23), d.1204; Erik II Magnusson (#47), d.1299; Haakon III (#37), d.1204; his son, Haakon IV (43), d.1263; Sigurd Magnusson (#35), d.1194; Erik II Magnusson (#47), d.1199; Haakon Galen; and Hallkel Johnsson.

GRENLAND. The district south of Vestfold. (Not to be confused with Greenland).

GREENLAND. Large island northwest of Norway.

HAAKONSHALLEN. A great feating hall of the Vikings. In Bergen Cathedral in Bergen.

HAALOGALAND. Between Tromso and Molde. Home of the Jarls of Lade. Harald I Fairhair (#1) ruled here at the beginning of his reign. Home of Ozur Toti, foster-father of Gunnhild, Eric Bloodaxe's (#2) wife.

HAFRSFJORD. Near Stavanger. Where Battle of Hafresfjord was fought.

HALLVARD. St. Hallvard Cathedral. Oslo. First to be buried here: Sigurd the Crusader (#21) in 1130. Also buried here: Crown Prince Haakon, son of Haakon IV (#43) in 1257, and Inge I Hunchback (#25).

HARTHANGERFJORD. A fjord in Iceland.

HATHALAND. Where Rognvald Rettilbeini perished.

HEBRIDES ISLANDS. A group of islands lying off the the western shore of the northern coast of Scotland.

HEDEBY. In S. Denmark, at the foot of the fjord leading into the Baltic and within 10½ miles of a river entering into the north Sea. This made it an ideal center for east/west traffic, which at the cost of some river-rowing and a single portage could avoid the arduous passage round the Skaw. Important for its long distance commerce. Before 1050 Hedeby was burnt down, perhaps on the occassion of its capture by King Harald the Hard (#13).

HEDMARK. A Province in E. Norway. Towns: Hamar, Kongsvinger.

HEITHMORK. Where Ragnar Rykkil ruled.

HELGOY. An island on Lake Mjosa. Inge Magnusson (#36) was slain here.

HLATHIR. Main estate of Harald I Fairhair (#1) in Trondheim.

HORDALAND. A Province in W. Norway. Towns: Bergen.

HORTEN. On western shore of Oslofjord.

HORTHALAND. Sweden. Swedish King Erik was king here. He was father of Gyda, Harald I Fairhair's (#1) wife.

HORUNDARFJORD. A fjord in Trondheim area .

HRINGARIKI. See Raumariki.

HVINIR. Home of Thjotholf, foster-fahter of Guthroth Ljomi "The Radiant."

ISLE OF MANN. An island in the Irish Sea between N. Ireland and England.

JAREN (Jren). Where Olaf Tryggvason's mother is from. Jon Kuvlund (#34) was defeated here in 1187.

JUTLAND (Denmark). An independend kingdom until it was captured by the Danish King, Gorm the Old in the early 10th century. King Erik, father of Ragnhild, Harald Fairhair's wife, was king here.

KALVSKINNET (Battle of Kalvskinnet). Tronheim. Erling Skakke fell in this battle.

KAUPANG. A Viking trading place close to the mouth of the Oslo Fjord. South of Oslo.

KENT. In SE England.

KIEV. Now Russia.

KVITESY. Island of Kvitesy. Near Stavanger.

LAURENCE. St. Laurence Church in Tønsberg. Built in about 1120.

MARGRETA CHURCH. In Trondheim. Built by Olav III Kyrre in the 11th century. Much of the town burned in 1328, including the church.

MARIA. Royal Chapel of Maria. Oslo. Buried here: King Haakon V (#49) on May 8, 1319; Magnus VII (#48) alongside his wife, Blanca; and King Haakin VI (#50).

MARIA CHURCH. Bergen. It survived the great fire that destroyed the major part of Bergen on July 4, 1248. Mass grave of the "island-beards" is here. Jon Kuvlung (#34) buried here.

MARIA CHURCH. Tønsberg. Michael. St. Michael's Church, Tønsberg. St. Michaels was made a Royal Church by Haakon V (#50). This church is at Slottsfjellet.

MJØSE. Lake Mjøse. About 50 miles north of Oslo. The largest lake in Norway.

MORE OG ROMSDAL. More Og Romsdal. Province in W. Norway. Towns: Alesund, Molde, Kristiansund.

MORSTR. The Island of Morstr. Home of the kin of Thora.

MUNKELIV ABBEY. In Bergen. An abbey founded by Eystein (#20). Princess Ingeborg, wife of Magnus VI the Lawmender (#46) stayed here before her coronation.

NAMUR. In Sweden.

NID RIVER. See Nith.

NIDAROS. Former name for Trondheim.

NIDAROS CATHEDRAL. Trondheim. On Easter Sunday in 1328 a devastating fire broke out and the nearly completed Cathedral burnt to the ground. Rebuilt many years later. Built by St. Olav's nephew, Olav Kyrre (#15). It was built over St. Olav's grave. Kings buried here: St. Olav (#9), d.1030; Magnus the Good (#12), d.1047; Olav Kyrre (#12), d.1093; Haakon Magnusson (#16), d.1095; Olav (IV) Magnusson (#19), d.1115; Eystein Magnusson (20), d.1122; Haakon Broadshoulder (#28), d.1162; Guttorm Sigurdsson (#40), d.1204; Inge II Bardsson (#39), d.1217; and Skule Bardsson (#45), d.1240.

NITHAROS. See Nidaros.

NITH RIVER. In Tronheim. Also called Nid.

NORDLAND. Province in N. Norway. towns: Bod, Narvik.

NORD. Trondelag. Province in N. Norway. towns: Steinkjer, Namos.

NORNES. On shore of Sognfjord. Across fjord from Fimreite.

NORTHUMBERLAND. NW England.

OLAV. St. Olav's Abbey. At Tønsberg. Sigurd II the Mouth's (#26) son, Erik, and his wife were poisoned here. Shrine of St. Olav is here.

OLD CHRIST CHURCH. See Great Christ Church. Trondheim.

OLAV'S PREMONSTRATENSION ABBEY. Mentioned by Danish Crusaders in 1191. The church was the largest round church in all of the north.

OPPLAND. Province in S. Central Norway. Towns: Lillihammer, Gjøvik. "The East Norway Kingdom."

ORKNEY ISLANDS. A group of about 90 islands situated about 6 miles north of the coast of Scotland.

OSEBERG. Vestfold. On western side of Oslo fjord. Oseberg ship excavated here in 1904. Queen Asa, wife of Guthroth the Hunting King (#-2) buried here.

OSLO. Province in S. Norway. Town: Oslo.

OSLO. The capital of Norway since 1286. Called Kristiania or Christiania from 1624 to 1924. The old city of Oslo was founded by Harald the Hard (#13) in 1048–1050. Several times burned and plundered. Finally destroyed by fire in 1624. Present Oslo built on nearby site. Heavily damanged in World War II. Rebuilt.

OSLOFJORD. The long fjord running south of Oslo. Foldenfjord was an earlier name for Oslofjord.

ØSTFOLD. Province in SE Norway. Towns: Halden, Sarscorp, Fredrikstad, Moss.

ØSTLANDET. Eastern Norway.

RANDEBERG. The burial place of the husband of Erling Skakke's daughter, Ragnhild.

RANRIKE. Between the Gulf-Elf River and Svina sound.

RAUMARIKI . Old name for present city of Romeriki. See Romeriki.

RINGERIKI. See Romeriki.

ROGALAND. Province in SW Norway. Towns: Eigersund, Sandness, Stavanger, Haugesund. Where King Harald Fairhair (#1) is buried.

ROGNVALD OVER MORE. In NW Norway. Where Jarl Thorir ruled.

ROMERIKI. Old name is Raumariki. An area to the south of Lake Mjøsa, and northwest of the present city of Oslo. Was also called Hringeriki and Ringeriki.

ROUEN. In Normandy. Where Saint Olav (#9) was baptized.

SARPSBORG. On Orkney Islands. Now part of Scotland. Haakon IV (#43) was born here.

SAXLAND. The old Norse name for Germany.

SAXONY. A Province in E. Central Germany. Orduld was Duke of Saxony.

SKIBBY, Denmark. Magnus I the Good died here.

SKIRINGSAL. In Vestfold. A great trade center. Halvdan Whiteleg (#-5) and his son, Eystein (#-4), are buried near the temple at Skiringsal.

SLESVIG. In Denmark. Battle of Lyrskov fought near here.

SLOTTSFJELLET. Tønsberg. The Royal residence of early Viking kings. In 1230 Haakon IV (#43) built gatehouse and his residence here. It was fortified in the 1160's.

SOGN. The land around the Sognfjord in wesern Norway. Harald Goldenbeard was king here.

SOGN OG FJORDANE. A Province in W. Norway. Towns: Flora. Soknar sound. Near the Island of Bokn.

SOLEYAR (Also Solyar, Sølayar, Solor, Solayar, Søleyar). West of Varmaland, Sweden. .

SØR. Trondelag. Province in N. Norway. Towns: Trondheim.

ST. OLAV'S ABBEY. See Olav's Abbey.

STEIN. Ringerike. Halfdan the Black (#-1) is buried here.

STIFLU SOUND. On the shore of Vestfold.

SUDROANE. Ireland. Boyhood home of Harald Gilchrist (#23).

SVALBARD. Also called Spitzbergen. Province of Norway. Towns: Longyersyen. An archipelago north of Norway in the Artic Ocean. These islands were known to the Vikings.

SVERRESBORG. Trondheim. Sverre's (#33) home.

SVERRESBORG. In Bergen after Sverresborg in Trondheim was demolished. Where Sverre (#33) lived. Burnt to the ground on July 4, 1248, during reign of Haakon IV (#43).

SVOLD. Near Rugen Island in the Baltic Sea.

SVINA SOUND. Forms part of the boundary between southern Sweden and Norway.

TELEMARK. Province in SE Norway. Towns: Porsgruan, Skien, Notodden.

TØNSBERG (Tønsberg). On the western shore of Oslofjord. Oseberg ship excavated here.

TROMS. Province in N. Norway. Towns: Harstad, Troms.

TRONDELAG. In the region surrounding the Trondheim Fjord. The eight shires inhabited by Tronder formed Trondelag.

TRONDHEIM. A city in northwestern Norway. Founded by Olav Tryvasson (#6). Third largest city in Norway. King Haakon VII crowned here in 1906.

UPPLAND. Province in NE Sweden.

UPPSALA or Old Uppsala. In northeastern Sweden.

VARTEIG. Small community in SE Norway.

VALDRES. Sweden. Gyda Eriksdatter, one of Harald I Fairhair's (#1) wives, was fostered here.

VARMALAND (Vaermland, Vermland). The western part of Sweden.

VARMLAND. Area next to Vestfold in Norway.

VARNA. In Eastfold on the eastern side of Oslo Fjord. Across the fjord from Vestfold.

VENDLAND. Germany. The present Pomerania (Prussia). Olav Trygvasson's first and second wives came from here.

VESTFOLD. A Province in S. Norway. Towns: Holmestrand, Horten, Tønsberg, Sanefjord, Larvik, Stavern. South of Oslo, on the western shore of the Oslo Fjord. The smallest province in Norway, however rich in history. Tønsberg, the oldest city in Norway located here. The largest group of royal graves, and nine huge mounds and fifteen smaller ones are located at Borre in Vestfold. South of the Borre group are two Yngling graves. The Oseberg and Gokstad mounds are also here.

VEST. Agder. Province in SE Norway. Towns: Kristiansand, Mandal, Farsund, Flekefjord.

VESTLANDET. Western Norway. King Harald I Fairhair (#1) appointed Erik Bloodaxe (#2) to rule with him in Vestlandet.

VIK. The region around the Folden Fjord, or the Oslo Fjord as it is called today.

VIKA. An early name for Oslo. Harbor district of Oslo.

VINGULMARK. Where Olaf Geirstatha-Alf II ruled.

WENDLAND. See Vendland.

WESTFOLD. See Vestfold.

WESTMARIR. Another name for Vestfold.

YORK. In NE England. The capital of Northrumbia.

Norway

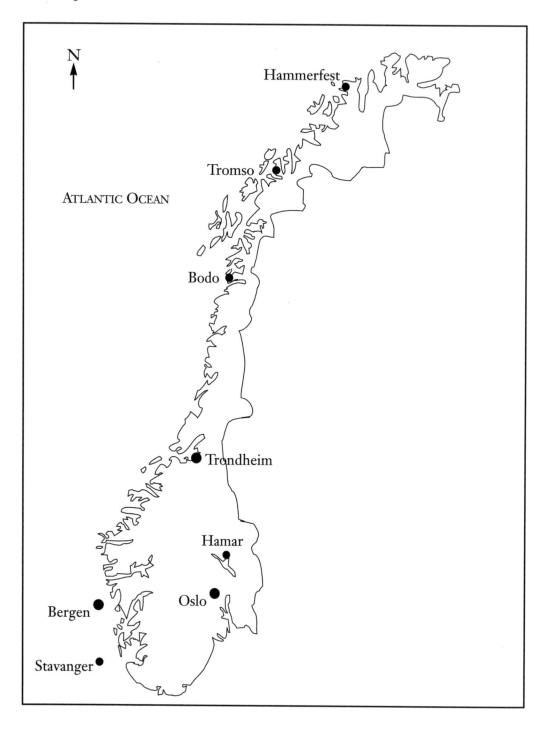

N

Hammerfest

Tromso

ATLANTIC OCEAN

Bodo

Trondheim

Hamar

Bergen

Oslo

Stavanger

Southern Norway

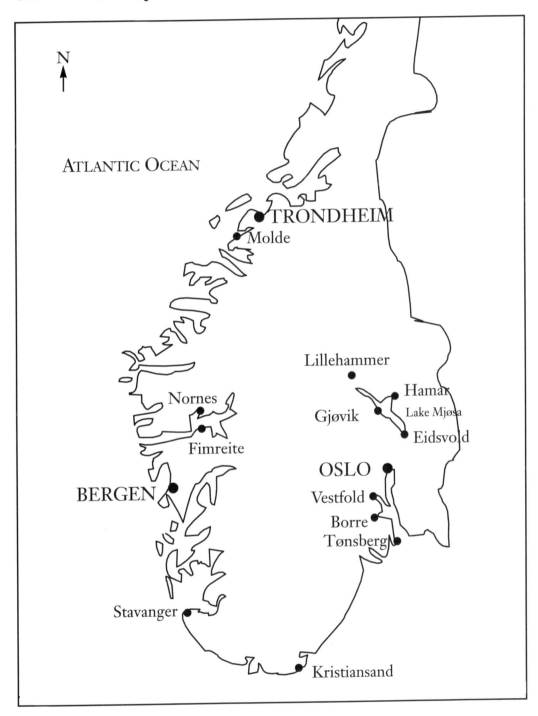

N

ATLANTIC OCEAN

TRONDHEIM
Molde

Lillehammer

Nornes

Gjøvik

Hamar
Lake Mjøsa
Eidsvold

Fimreite

OSLO

BERGEN

Vestfold

Borre
Tønsberg

Stavanger

Kristiansand

Scandinavia and the British Isles

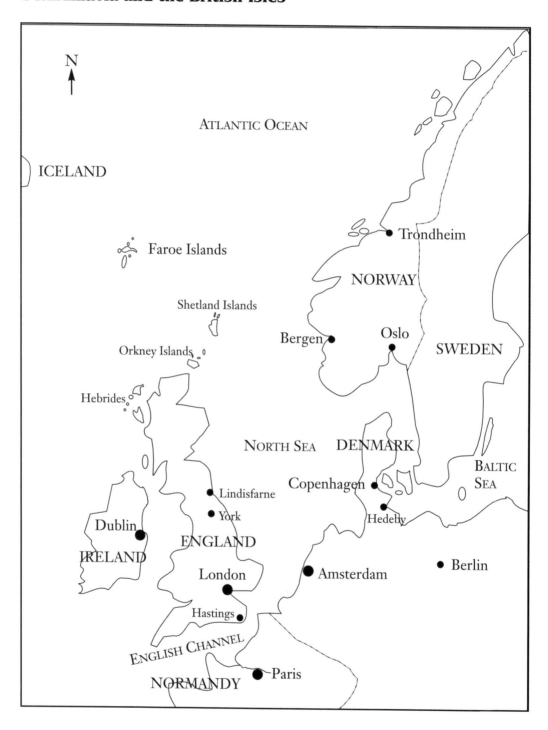